Nature's Spokesman

M. Krishnan photographing the twelfth-century frescoes at
Sittannavasal, Pudukottai District. (Photo: Gopal Gandhi)

Nature's Spokesman

M. KRISHNAN
AND INDIAN WILDLIFE

edited by

RAMACHANDRA GUHA

OXFORD
UNIVERSITY PRESS

OXFORD
UNIVERSITY PRESS

YMCA Library Building, Jai Singh Road, New Delhi 110 001

Oxford University Press is a department of the University of Oxford. It furthers the
University's objective of excellence in research, scholarship, and education
by publishing worldwide in

Oxford   New York

Athens   Auckland   Bangkok   Bogota   Buenos Aires   Cape Town
Chennai   Dar es Salaam   Delhi   Florence   Hong Kong   Istanbul   Karachi
Kolkata   Kuala Lumpur   Madrid   Melbourne   Mexico City   Mumbai
Nairobi   Paris   São Paulo   Shanghai   Singapore   Taipei   Tokyo   Toronto   Warsaw

with associated companies in   Berlin   Ibadan

Oxford is a registered trade mark of Oxford University Press
in the UK and in certain other countries

Published in India
By Oxford University Press, New Delhi

First published 2000
Oxford India Paperbacks 2001

ISBN 019 565911 2

Typeset in Adobe Garamond
by Guru Typograph Technology, New Delhi 110 045
Printed in India by Pauls Press, New Delhi 110 020
Published by Manzar Khan, Oxford University Press
YMCA Library Building, Jai Singh Road, New Delhi 110 001

Acknowledgements

I AM GRATEFUL TO the family of M. Krishnan for their generous support to this project. His papers and clippings were made available to me in Chennai by his wife, Indumathi, and his daughter-in-law, Dr Meenakshi Harikrishnan. His son, M. Harikrishnan, provided fascinating insights into the character and beliefs of his father. From distant Cambridge (Mass.) his granddaughter, Dr Asha Harikrishnan, sent across a copy of the delightful 'animal alphabet' that Krishnan had made for her. A selection of those verses, with the illustrations that accompany them, serve as 'section-breaks' in this book.

The family's support was strengthened by the vital assistance provided by A. Madhavan, Krishnan's kinsman and mine; and by Gopal Gandhi, Krishnan's friend and mine. Both allowed me to raid their personal archives of Krishnan lore. I would also like to thank S. Seshadri, former Regional Director of the Oxford University Press, Chennai, without whose early encouragement this project would not have got off the ground.

Contents

A

Orycteropus afer: Nocturnal burrowing mammal of Central and South Africa, order Tubulidentata. Long snout, extensile sticky tongue, diet of ants, termites. Also known as earth pig.
—Collins Family Encyclopaedia

THE AARDVARK

Behind the kopjes of his land
this curious, unfamiliar brute
gambols, and frisks — and pants.

His coat is much like rain-wet sand,
he lives in burrows under-root
and mainly feeds on ants.

Introduction

The Worlds of M. Krishnan

I HAVE BEFORE ME a New Year's card for 1994. It has been made by an eighty-one-year-old man for his ninety-one-year-old sister. He lives in steamy Madras, she in Mysore, the town on the Carnatic Plateau which (he remembers) 'can be Arctic in December–January'. He is an artist, and so is she. To mark this, and the weather in Mysore, the card begins with his portrait of a bird in flight, its red beak and red legs and white-and-black wings etched against a blue sky. It is the White Stork, says the artist, helpfully providing its Latin and Tamil names too.

And why the White Stork? 'Can't you see the connection,' asks the artist of his sister. He reminds her of the address, offered some fourteen centuries previously, by the poet Saththi-muththap-pulavar to the bird as it passed Madurai en route to its winter-grounds in Kanyakumari. One column then prints the poem in Tamil, the letters and words flawlessly formed; the other column offers a translation in English, in a typed draft scored over with handwritten corrections. The poet had asked the stork 'with coral-red beak sharp-tapered like a split palmyra stalk' that if it should halt, on its return journey northwards, at the tank of his home village, Saththimuthththam, it should seek out his wife in her 'wet-walled leaky' hut, there listening 'to the gecko's whinnying voice for augury of my return', and

> Tell her that you saw this abject being
> In Madurai, capital of the Pandya king,
> Grown thin with no clothes against the north wind's bite,
> Hugging his torso with his arms,
> Clasping his body with up-bent legs,
> Barely existing
> Like the snake within its basket.

Some family news follows, and then, at the end of the card, is a portrait in colour of the unhappy Saththi-muththap-pulavar. 'The stork is quite accurate,' comments the artist, but 'I should not have attempted an impression of the poet—in my depiction, he looks more like a toad in a hole than a snake in a basket, though the foetal position must be correct.'

This New Year's card was sent by M. Krishnan to his sister Muthu. It is a period piece, in the precise sense of the term—'an object or work whose main interest lies in its historical etc. associations' (as defined by the Concise Oxford Dictionary)—an object or work that could only be sent or received by one born before the First World War. The card continues a conversation conducted over decades between two old people of culture, learning, sensitivity, and *style*. It is also a handsome demonstration of the talents that made Krishnan the finest naturalist and nature writer in the land. In this private communication, as in his printed oeuvre, we find a distinctive combination of great skill, exceptional self-confidence, and obsessive perfectionism. We see at work the artist, scholar and writer, the man who would single-handedly annul the distinctions made by academics between nature and culture or literature and science. Even the showing-off—the pedantic precision of the stork's Latin name, *Ciconia ciconia ciconia*—is in character.

Perhaps the most remarkable thing about this card, however, is that Krishnan made it in the knowledge that it might never reach Mysore. For there was a postal strike on in December 1993, and, as he told Muthu, 'only the good god knows when you will get it or, with unskilled replacements for the regular postal workers, if you will get it at all'. The card was produced out of affection for his sister, certainly, but also for the sheer joy of it. It was made by a man in love with his calling, a man with a supreme unconcern for what the world thought of him.

II

M. Krishnan was born in Tirunelveli on the 30 June 1912, the youngest of the eight children of the Tamil writer and reformer A. Madhaviah (1872–1925). Madhaviah was employed in the Salt and Abkari Department of the Government of Madras. Posted in small towns, his work involved much riding on horse-back, cross-country, in search of smugglers and drug pedlars. In his spare time he read, and wrote. His vast output includes the first realistic novel published in Tamil (*Padmavathi Charithram*, 1898), an English novel published in London (*Thillai Govindan*,

1916), as well as essays, short stories, poems, and skits. In about the year 1920 he took premature retirement, commuted his pension, and with the proceeds built a house in the Madras locality of Mylapore. Adjoining the new family home was a shed where he installed a press to print his magazine, *Panchamirtham*. Madhaviah had resolved to devote the rest of his life to literature, but not much was left of it. He died at the age of fifty-five, in the Madras Senate House, immediately after making an impassioned speech on the need to introduce Tamil (or the equivalent mother tongue) as a compulsory subject for the BA.

Madhaviah was a remarkable man, made more remarkable in the recollections of Krishnan. In a 'verified factual record' he compiled in 1990, the adoration is unquestioned and uncharacteristically unqualified, with a gloss and glow put on imperfect memory by a devoted son. The father, in this telling, was always at odds with authority, always ahead of the social and political currents of the time. In a more personal vein, Krishnan remembers the early horse-rides with his father and the daily walks they took together before sunrise, to Marina Beach and back. He writes of how in the last four years of his life Madhaviah ate his meals with his last-born, and how at night his own cot was placed next to his.

When his father died, the care and financial responsibility for the younger siblings was assumed by the second child, Lakshmi. Born in 1896, married in 1905, she had been cast away by her husband's family. Madhaviah took Lakshmi back and educated her. At the time of his death she was teaching at the prestigious Queen Mary's College, of which she was later to be Principal. Krishnan was now studying at the Hindu High School; although not what we would term a 'prize' student, he read widely, and had developed an interest in art. Also in nature, for as he relates in an essay published in this volume ('A City's Bird Life'), Mylapore in the twenties was something of a frontier settlement, stray houses with acres of shrub and pasture in between. The area was home to a teeming bird life and the odd jackal and blackbuck as well. The environment rubbed off: at the age of eleven this son of a scholarly Brahmin had as his pet a grown mongoose.

In 1927 Krishnan joined the Presidency College, a since decayed institution then in its pomp. He appeared for the Intermediate examination and, in 1931, for the BA, one of his subjects the Tamil for which his father had so vigorously fought. The subject he most enjoyed was Botany, taught by Professor P.F. Fyson. Fyson was a fine and devoted field scientist who (judging from Krishnan's references to him in later life) deeply impressed the young student. He accompanied the Fysons on trips to the Nilgiri and Kodaikanal hills, learning science from the Professor and discussing the techniques of water colour painting with his wife.

The friendship with the Fysons did not come in the way of Krishnan getting a Third Class in his BA. Job prospects were bleak, but an elder brother, M. Anantanarayanan, was in the Indian Civil Service,[1] and he had a father-in-law more eminent still. This was R. Narayana Aiyar, one of the first Tamilians to get into the ICS. Narayana Aiyar took Krishnan to an even bigger man, a knight no less, Sir T. Vijiaraghavachari, who had among his many charges the Agricultural Research Institute in Pusa, a likely resting-place for a young fellow with an indifferent academic record but a serious interest in plants. When Sir T.V. was told of Krishnan's 'achievement' he advised him to do an MA and come back. Two years later the journey was repeated. In a letter written fifty-five years after this meeting the supplicant remembered the scene: 'The knight in an easy chair; me, next to him, in a bentwood chair; Mr R.N. in a sofa farther away.' 'Another Third Class,' burst out the knight in a storm of protest, 'Now if you had only got a First Class in either the BA or the MA. I could have done something for you.' 'If that were the case there would have been no need to come here at all,' remarked Narayana Aiyar, and departed taking Krishnan with him.

At the family's behest Krishnan then spent two years obtaining a law degree. He graduated in 1936, but there is no record of any subsequent briefs or court appearances. In those days the lack of an income was no bar to matrimony. Thus on 26 March 1937 Krishnan married Indumati Hasabnis, from Bangalore, only fifteen, but in spirit and strength of will already a match for her husband.

The first 'verified factual record' I have of any paid employment dates to 1937, when Krishnan published some drawings and caricatures in the *Madras Mail.* The next year he was publishing essays on book-design in the low-circulation but high-prestige *Indian Affairs* and, more consequentially, nature notes in *The Statesman* and *The Hindu.* These early notes (a couple printed in this book) display the close observation and spare style that was to distinguish all his work. But as the aspirant novelist

---

[1] And later the author, in *his* spare time, of a well-regarded novel, *The Silver Pilgrimage,* originally published by Criterion Books, New York, in 1961, and reprinted in 1993 by Penguin India.

R.K. Narayan was finding out at about the same time, the concept of the freelancer was unknown to the moral and pecuniary universe of Tamil Brahminism. Thus in the early years of his marriage Krishnan irregularly held a 'regular' job—working initially with the Associated Printers, then with the Madras School of Art, and finally as the Publicity Officer of the local station of All India Radio.

In 1942, at his family's urging and with the help of whatever influence they could command, Krishnan was given employment by the Maharaja of Sandur, a small princely state in the northern part of present-day Karnataka. Employment was, it seems, a somewhat incidental consideration, the main reason for the move being that his wife's doctor had advised them to relocate to a drier place. Krishnan was to spend eight years in the state—eight years under one paymaster but, true to form, in many jobs. In Sandur Krishnan served successively as schoolteacher, judge, publicity officer and Political Secretary to the Maharaja. The work was dreary, but there was always the possibility of escape. For in his tours through Sandur the naturalist would come across the sambhar and the wild boar, jackals, jungle cats, porcupines and leopards. In this valley ringed by hills and forests, fields and shrub jungle within and the Tungabhadra flowing through them, the great ruined city of Hampi but a day's bullock-cart journey away, Krishnan could nurture his love of nature and cultural history. He raised goats, occasionally grazing them himself; bred pigeons, running an experimental pigeon-post with the state's Boy Scouts; and walked in the wild and among the Hampi temples, returning home to read by lantern-light the Tamil poets once patronized by the Vijayanagara kings. He also developed an abiding fondness for *Mandalu-menasinakai*, chillies fried in oil, a culinary gem of the interior Deccan.

Krishnan was temperamentally well suited to the informal paternalism of the princely state. He could fit in here as he would never have 'adjusted' to the rule-bound impartiality of the administration of British India. Sandur was Krishnan's finishing school or, to vary the metaphor slightly, the laboratory where he conducted the research for his unacknowledged doctoral degree. What he learnt there was communicated in the nature essays, cultural profiles, and short stories he published in the forties, under his own name in *The Illustrated Weekly of India* and under the *nom-de-plume* 'Z' in *The Hindu*. For years afterwards, as this anthology will reveal, he would embellish his articles with a fact or anecdote from his Sandur days. The state meant much to him, and he to it. Half-a-century after Krishnan left Sandur one of his students there recalled:

. . . one particular lecture on protective coloration, where the science and nature study teacher, who was also a talented artist, drew a zebra and a monkey on a portable blackboard, which was moved farther and farther away from us, to demonstrate that, at a distance, the zebra with its broken pattern looked less prominent to the eye than the donkey in a block of single colour; though, at close quarters, it would be difficult to imagine how the vivid, black and white stripes of the zebra could ever look hazier than the dull, uniform brown of the donkey. My teacher was none other than M. Krishnan.[2]

In 1949, when the state of Sandur disappeared along with 520 others into the Union of India, Krishnan returned to Madras, taking up residence in the tiled cottage his father had built for his press. He never took a job again, for the next forty-seven years making a precarious but always honest living as a writer and photographer. In 1950 he began a fortnightly 'Country Notebook' for *The Statesman* of Calcutta; his last column was printed the day he died. Alert and alive, at once scientific and speculative, peppered with allusions to literature and myth, opinionated, and acid in its wit, the column must rank as one of the remarkable achievements of English-language journalism in this country (or any other). While *The Statesman* was his mainstay, Krishnan also wrote for *The Hindu, The Indian Express, The Illustrated Weekly of India, Shankar's Weekly, et al.,* and on a staggering variety of subjects. Krishnan is known above all as a great pioneering naturalist, as he should be. But in his day he had also served notice as art critic, writer of fiction, poet, translator and literary historian. In January 1952 he even reported for *The Statesman* on the five days of the Madras Test of that year, the match in which Vinoo Mankad took twelve wickets as India beat England for the first time. These reports were said to be 'From a *Special* Cricket Correspondent', a seemingly curious description more true than the newspaper knew.

I once wrote of the opening batsman Krishnamachari Srikkanth that he was the only Tamil Brahmin who did not have security as his watchword. I had forgotten about Krishnan. His brother was in the ICS, ending up as Chief Justice of Madras; his son in the Indian Forest Service, his final posting as the Principal Chief Conservator of Forests, Tamil Nadu; a nephew in the Indian Foreign Service, Ambassador to Germany and to Japan. But Krishnan would be his own man, and not just in the matter of regular employment.

[2] M. Y. Ghorpade, writing in *Blackbuck*, quarterly journal of the Madras Naturalists Society, vol. 12., no. 2, 1996. I am grateful to T. R. Shankar Raman for alerting me to this special Krishnan issue of *Blackbuck*.

III

The library of natural history is dominated by spectacular habitats—oceans, mountains and deserts—and by charismatic megavertebrates—the whale, the lion, the tiger. Krishnan wrote, by choice, of the humdrum landscape of peninsular India, a countryside 'broken up with ridges and depressions, stones and burrows, wiry, much-branched shrubs and thorn and dessicated grasses, and an occasional patch of sand or rock or some succulent xerophyte'. It was his special gift to make this land come alive, to write about its apparent lack of colour in understated but wryly effective prose. While he knew the tiger and the elephant, he wrote as lovingly of the jackal, the ghorpad, and the spotted owlet, the small, homely, unglamorous denizens of the Indian countryside. That he wrote of the blackbuck in Ranibennur instead of the tiger in the Himalaya is one reason why he is not as well-known as Jim Corbett, a state of affairs that does not properly reflect their respective skills as writers or naturalists. While we are in the business of comparison, let me also say that Krishnan had a sharply developed visual sense unmatched by other Indian nature writers.

Krishnan never talked down to his readers, assuming in them a knowledge and range of interests equal to his own. If they had not read Blake (and committed his poems to memory) or did not know who 'Eha' was, they could always go to the library and find out. In what I regard as his finest period (which ran, roughly, from 1948 to 1961), the learning was carried lightly, leavened by the more-than-occasional flash of humour, which in the best Anglophone fashion was generally directed at himself. But as he grew older the tone grew more sombre. The essays were still beautifully crafted and rich in detailed information. However, they were no longer so attentive to the human or cultural context, being natural history in a more straightforward sense. Krishnan changed, so to say, with the times: if from the 1970s we find an intensity of tone and even an impatient hectoring in his essays this was not unrelated to the rapid disappearance of forests and wildlife all over India.

The ecologist Raman Sukumar has pointed out that Krishnan worked at a time when the 'environment' was not a glamorous subject attracting millions of dollars of research funding. This naturalist did most of his fieldwork, and took all of his photographs, from his own funds. When Sukumar started his own research he went to Krishnan, who told him, 'When watching elephants for heaven's sake keep looking behind your back', thus alerting the novice to the straggler to the herd, who would come up suddenly after the rest of his mates had passed you by. Sukumar, who is now a world authority on the elephant, tells me that in a little-known note of 1972 the naturalist had anticipated high-tech science in two respects. Here Krishnan had observed that elephants communicated at sound frequencies not easily audible to humans, sounds he described as 'throaty, hardly audible, a throbbing purr'. Twelve years later, three scientists at Portland Zoo, working with fancy equipment among capt-ive elephants, gave the phenomenon a name, 'infrasound', and a number, 14 hertz, a decibel level way below the range of the human ear. Krishnan also speculated that female elephants sometimes chose their partners, a claim that then flew in the face of a consensus among scientists that mating was determined by dominance hierarchies among males, but is seemingly confirmed by recent work on the African elephant. It is not unlikely that other theories of Krishnan's, likewise based on close obser-vation in the field, shall in time be certified by technology-driven re-search.

Krishnan had also told the beginner 'to study the elephant for its own sake. Don't expect anything to come of it.' Brave advice, even if he didn't always follow it himself. This man outside the system occasionally tried to manipulate it, as a member of the Indian Board for Wildlife (for more than three decades) and the Steering Committee for Project Tiger. Now and then he sounded the tocsin, the chronicler of nature becoming the crusader for its protection. A 1970 essay on 'The Dwindling Animals of the Forest' (reprinted in this collection) complained that 'neither at the level of the illiterate poor nor among the educated people is there any popular feeling for wild life in India today'. He wondered why 'the centre cannot prevail upon the states to adopt a more conservationist attitude towards its wild life'. His last column, printed on 18 February 1996, pro-vided part of the answer: the snag 'seems to lie in our Constitution, evolv-ed by men with formidable knowledge of legal and political matters and hardly any of the unique biotic richness of India—they do not even seem to have realized that the identity of a country depended not so much on its mutable human culture as on its geomorphology, flora and fauna, its *natural* basis'.

Krishnan was an ecological patriot, who believed (to quote from a 1974 piece not included here) that only if 'we can save India and her magnificent heritage of nature for the generations of Indians to come, and safeguard the physical and organic integrity of our country, threatened today'—only then can we 'give them a country to be truly proud of'. This meant pushing back the forces that would destroy nature—dams, mines, commercial forestry, cattle, exotic species—to thus maintain 'the equipoise of nature and to do nothing to upset it'. It is time, he wrote, that 'we cultivated a narrow sort of patriotism in our floral preferences'. He could be ruthless in his opposition to species introduced from outside. He was once asked to speak at the Indian Institute of Science in Bangalore, by common consent the most beautiful of our university campuses. It was late February, and the avenues were set alight by the *tabebuia*, whose spectacular yellow flowers were in blossom. The planting of this Central American tree, as of the other species that adorn the Institute, was the handiwork of the wife of the Director. At a reception the lady asked Krishnan what he thought of the campus. 'Disgraceful', he answered, 'You should uproot all those foreign trees, and plant some of our own.' On another occasion, when a kinsman wrote of the death by felling of a gul mohar tree near his house, Krishnan shot back: 'Anyway, why regret the demise of a gul mohar—an exotic that litters the ground beneath with fallen, faded flowers—a vermilion strumpet from Madagascar? If you want to see a truly impressive crown of red flowers, you should see the flame-of-the forest, *Butea monosperma*, entirely our own, early in summer—3 or 4 trees close together setting the horizon ablaze.'[3]

Krishnan liked to contrast two authentically indigenous traditions of nature conservation, the traditions of Vedanthangal and of Ashoka. The first referred to a village near Chinglepet, where custom and religious tradition had saved, for generations, breeding birds from the hunter's arrow and the shikari's shotgun; the latter to the Mauryan emperor whose edicts commanded his people to protect rare animals and plants. Krishnan first visited Vedanthangal in the early 1950s (as he writes in this collection), studying its avian life and history of protection, and succeeding in having it designated as a formal 'sanctuary'. He knew that cultural traditions could be in harmony with nature—consider also the essay on Bishnoi and blackbuck printed here, which was written years before the Salman Khan incident had made this a topic for cover stories in up-market magazines. But he also sensed that in an altered modern context, with rapid economic growth and human population growth as well, traditional restraint had in many cases given way to greed. There would, he hoped, come a time when local traditions could once more contribute creatively to wildlife

[3] On this theme, of imported versus native floras, see also the essays 'Gilding the Lily' and 'Nature Study' in this volume.

conservation. Meanwhile, the state had to take a proactive role in effect-ively protecting the habitats and species that remained.

As a naturalist Krishnan was singular in many respects, as will become clear to the reader who reads through this volume. What will not be so immediately apparent, however, is that he was a vegetarian who never held a rifle, a man who was exceptional in his generation for being a con-servationist *qua* conservationist, not a shikari-turned-protector and mem-ber of the repentant butchers' club. The finest students of our natural history have either been Europeans, or Hindus and Christians of work-ing-caste origin, or members of the Rajput and Muslim nobility. Europ-eans have been inspired to more serious study by their experience of the wild and their adherence to a post-Enlightenment scientific rationality; naturalists of plebeian background familiarized by an occupational tra-dition of working with animals or plants; thakurs and nawabs challenged by their aristocratic lineage to move from hunting to conservation. And yet, it fell to a *rasam*-drinking, gun-loathing Tamil Brahmin to become the ablest naturalist of them all.

IV

This book will give one a fair idea of Krishnan the naturalist and writer, but what kind of man was he? His character is, I think, nicely revealed in the technical apparatus of his photography. He came to the craft late, when he was past forty, but brought to it a ferocity of commitment that was all his own. He strongly preferred black-and-white film to colour, and roll film to 35mm, for it enabled him to make large prints (36" by 24" or bigger still) that showed up animals in the wild in proper detail. How-ever, these preferences ruled out the use of any of the makes of camera then available in the Indian market. This man, who in his lifetime was un-questionably the 'biggest name in India's wildlife photography', had more-or-less to manufacture a camera himself. This was, to quote his fellow naturalist E. P. Gee, 'a large, composite affair, with the body of one make and the tele lens of another, and other parts and accessories all in-geniously mounted together by himself. I cannot swear that I saw prover-bial bootlace used to fix them all together, but I am sure there must have been some wire and hoop somewhere!'

This contraption was known, to master and acolyte alike, as the 'Su-per-Ponderosa'. In 1974 the body needed to be changed; the problem was that it was a German make, an *East* German make. If Krishnan wanted to import a Pentacon Six body without the accompanying lenses he had to overcome both the Iron Curtain and the *swadeshi*-minded Indian government. He wrote for a replacement to 120 suppliers of photo equipment in Europe, Asia and the Americas. Only one replied, Andrews and Company in Hong Kong. This, he thought, was actually a slice of luck, for his nephew had just been appointed to the Indian mission in the colony. He could, when required, pay up, collect the box, and send it along to Madras. Krishnan now flew to Delhi, and 'after a specially unpleasant series of engagements with the bitter cold [it was December] and Sardul Singh, Deputy Chief Controller of Import and Export', succeeded in getting a license allowing him to import two camera bodies alone.

Meanwhile, back behind the Iron Curtain, the East Germans had stopped production of the P-6. Andrews and Company, who had promised to supply Krishnan a box, now wrote to him saying they were 'temporarily out of stock', and would send the item later in the year. The truth was that having heard of the brand's demise, the canny Chinamen had no wish to sell the box on its own—how then would they dispose of the lenses (which this particular customer had no use for?) The story has a tame and typically Indian ending—a P-6 box was donated to the photographer by some friends in England.

Even when he could afford it, Krishnan never bought a car or a motor scooter. In the late sixties, his son Hari briefly contemplated buying a car, for as a forest officer he had much roaming to do. Father and son worked out the economics, and decided that each could afford a four-wheeler. No longer, it seemed, would the naturalist have to trust to his feet or a bicycle in negotiating the roaring Madras traffic. Days before the order was to be placed, recalls Hari, 'rescue arrived swiftly and unexpectedly from the Union Finance Minister in the form of an "upward revision" in the price of petrol', that (for both of them) put the issue beyond doubt for good.

It is also in character that in 1995 Krishnan was still using the Swan Signature fountain pen with which he had written his BA examination. His attitude to the 'latest' in technology can be usefully contrasted to that of the poet Vladimir Mayakovsky. Born in a Georgian valley, Mayakovsky was unmoved by the glories of the Caucasus. He grew up in the woods, with a father who was a forest ranger. Accompanying his father on a round one night, the boy saw a factory on the far side of a river, gloriously illuminated. 'After seeing electricity', recalled Mayakovsky in his memoirs, 'I lost interest in Nature. Not up-to-date enough.'

Krishnan happened to be in the crowd that saw the display of India's first jet aircraft. But he came away unimpressed—it was not natural enough. For these were 'just big, loud engines', whose power and speed was 'mechanical, chemical, inhuman'. What moved him was the 'living, muscular speed of animals', a quickness he could marvel at. 'If you like speed', he told his readers, 'and want to see something sustained in its effortless, rhythmic impetuosity, you should watch a herd of blackbuck going all out for a few miles—there is tangible, real speed for you.'

A younger friend who knew him well writes that while 'never guilty of under-estimating his exceptional talent, Krishnan nonetheless lived a life of self-imposed obscurity. When not in the forests, he hibernated in the bush cover of his home-cum-studio in Madras.' There, when he was not developing film, painting a sketch or typing a column, Krishnan indulged in his *un*-natural interests—detective fiction, Carnatic music, and cricket. Of these I share only the last, but can certify here to a high degree of understanding. In a family history he once wrote ('The Descent of the P.H. ites', 1991), against the name of his brother P.M.Y. Narayanan— a medical doctor who died young—he had entered this significant detail—'Was a lefthand batsman and bowler and could bowl the Chinaman.'[4]

'Krishnan's reclusion was notorious', remarks the same friend, and two stories testify to this. In the mid sixties, when Air India started a non-stop service to London, they offered to a select group of 'eminent Indians' free tickets for the inaugural flight, with a week of travel in the United Kingdom thrown in. A Tamil manager with Air India, devoted to Krishnan and his works, knew the way things were ordered in India Krishnan would not be put on the list. Yet who could be more properly deserving than this scholar of English literature and this master of English prose? What could more become a *public* sector airline than to pay for Krishnan to walk in the Lake District and examine the collections in the British Museum? After special pleading the manager got Krishnan's name put on the list, and himself flew to Madras with the offer. It was refused, as was an all-expenses paid invitation from the Smithsonian Institution soon afterwards, the money to come this time from the United States treasury. It

---

[4] On the field of play Krishnan was a fiery fast bowler, with a temper to match. My friend Anand Doraswami tells the story of a match in which Krishnan took two wickets in the opening over. Out came the next batsman, wearing a blue shirt and brown trousers, his leg-guards tied up with handkerchiefs. It was too much for the fastidious Krishnan. 'What is your name', he demanded of the batsman. 'Thirunavakkarasu', came the answer. 'I refuse to bowl to a man with that name', said Krishnan, and tossing the ball to his captain, left the field.

was not that this patriot could not cross the *Kala Paani*, but that the self-reliant, Thoreauvian individualist would not allow a mere government to pay for him.[5]

Then, in the last months of 1969, when Krishnan was away in a forest, his wife Indu received a telegram from the Government of India, asking whether he would consent to being awarded the Padma Shri. Indu thought on her feet—who knew when her man would be back, and how he would respond to such a request. She wired his acceptance immediately. Once Krishnan returned he saw there could be no second thoughts, and accepted the honour with grace.

V

Krishnan once told a friend that he was better known in West Bengal than his native Tamil Nadu (this was said with some regret, for he was, after all, Madhaviah's son). Copies of *The Statesman* rarely reach the city of Madras, but its Delhi edition found its way to the small sub-Himalayan town where I grew up. My father read *The Statesman* for much the same reason that Krishnan wrote for it (it had fewer misprints). The photograph that introduced his column did not hold me—newsprint could scarcely do justice to this master of the black-and-white art—but the writing did. In those days 'Country Notebook' alternated with a column by the politician Minoo Masani, likewise a man of strong opinions, but not his own (these came from Milton Friedman and Margaret Thatcher). I closely read the *Sunday Statesman* one week and stamped on it the next. (At least that is how I wish to remember it; in fact I probably snatched the paper from my father one Sunday and allowed him first shot the next.)

While visiting Madras in the summer of 1979 I found that I was connected to Krishnan. The connection was tenuous—his brother the Chief Justice was married to my mother's cousin—and all I knew of his house was that it was 'somewhere near Rajeshwari Kalyana Mandapam'. That was enough, for the Tamil is the best short-distance cartographer in the world. Walking down Edward Elliots' Road, I was quickly directed to where Krishnan lived. His home was nondescript; a grey cement block tucked away behind an old Madras bungalow. It was late evening when I got there, catching the naturalist as he emerged from his darkroom, wearing a red checked *lungi*, a roll of film, dripping wet, in his hands.

On Christmas Day, 1995, I was on Edward Elliots' Road once more.

[5] I owe this information to S. Theodore Baskaran.

Except that it is now Radhakrishnan Salai, and I was visiting, by appointment, another Madras institution, the son of the man who gave the road its (new) name. My visit ended, I walked out onto the pavement and saw, in the near distance, the board of the Rajeshwari Kalyana Mandapam. In minutes I was with Krishnan. He had forgotten our last meeting, but took me into his study. Surrounded by books, a half-filled page scrolled into his typewriter, a cigarette in his hand, he talked for an hour. He still wore the red lungi, a dress which, in retrospect, seems to have mocked the pieties of Tamil Brahminism, the safe middle road of the white starched *veshti*, the white *banyān*, and the off-white *poonal.* Six weeks after this second meeting Krishnan was dead.

Krishnan could be savagely dismissive of those who failed by his own standards. Consider these three judgements, which I recall from our two conversations. On a famous Tamil writer: 'That man was so unsure of his worth that he wrote under twelve pen-names, using one to write a book and another to review it.' On a well-known ornithologist: 'I told him when the Government appointed him to the high-powered committee on environmental protection, "Don't join, you'll make a fool of yourself. You may know something about birds, that does not make you an ecologist".' On a respected editor who dared change one word of his copy: 'I had written of my father A. Madhaviah as "the Tamil scholar, poet and novelist"; it was changed to "a Tamil scholar, poet and novelist". My father was the most celebrated Tamil writer of his day, better known even than [Subramania] Bharati; this fellow in Delhi has made him an also-ran.' And also one, in print, on the observational skills of a once celebrated poet: 'According to Sarojini Naidu the koel sings "Lira! liree! Lira! Liree!" I have not heard this call. Nor has anyone else.'

The contemporary meaning of 'civilized', writes Krishnan in one of his essays, is 'hypocritical and polite'. Here are some more delightfully uncivilized remarks, gleaned from his letters:

[Writing to the newly appointed Director of the India International Centre in New Delhi]

I remember the India International Centre as a rather heavily built boarding house with a large lecture hall attached, frequented by all sorts and conditions of culture vultures and bores. I sincerely hope it has improved since.

[After reading a pamphlet, in Tamil, on the sayings of Mahatma Gandhi]

The rendering does not mask the dictatorial tone of the pronouncements.

[Commiserating with a friend posted to Japan]

I believe that Japanese English is a language even more difficult to follow than Jap Japanese.

[On an influential environmental organization]

The World Wildlife Fund, that hotchpotch of truly fine and truly distinguished wildlifers and pretentious charlatans, to which both Peter Scott and Duleep Matthai belonged.

VI

That Krishnan cared nothing for what the world thought of him must be a matter of regret. A Jawaharlal Nehru Fellowship (the first), a Padma Shri, a place in the Global 500 Roll of Honour of the United Nations Environment Programme—all these meant naught to him; but a dozen collections of his work could have meant a lot to us. As a chronicler of the natural world he was unequalled, yet his work is to be found, for the most part, only in his now inaccessible newspaper columns. He published only two slim collections: *Jungle and Backyard* (National Book Trust, 1963: reprinted in 1993 by Oxford University Press), and *Nights and Days* (Vikas, 1985), the text embellished in the first instance by his superb pen-and-ink drawings, in the second instance by his photographs. He also wrote a book on elephants for children, as well as an ecological survey of the mammals of peninsular India, *Indian Wildlife, 1959–70* (Bombay Natural History Society, 1975), the fruit of his Nehru Fellowship. There were also some charming stories about a forest contractor named Dawood Khan, but the book where these appeared is not with me now. His last book, an original detective novel in Tamil, was published in 1995.

When I was introduced to his sister Muthu (the recipient of that 1994 New Year card) as someone interested in Krishnan, the sprightly old lady demanded, '*Which* Krishnan? The artist, the writer, the photographer, the story-teller, the scholar, or the naturalist? You must know all the Krishnans if you wish to understand the man.' This anthology, alas, has to make do with only some of those Krishnans. The twin burdens of technology and finance allow it to reproduce but a handful of his sketches, and none of his photographs. But the book does, I believe, provide a wide-ranging and on the whole representative selection of the work of the writer, the story-teller, the scholar and the naturalist. I have chosen sixty-eight pieces, out of more than 2000 that he wrote (and I, with an indescribable pleasure, later read). These range in length from 500 words to 5000.

The earliest of these essays was published in 1938; the latest, posthumously, in 1997. To the best of my knowledge, not a single piece has previously appeared in another book.

To 'edit' the works of Madhaviah Krishnan is an assignment fraught with hazard. In the 1980s, when a group of naturalists in Madras wished to begin a journal, they asked the doyen for a contribution to the first issue. He set one condition: 'Do not edit or change a comma in the text.' They didn't, but now that he is gone, I have been more meddlesome. By contemporary standards my editing has been light, but were I to have done in his lifetime what I have done here he would never have spoken to me again. I thought it pointless to gloss every Tamil word or literary allusion likely to escape the younger generation. But about a fifth of the essay-titles are mine, not his. I have corrected some misspellings and inserted some necessary commas, reassuring myself that these errors were those of some incompetent sub-editor, not his. I have corrected one of his own common mistakes, which was to insert a redundant concluding 's' to Himalaya (I have not dared, however, to insert a definitive 'i' at the end of that once widespread but now antiquated usage, 'Madura'.)

A word also about the sections into which the book has been structured. 'Nature Venerated' brings together essays on the representations of animals in our religious and cultural life. 'Nature's Marvels' highlights encounters in the wild with large, 'sexy' species such as the tiger and the python. 'Nature in Miniature' turns the spotlight (and microscope) on dainty or dangerous little things such as lizards and butterflies. 'Nature's Wars' features battles both inter- and intra-specific, small cats fighting each other and big cats being beaten back by a buffalo. 'Nature Theorized' illustrates the analytical side of Krishnan, as he punctures widely held theories of the vengefulness of cobras and the larger size of north Indian animals. 'Nature Domesticated' displays Krishnan's interest in and knowledge of the plants and animals that live with humans: goats, cows, dogs, the neem tree and others. 'Nature Desecrated' showcases some particularly gross examples of man's destruction of species and habitats. 'Nature Protected' prints documentary and exhortative essays on the methods by which Indians may come to cherish and conserve their unparalleled richness of natural diversity. The concluding section, 'Nature Transcended', selects examples of the 'non-nature' Krishnan, essays and stories placed wholly in the world of humans.

The selection of articles for this anthology was difficult, given the number of options and their consistently high quality. In my choices I have exercised a slight bias in favour of literary quality over scientific worth, but the reader will find plenty of both. Their organization into named sections was equally problematic. The sorting has been done according to the dominant theme of individual essays, but the polymathic Krishnan resists being sorted anyhow. The pieces slotted under 'veneration' speak also of domestication and desecration, and *vice versa*. The only truly sustainable distinction one can make is between the first three-fourths of the book, which deals in one way or another with the natural world, and the last quarter, which does not. These essays can be read in any order. The reader might start with nature's marvels, if he so wishes, then move backwards to nature's veneration or forwards to its desecration.

Begin wherever you want, and wander which way you wish. The anthology can be read at one sitting or piecemeal. It begins with a short piece, from 1952, on the landscape of love in ancient Tamil poetry. It ends with a long disquisition of 1995 on the culture of patronage in late medieval Tamil poetry. This choice of bookends has a twin rationale; to push the argument that while Krishnan was a great naturalist he was also an outstanding writer, and to underline that while his natural allegiances lay with India as a whole, his cultural affinities were more circumscribed. Krishnan himself felt of this last essay that it was 'one of the best things I have written and wholly original'. The men and women he was writing about were, in fact, 'my personal literary ancestors'. Might we not single out among them the figure of Kaalameghappulavar, an 'out-and-out free-lancer' who seldom approached a patron, a man 'renowned for the spontaneity of his poetic verse', an 'acknowledged master of instant repartee [who] has written some foul-mouthed insults and curses in immaculate metres'. Krishnan's compliments and insults were offered in prose and by photograph, but otherwise the resemblances are striking. May his work live as long as that of his adored poets of the Tamil country.[6]

RAMACHANDRA GUHA

---

[6] This introduction has greatly benefited from the comments and criticisms of M. Harikrishnan, A. Madhavan, and Gopal Gandhi. I remain, of course, responsible for any remaining errors of fact and interpretation.

Arctitis binturong: Binturong — also called bear-cat. East Indian prehensile tailed carnivore, akin to the civet.
—Chamber's Twentieth Century Dictionary

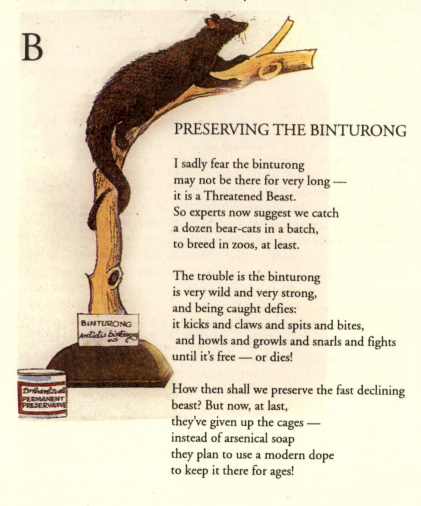

B

PRESERVING THE BINTURONG

I sadly fear the binturong
may not be there for very long —
it is a Threatened Beast.
So experts now suggest we catch
a dozen bear-cats in a batch,
to breed in zoos, at least.

The trouble is the binturong
is very wild and very strong,
and being caught defies:
it kicks and claws and spits and bites,
and howls and growls and snarls and fights
until it's free — or dies!

How then shall we preserve the fast declining
beast? But now, at last,
they've given up the cages —
instead of arsenical soap
they plan to use a modern dope
to keep it there for ages!

Nature Venerated

1

The Landscape of Love

I N ENGLISH POETRY of the recent past, love has a lowland bias. Tennyson's shepherd sings, 'What pleasure lives in height, in height and cold, the splendour of the hills?' and, redundantly again, 'Come, for Love is of the valley, come, for Love is of the valley, come thou down', and Meredith's *Love in the Valley* will endure when his lesser poems are forgotten.

Climatic differences may account for it, but in the traditions of classical Tamil love belongs predominantly to the hills and mountain slopes. Not that there was no love in the sun-baked plains and coast-lines of the Tamil country, but it attains its fulfilment most typically in the hills. In fact, love has a specific ecology in the poetic traditions of Tamil, almost as old as the language itself, and it is of this that I write.

Classical Tamil is peculiar in its division of the land and specification of the attributes of each terrain. No doubt other languages, too, have such territorial leanings in their literature, but Tamil is unique in the detail of its literary ecology. The land was divided into five main tracts, in this order—hill crests and hill-sides, plain-land jungles (including scrub jungle), agricultural tracts, the coastland, and lastly the barren, parched strips that lie between these four. Anyone who has studied Indian plant ecology will appreciate the justice of these divisions.

Traditions set out in elaborate detail the appurtenances of each tract. The soil and the water, the fauna and flora, the people belonging, their occupations and recreations, the food crops and other natural resources, the season most typical of the place, the characteristic melodies and drums, the presiding deity, the trend of young love there—all these are listed, and were followed by classical poets with studious regard.

Many of these details are physical and based on actuality. Therefore their specification did not impose an insufferable limitation on poetry—

on the other hand it invested amatory poetry with a conventional but naturalistic realism.

We are here concerned only with the course of love in these tracts, but, where they will help to provide the setting, I shall mention physical features very briefly.

Love was, in those days and in poetry, mainly an open-air pursuit. The land was less congested then, and lovers could find privacy not too far from the settlement.

In the first tract, in the hills, love was illicit and triumphant. Here, where there was adequate cover in the rank grasses and under-shrubs of the slopes and in the abiding gloom of rain-forests, a young man and his lass met and loved, in secret. It was a literary feature of their love that it was illicit, but do not imagine, in terms of contemporary law, that it was adulterous. It was just that they took the law into their hands and consummated their love without the sanction of social codes and regulations.

It was not sanctimonious, married love, but the more puritanical of my readers might feel relieved to know that marriage was less formal, and more varied and factual, in those days. To the ingenuous question, 'But why should youthful love have been illicit in its climax?' I can only say that the Tamilian grammarians of ancient times had a fine feeling for the poetic—and knew human nature, as many ancients did. 'Stolen waters are sweet, and bread eaten in secret is pleasant.'

Think of the setting envisaged by tradition. The hill-sides were clad in great forests of teak and eagle-wood, red-streaked kino and the graceful, dark-leaved sandalwood—the time of the year was October and November, with the monsoons spent, when the air is cold and the dew early. The lovers met by assignation after daylight had failed; it was dark and cold and dangerous. Could legalized, domestic love have been in place here?

One English poet has had the imagination to visualize a similar setting, though he could have known nothing of the erotic grammar of Tamil. I admire Browning more for his cunning with words than for his poetry, but no one can deny the authentic poetry in this passage, where Ottima recalls to her paramour an illicit assignation in the pine-forests:

Buried in the woods we lay, you recollect:
Swift ran the searching tempest overhead:
And ever and anon some bright white shaft

Burnt thro' the pine-tree roof . . .
As if God's messenger thro' the close wood screen
Plunged and replunged his weapon at a venture,
Feeling for guilty thee and me . . .

In the lowland jungles, shepherds grazed their cattle and grew pulses and millet and a fine feral sort of rice. The setting was much less open than in English pastoral poetry—it has been specified, by the learned author of a Tamil-English dictionary published in 1908, as 'woodland', but I think he is mistaken. The South Indian level-land jungles, where cassias and the blue-flowered *Memecylon edule*, the savage-red lily, *Gloriosa superba*, and the sweet-scented jasmine grow (as they still do, conforming to classical description), is not my conception of tranquil woodland.

Anyone who has ventured into the jungle's outlying life in the plains will know the tract—goatherds and cowherds still graze their herds here. Rainy August and September were the months, and evening the time of day, chosen by literary traditions for love here, and here love was chaste and forlorn. I cannot describe the situation better than in the words of the lexicographer mentioned above: he terms it 'continuing solitary'. Especially did the young shepherdess continue solitary, waiting for her lover's return, while youth danced hand in hand around her or played the flute (traditional recreations belonging to the place).

Perhaps some gawky goatling nuzzled up to her as she sat by herself in the twilight, with that wonderful, spontaneous sympathy of beasts for forlorn humanity. There are many passages about the expectancy of the waiting maid (often she was a newly-married bride, awaiting her husband's return), but it is futile attempting translation; they allude to literary conventions that need tedious explanation in English, and nothing so explained can be poetry.

The agricultural tracts featured disharmony in love—lovers' tiffs, partings in a huff, accusations. Often enough the situation was triangular, for then, too, there were ladies of easy virtue waiting to ensnare the errant lover or young husband, and at times it happened that news of such snaring got abroad.

Translations from classical Tamil of pieces about such lovers' quarrels cannot convey their poetic worth. But I must give one little piece (or rather a fragment from a piece) that tells the story from an unusual angle, the third angle, and which displays a certain devilry and *elan* too rare, unfortunately, these days. This was written by Paranar, some 1800 years ago, and is an anecdotal address by one of the aforementioned ladies to her *thozhi* (a feminine friend, in whom one confided), telling of a tiff between herself and her youthful, married paramour:

> Whenever I think of it, my dear, I laugh—
> And I said to him, levelly.
> 'I will go and tell your wife'—
> How he trembled then,
> Like the binding of earth on a drum!
> Whenever I think of it, I laugh.

The translation is loose, but still fails to convey the zest of the original. Next time you see the *tabla* or *mridangam* or some similar drum being played, watch the way the binding of earth on the tympanum quivers, and you will know just how that unfortunate man must have trembled!

Love has many moods on the sea-coast, but most typically it is sombre and tragic—a man bemoaning his dead love. The finality and deprivation of death have been powerfully realised in Tamil poetry with a maritime setting.

The barren waste lands had their own, tough vegetation—spiky, dwarfed trees and the much-branched, cylindrical cladodes of the *Kalli (Euphorbia tirucalli)* and other xerophytes. Here lovers parted, not in anger, but with many promises as the truest of lovers must part when their love cannot be publicised. The setting is particularly apposite for such farewells, but again it is futile to try and explain its poetic virtue in English, because of its allusiveness. Moreover, it is neither artistic nor even decent to go too deeply into these highly personal and fond farewells.

1954

2

Fabular Fauna

STRIKING PECULIARITY OF the birds and beasts of Indian legends is their realism. No unicorns and rocs, no griffin or phoenix or basilisk, is common in our literature, oral, written or carved. There are, it is true, just a few wholly fabulous creatures, which I shall mention later, but for the best part the legendary fauna is extremely naturalistic.

It is the common animals of the countryside that figure in the old tales, with only the difference that they confab and plot and indulge in soliloquies. There are a number of supernatural creatures, gnomes, sprites and demons of many kinds, but these are not animals. And our legendary animals are more unnatural in the characters that are ascribed to them than in their ability to talk, when you look at them narrowly. The jackal, for instance, is always cunning and thinks out infamous schemes (note that the fox, a close cousin, is also a shady character in Western folklore), the tiger is cruel and fond of human flesh, the lion is the noble and warlike King of Beasts (as lions in stories are universally), the cat is a sanctimonious humbug, crows are fond of council meetings, the hare is crafty, the deer ingenuous and timid, and the crocodile villainous.

The ancient Panchatantra tales, so long and so widely known to every Indian language, are typical of our stories. All the characters I have mentioned, and many more figure in them, but it is only fair to point out, in an aside, that though naturalists may think these characters highly fictitious, there is also much observation of nature in the tales. Skipping rapidly through the pages of my copy of the Panchatantra, I find there close observations of nature leavening the anthropomorphism of the narrative: monkeys suffer much from the cold and elephants from drought; snakes are much given to egg-stealing and heat is quickly lethal to them: pigeons are deeply attached to one another and grow miserable when separated from their mates: rock-owls are the enemies of crows, which they kill by night. These are only examples chosen at random, but, frankly, did you know that these things are true?

However, it is far stranger and less factual observation that we must look for in any legendary natural history. Although our old tales cannot produce much in the form of such lore, our art and poetry can, and there is also some strange natural history to be culled from popular superstition.

Taking the last first, the Abominable Snowman of the Himalaya and the Biscobra of the Deccan are known well beyond their territories. No one really knows the truth about the Yeti, but 'Eha' discovered the identity of the latter. The Biscobra, as the name implies, is twice as terrible as the cobra, and since it can fly through the air in attack, the man who provokes it has practically no chance. 'Eha' found that the dreaded Biscobra was nothing more than a very young common monitor, while it was still slim and agile and banded. Why a lizard innocent of all poison should have achieved this reputation is hard to say, but the fact remains that it did, and that another harmless lizard, the sinuous little skink, is also dreaded for its venom. True that the skink does not bite humanity, but it darts its slick little tongue in and out of its straight jaws, and its lick is sure death. However, it has a forgetful nature, and often it forgets, when it sets out to lick one, why it set out at all and turns back. Because of this, very few men have been skink-licked, but I have been, and, believe me, I didn't die.

Poetry, especially the more romantic type of lyric, gives us some definite *rara avis*. There is the Chuckor or Chakoram, which languishes when the moon that it loves is away—the bird has been identified, by pundits, with the Chuckor partridge of the Himalaya. Then there is the Crownchapakshi of the classics, which is always seen in inseparable pairs, one of the pair pining to death if the other is killed. Some years ago, a pundit of the most formidable scholarship in Sanskrit, and I joined forces in an attempt to establish the identity of this bird, he supplying details from all references to it in the classics, which I collated and compared to the likeliest birds of Indian ornithology. We were both satisfied at the end of this, that the Crowncha-pakshi (which is tall and red-headed, and so utterly devoted to its mate) could only be the Sarus, stateliest of our cranes. Let me quote Hume and Marshall on the Sarus, in this context:

Whether in large or small numbers, they are always in pairs, each pair acting independently of the other pairs. They certainly pair for life, and palpably exhibit great grief for the loss of their mate. On two occasions I have actually known the widowed bird to pine away and die.

Not all legendary fowl can be so certainly identified, though. What, for instance, is the two-headed 'Gandaberandam' known to Tamil? Unquestionably it is the two-headed bird of that same name that figures in the coat of arms of the Maharajas of Mysore, but that takes us no nearer its identity, though I think there is a resemblance to the Crested Serpent-Eagle. And what is the Anril, beloved of Tamil poets? Or the Eight-legged Bird?

The fauna of our art is usually naturalistic, if puns in stone are excepted. I should explain just what I mean by 'puns in stone' for the description has not been used in any comment on Indian art so far, and yet is so apt. In Hampi, over a gateway, there is a bas-relief showing a bull and an elephant engaged in a mighty butting contest, head to head. The bodies are distinct, but the head is common to both combatants, and is in the form of a clever play upon contours that allows the onlooker to see it unmistakably as the head of the elephant, joined on to the elephantine body, or as the bull's head, in conjunction with the bull's body. Again, at the Meenakshi Temple in Madura, there is a monkey with three bodies but only one head—the onlooker may see this monkey in three different postures, depending on which body he chooses to view with the head.

Well, apart from such carvings, the fauna of our stone is highly realistic. However there are the snake-people and the Yali, genuinely fabulous both. The Nagas and Naginis, subterranean and semi-serpentine, snakes really with the heads and torsos of human beings, are well known to our art all over the country. Along with these creatures, a truer snake whose features are rigidly prescribed by iconology may also be mentioned, the eight-headed Adhi-Sesha, also known all over India. But the Yali, for some reason that is quite beyond me, is less celebrated by our art critics.

Actually, I think the Yali is the most genuinely fabulous of our legendary beasts. It belongs both to the literature and the art of the South and is half elephant, half lion, as per the written and oral literature of Tamil. It is the mightiest of all creatures, and preys freely on the lion—the lion, according to literary and artistic traditions all over India, is the King of Beasts and kills elephants with ease (in those traditions, of course). Imagine an animal, then, so powerful that it subsists largely on the elephant-slaying King of Beasts! Literary traditions are discreetly reticent over the Yali, for they know well that when dealing with such a terrible beast, the power of suggestion is defeated by detail. But in South Indian stone, the Yali is a familiar figure, lacking the idiomorphic integrity and dreadful mystery that it has in verse and folklore—Yalis, carved in florid detail and often with formal scroll-work delineating their features, are quite common in southern temples, where they squat timelessly supporting a corner-stone, or rear like a circus horse beside a pillar, or even prance in packs across lintels!

The orthodox Yali (I mean the beast which conforms to literary and folk traditions) has the trunk, face and even the forelegs of the elephant, but is otherwise leonine, particularly in its wavy mane and ears. But many temple Yalis are strikingly different—some have strongly-clawed forelegs, like a lion, and many lack the trunk, the head being part leonine, part canine. One peculiarity of those 'unorthodox' Yalis is that their tushes seem to start from the sides of their jaws, more like a boar's (though they do not curve up) than an elephant's or a lion's. Sometimes it is hard to tell, especially in weathered stone, whether the sculptor intended a Yali or a lion. I am unable to find any specific literature on the Yali in the writing of art critics like Vincent Smith, Favell and others—a surprising omission, considering the profusion of Yalis in southern temples. For this reason, I do not know by what tokens the pundits determine that a particular carving is a Yali and not a lion, but if the somewhat canine cast of countenance is what guides them, it is unreliable. The following excerpt, from Dr Rajendralal Mitra's *Indo-Aryans* (1881), on the sculpture of Orissa, may be cited here.

The lion among animals is however, invariably ill-carved. It has everywhere a conventional, unnatural half-dog half-wolf look about it.

Some day, perhaps, a more systematic natural history of our literature and oral traditions and art will be attempted, but there is so much scope for work here that whoever takes it on should be prepared to devote a lifetime to the study, and to write a ponderous tome at the end of his researches. Thereafter, of course, there will be sufficient scope for several further books of even larger size, by way of dissent. But that is as it should be, for what study is worth the undertaking if it has no room for argument?

1955

3

Ancient Depictions of Hanuman

WHEN I WAS a boy I was taken to a zoo and shown the 'Hanuman-monkey', a full-grown, male mandrill with vivid grooves of vermilion and azure over its nose. I protested that it could not be Hanuman for all its blatant 'naamam', for even then I knew that the mandrill was a native of Africa whereas Hanuman belonged solely to our traditions. Thereupon I was promptly snubbed and asked to hold my tongue, and had to submit to the authority of the elder in whose company I was, for in those days I thought that knowledge went with years.

In writing this I am fulfilling neither a long suppressed childhood desire for retribution, nor an adult, spiteful wish to shock those that are orthodox. This discussion need hurt no one's susceptibilities, however traditionally religious: in fact, it cannot. There is nothing sacrilegious in a theoretical inquiry into the mundane identity assumed by any divine character. Granted that Vishnu did take on the form of a fish and a tortoise in the course of the *Dasavathara,* it is perfectly in order to seek to know which particular fish and tortoise were so honoured. Similarly, it is quite proper to ask which species it was to which the monkey-god belonged.

Several lines of inquiry suggest themselves at once. One could refer to classical *Ramayana* literature or to iconography: one can look into folklore or else study our highly depictive sculpture.

We need not go into literature or iconography here. For one thing, a cursory consultation with pundits has yielded little information that is taxonomically significant. But I would like to point out that it is generally conceded that the canto of the *Ramayana* that refers to Hanuman, Vaali and Sugriva is laid well in the South and that Lanka is Ceylon.

I make this point because in North India, which was not the home of the monkey characters of the *Ramayana*, the Common Langur is called 'Hanuman'. So far as I know, there is no reliable evidence in southern folklore that points to a langur, or any other kind of monkey, being of the caste and tribe of Hanuman. But I may add that the Tamil word 'kurangu' is usually used of the macaques, 'sengurangu' denoting the common 'red monkey' (Bonnet Monkey) that adds so much to the zest of life in southern shrines and railway stations and 'karungurangu' denoting the black Lion-tailed Macaque of the far South: this macaque, is also called 'arakkan'. The langurs are usually called 'manthi', a word that also indicates she-monkeys generally, the Common Langur being known as 'ven-manthi' and the Nilgiri Black Langur as 'karu-manthi'. I should make it clear that I speak of the common far southern Tamil names for these monkeys. I have not looked into the *Kamba Ramayana* for my terminology, for while I have the most genuine respect for the acute observation of nature that occasionally inspires the poetry of the Sangam period, I am not prepared to trust Kamban's natural history an inch.

Of course we cannot now say that the monkeys of the South in *Puranic* days must have been identical with those found here today, but it seems unlikely that any northern species then inhabited this area, and anyway it is safe to rule out all exotic species, such as the mandrill. The question, then, is quite straightforward and is merely this: Was Hanuman a langur or a macaque?

The langurs are tall, slim, arboreal and long-tailed. The langurs that might have lived here in *Puranic* days still live here—the grey or silver-grey Common Langur, with a prominent peak of hair shading the eyes, white whiskers around a flat, black face and dark hands and feet, and the Black Langur, with a rich black pelage and black all over except for a tawny cap and whiskers. The macaques are shorter, thicker set and less arboreal. The common macaque of the South is the Bonnet Monkey, red-faced, grey-coated and very agile. The Lion-tailed Macaque is black all over, except for a great, grizzled mane framing the black face; even if the Northern Rhesus had lived here in *Puranic* days (it is rather like the Bonnet Monkey but lacks the crown of radiating hair and is thicker-built), both the Lion-tailed Macaque and this have short tails and are not particularly good at aerial acrobatics. Hanuman, as everyone knows, had a very long tail and was famed for his powers of leaping. The Bonnet Monkey has a long tail.

We may safely go by our art in deciding this question, for it is very depictive. Ravi Varma, the Kerala painter of scenes from the *Puranas* shows an unmistakable Bonnet Monkey in his pictures of Hanuman. But Ravi Varma, painstaking as he was in his details, was recent and might have fallen into an error. The traditional folk-art of the country-side is more reliable. Clay figures of Hanuman and crude frescoes on walls depicting the god always show a Bonnet Monkey, and the face is invariably pale red. However, folk-art is also susceptible to recent corruptive trends and so let us look at our old traditional stone.

The Hanuman of our classical stone has a muscular, patently macaque build, a very long tail and features that suggest, in their lack of heavy whiskers and the lack of a peak of hair shading the eyes, in the displayed ears and the strong profile of the nose and muzzle, a definite macaque affinity. Incidentally, Hanuman's tail is frequently much longer than that of any Indian monkey, but both the Bonnet Monkey and the langurs have long tails, though the latter have longer tails.

The heroic-sized Hanuman at Hampi are typical of the figure of the monkey-god in our classical stone, and are obviously Bonnet Monkeys. I should add that the carvers of Hampi could not have been led by lack of choice in their models, as langurs are as common there, or commoner, than Bonnet Monkeys.

I have no doubt that it is the Bonnet Monkey, and no other that has been depicted in old representations of Hanuman. But of course this identification is purely of theoretical interest, and it would be valid to argue that Hanuman was a special kind of Puranic super-monkey, unrelated to existing species. That, however, would not explain the almost reverential tolerance that the Common Langur and the Bonnet Monkey (and even the Rhesus) have enjoyed in our country from time immemorial till yesterday.

1955

4

The Shawk

FEW MILES FROM Mahabalipuram, celebrated for the richness of its carvings, is a shrine no less celebrated among the pious. Tirukkalukunram (I follow the spelling of the railway guide) is one of the 16 (or is it 60?) holy places of the South.

It is a temple perched on top of a small, rocky hill, lacking the rugged grandeur of other southern hill-top shrines. But every day it is graced by the visit of two saints in avian garb.

Rain or shine, shortly after the noon invocation, a portion of the sweet, opulent *prasad*, of jaggery and milk, ghee and rice, is brought out by the priest and placed on a shelf of rock. And two large, white birds materialize from the skies and partake of the offering. They are, of course, not birds at all but saints in feathers, most rigorous in their penances and rites.

Each morning they wing their northern way to the Ganges, for a dip in its purifying waters, then they fly all the way back to Rameswaram for a further dip in sanctity, visiting Tirukkalukunram in time for lunch. Local traditions give the names of these two punctilious saints, and further particulars.

Unfortunately for those with romantic inclinations, these birds have no claims to looks, in spite of their whiteness and the sail-like spread of their black-pinioned wings. They are not even kites, as the railway guide calls them, but are Scavenger Vultures, perhaps the least prepossessing of our birds. On the wing they look handsome enough, circling with effortless ease or swooping along the skyline at a terrific pace, breeze-borne. But the weak, yellow beak and face, the dirty hackles and the clumsy, waddling gait proclaim their ugliness when they are on the ground and near. In their youth they are less hideous, a decent, dark-brown all over, but even then you can tell them apart from kites and other brown birds of the sky by their wedge-shaped tail. I do not remember the saint-names given to them at Tirukkalukunram, but can give you their other aliases—

the neophron, or, more specifically *Neophron percnopterus ginginanus*, Pharaoh's Chicken, the Lesser White Scavenger Vulture, and, according to Eha, the bird known to Mr Thomas Atkins as 'The Shawk'.

The last name, I think, is derived from the bird's habit of frequenting heaps of garbage and ordure. If I am right in my etymology, it is a name truly indicative of this vulture's disposition. Wherever there are mounds of manure or other assorted filth, offal and refuse lying around, you are likely to find the neophron. It is commonest outside the city and industrial centre, where there are broad acres of what the engineers call 'rubbish', and around hill-top shrines and country market-places. It is a very useful bird, indeed, and no one who realizes the public good that scavengers do will ever dream of looking down upon it.

Incidentally, it is not only at Tirukkalukunram that it is held sacred: it was venerated in ancient Egypt. Unlike most other birds of its profession, it is not gregarious, but usually goes about with its mate, in a close pair. Like all vultures, it is long-lived and has wonderful powers of sight and flight.

It is likely that the pair at Tirukkalukunram have long been in residence, and it is a fact that they are most punctual in their attendance at the shrine. But there is nothing remarkable in all this. Many birds have an instinctive sense of time, and these vultures deeply appreciate regular provision of food. I have seen several pairs of these birds in and around Tirukkalukunram, so that it is quite conceivable that when the seniormost pair dies, their territory and 'prasad' is taken over by the pair next in the order of precedence among local neophrons—that way one can understand how for generations these birds have been attending at the shrine each day, and set up the tradition of immortality.

I can even testify to the fallibility of the daily visits of the pious birds. One day, in the winter of 1935, no birds turned up at the feeding rock, in spite of the priest's loud invitations and widely waved arms. No vulture of any sort was visible in the skies, and I concluded that a cow must have died on the hillside beyond, that day. The priest made no comment, beyond pointing to the slight drizzle that there was, but an elderly gentleman by my side volunteered a complete explanation. He was a native, and assured us that the absence of the birds was most exceptional; in fact, they were absent only when some major sinner, who should never have been admitted to the precincts, was there. And I must say I did not like the rather pointed look he gave me.

1956

5

The Southern Lions

I N TEMPLES AND places famous for their stone carvings in South India, you will find as many lions in the round and in bas-relief as in the North. All of them are both realistic and formalized—that is, in their proportions, especially in the relative size of the head to the body and the massive but quite natural conformation of the body and limbs, they are realistic; and in the surface treatment of the lineaments of the face, and particularly in the rendering of the mane in tight little spirals or close wavy lines, they are formal, even stylized. I have neither seen nor heard of a lioness in old southern stone, nor, so far as I know, are there any in the North. Moreover, except for the lions of the Sarnath capital and related beasts (which are formalized even in build and clearly betray Hellenic influences in the surface treatment of the mane and paws), the lions of northern classical sculpture are very similar to those of the South.

From these facts, a naturalist seeking a clue to the distribution of lions in ancient India would reach altogether mistaken conclusions. The absence (or rarity) of lionesses he would ascribe to the more arresting looks of the male in this strongly dimorphic species, and from the plentiful representations of lions in the South, and their realism of build, he would conclude that long ago, long before the records of the lion-hunts of the Muslim Emperors in the North, there were lions in South India. How else would so many generations of carvers have rendered so faithfully a beast they had not seen?

The answer to that question is that the lion, the *vahana* of Durga, the beast that lends its visage to Narasimha, and the traditional emblem of sovereignty, belongs so much to the mythology and iconography of the land (undoubtedly the South absorbed much of its traditional culture from the North in early times), that the leonine form and features were well known to those carvers, though they had not seen the beast in the flesh. Perhaps some of them were even familiar with live lions, for there is evidence to show that in the distant past master-carvers from the North, and even from foreign countries, were 'imported' by southern potentates, and there is no reason to presume that such traffic could have been only one-way and that southern carvers of special renown could not have gone up North on a commission.

Let me tell you of a personal experience. Years ago, I met the son and apprentice of a traditional stone-mason (one of the few of his tribe still practising) in Nattarasankottai in the far South. While I waited (long and in vain) to meet his father, I questioned the boy on his attainments in the ancestral art. There is an old temple at this place, the stone pavilion of which is supported by pillars, each decorated with the figure of a rampant Yali, with smooth stone boluses rolling free within its jaws. The Yali is a wholly mythical beast, part-lion, part-elephant. Each Yali in that pavilion was exquisitely carved, and reared up in exuberant animation, and though the temple was old the pillars were recent and had been carved by the grandfather of the boy with me. The apprentice informed me that he too had learned, over painstaking years, to carve Yalis, though the cunning of the hand that enabled his father to insert a thin chisel between the slightly gaping jaws and fashion five perfectly spherical free-rolling balls from the stone within, eluded him—he showed me an almost finished Yali in miniature that he had carved himself, and except for the boluses it was an exact replica of the grandparental beast. There is nothing improbable in the hereditary transmission of fidelity of forms and figures through several generations of carvers.

In old literature we find better evidence. Of course the traditional lion occurs as freely in Tamilian literature and folklore as it does in Tamilian stone, but if one is familiar with the conceits and formalisms of the Sangam period, it is not hard to distinguish the realistic passages from the purely formal ones—and there are many such realistic passages in the literature of that period, some seventeen centuries old.

There are references to elephants in plenty, to tigers (one poet comments on the great strength of the tiger, that can kill a wild boar and carry away a bullock), panthers, wild pig, deer, antelope and all sorts of other creatures that lived, and still live, in the South. It is significant that there is no mention of beasts like the rhinoceros and nilgai that do not range so far south. There are many terse, vivid word-pictures that prove the acute personal observation of the poets—Paranar writes of the round-footed jungle cat waiting with hungry patience in the millet field in the evening, waiting for the village poultry to stray near; Nakkeerar has a line about monkeys huddled together and shivering in the cold and wet. Nowhere in all this wealth of naturalistic poetry can I find a reference to a lion.

Nor can I find it in the old prescriptive rules (based solidly on facts) that tell poets of the plants and animals peculiar to each of the five types of country. Nor even in the semi-formal adulatory passages addressed to famous chieftains, such as the one that tells of how the arrow of Val-vil Ori (literally, Ori of the Mighty Bow), the celebrated archer, pierced an elephant, then a tiger, then a boar, then a deer, and finally a monitor, slaying them all—such was the power of his arm!

It is futile trying to explain a conviction based on long familiarity with a language—it is like trying to set down logically something known empirically. Take it from me that the men who would most certainly have mentioned, and described, the lion, had it been known in the South two thousand years ago or afterwards, have not done so, and that this is sufficient proof that the lion was unknown in that part of India within this period.

1956

6

Asoka's Lions

T O ONE FAMILIAR with India's fauna the choice of the Sarnath lion capital as the national emblem must seem somewhat remote. Even to one familiar with Indian art and the Mauryan period this must seem far-fetched. Only those who know the political history of the country during the last decade can find justification for the choice.

Let us consider the aesthetics of the matter before its natural aptness, for there is no doubt that lions roamed the country in the past and that they have had an honoured place as symbols of kingly estate in our traditions. The lions of Asoka, however, do not belong to our traditions—they are foreign in build and feature.

One of the early critics of our art, E.B. Havell, thinks it likely that Persian craftsmen fashioned this capital. Another early writer, Vincent Smith, thinks it shows Hellenistic influences, prevalent in Asia Minor in Asoka's time. He says: 'The art of Asokan monoliths is essentially foreign with nothing Indian except details . . . I think that the brilliant work typified by the Sarnath capital may have been designed in its main lines by foreign artists acting under the orders of Asoka, while the details were left to the taste of the Indian workmen.'

Smith is positive in contradicting Marshall's view that Asiatic Greeks fashioned the Sarnath capital. Earlier in his book he says, of this capital: 'It would be difficult to find in any country an example of ancient animal sculpture superior or even equal to this beautiful work of art, which successfully combines realistic modelling with ideal dignity, and is finished in every detail with perfect accuracy. The bas-reliefs on the abacus are as good in their way as the noble lions in the round. The design, while obviously reminiscent of Assyrian and Persian prototypes, is modified by Indian sentiment, the bas-reliefs being purely Indian. Mr Marshall's conjecture that the composition may be the work of an Asiatic Greek is not supported by the style of the relief figures. The ability of an Asiatic Greek to represent Indian animals so well may be doubted.'

I must say I prefer Smith later to Smith earlier. The bull and the horse shown in relief on the abacus are typically Indian in style, but that does not establish the nationality of the lions (incidentally, Smith is out in his natural history in considering the animals shown alien to the habitat of an Asiatic Greek). The influence of foreign art and craftsmanship is manifest in the design and superfinish of this capital, and it is now accepted that while much of the Mauryan sculpture was indigenous, Asoka's edict pillars are in Persipolitan style.

I have cited the opinion of these experts only to say that we need not depend upon them. The lion is by no means an unfamiliar animal in Indian stone, and the lions of the South may be safely taken as typical of the Indian conception of the animal. That they are far removed in time or place from Sarnath and the Mauryan period does not detract from their value as types—there is sufficient fundamental affinity between South Indian and the undoubtedly indigenous Mauryan figures.

Strangely enough, none of the critics mentioned seems to have compared Asoka's lion with other lions in our art. Such a comparison reveals striking differences at once. The Sarnath lions are slimmer in build and have noticeably thin necks in a front view; their heads are smaller and the tongue-of-flame patterning of their manes is peculiar and foreign—the manes of typically Indian lions and Yalis are rendered in formal, circular curls, or else in parallel wavy lines. The large eyes with natural similitude, the unfurrowed forehead and nose, the pronounced down-face and the squarely angled lips are all foreign. The feet are even more revealing than the heads—in their taut modelling of muscle and tendon, and specific, detailed depiction of each toe and nail, they are very Greek. The innermost toe, raised laterally, somewhat in the manner of a dog's dew-claw, is a feature of the feet of the greater cats—this detail is displayed in the feet of the Sarnath lions, though the half-sheathed nails are semi-heroic and not natural. Show me a single undoubted Indian lion whose toes are anything like equally realistic, and I accept defeat.

As said already, lions were common in India, especially in North India, within historic recollection, and no doubt they were there in Asoka's time. There is no need to labour the point that the Indian lion, extinct except for a few carefully preserved families in the Gir Forests of Saurashtra, is an inopportune symbol for a new hopeful democracy with great aspirations.

Have we no animal more representative of the nation, more nobly rendered in our stone, that could have taken the place of Asoka's lions, which are not Indian in their art and which are third-rate as lions?

I may be hurting national feeling and outraging accepted aesthetic values in my condemnation of Asoka's lions as lions. I can only say that I intend no sort of affront, that I hope I am as patriotic as my readers, and that to accept the *realistic*, maned Cheetah-like lions of the Sarnath capital as just depictions of the noble beast requires more sophistry than I can command. A glossy perfection of finish and meticulous detail do not constitute art.

The lion is a magnificent animal. Its looks and proportions are so superb that art can do little to improve upon nature in adopting it as the symbol of kingly might and majesty. Many countries have exploited the leonine figure effectively in designing their symbols of State—but not the carvers responsible for the highly polished, svelte lions of Sarnath; they just had no appreciation at all of the beast.

Apart from all this, the lion, indicative of royal, totalitarian power in our traditions as in those of other countries, would seem an inapposite emblem for a democracy whose pride is its freedom for all.

Looking for other animals in our art that might have been nationally honoured, one must, reluctantly, give up the tiger, so inseparably associated with India in big-game lore. We do have depictions of tigers but none that is sufficiently masterly as a tiger for heraldic adaptation. Some of them might well be leopards—they are unmarked, and their size in comparison to the human figure in the relief is noncommittal, relative size being in no way indicative in a depiction where the human victor is shown, heroically, larger than the beast. Moreover it is possible that when the national government had to choose its animal emblem, some one of the Native States then independently sovereign had a tiger on its coat of arms.

Boars, horses, cattle and blackbuck (the last shabbily treated on the ten-rupee note, and frequently miscalled 'deer' by our art critics) are the other animals that commonly figure in our art, but perhaps they were not considered noble enough in looks.

How about the lordly Indian elephant, the unquestioned king of our forests, entirely Indian, anciently associated with power in our country, the most brilliantly rendered of all beasts in our art, magnificent in bulk, might and willingness to serve, august, lovable and universally beloved? It is impossible to think of an animal more representative of India or one with more imposing looks. What kept the elephant back, very likely, was the same political reason, that it figured already in the coats of arms of certain States. Is it now too late to take a broader view of its claims to represent the nation?

1953

7

A Bird Emblem for India

THE CHOICE OF a 'National Bird' for India was referred to the Indian Board for Wildlife which, at its recent session at Ootacamund, tentatively elected the peacock. My newspaper, reporting this, says 'the consensus of the board was in favour of the peacock, although some members had suggested the Indian Bustard, Brahminy Kite and the hansa (swan) for the honour. A final decision would be taken at the next meeting of the Board.' Earlier news reports said that the Sarus Crane had also been named.

I think the choice of the peacock, tentatively and probably finally, is almost inevitable. However, since the choice of a bird emblem for the nation is something that is of interest to every Indian, and since anyway the ultimate recommendation of the IBWL will need Governmental sanction before the bird is proclaimed a national emblem, it is quite in order to discuss the question here.

Whatever the comparative claims of these and other birds for the honour, it is highly desirable to do a spell of clear thinking first, and decide the criteria that should guide the choice, before going on to consider the actual birds themselves. Naturally the bird chosen must be an Indian bird, but should it be exclusively Indian? I think it need not—if it is typically Indian, that should do. This point is best made by analogy.

Asked to name an Indian beast for the same honour, I would unhesitatingly pick the Indian Elephant, though it is also to be found in many other south-eastern countries of Asia. (I must confess, in an aside, that the exclusively Indian Blackbuck seems almost as good a choice to me, but let us not bother about it—it weakens my argument!) That the elephant is very much at home in our forests, that it is to be found all over India, and that it has been associated with our life and culture from time immemorial are considerations that far outweigh the fact that it is also to be found in Burma, Ceylon, and other neighbouring countries. An exclusively Indian beast, like the Nilgiri Black Langur or Nilgiri Tahr, would be a bad choice, because it is restricted in its distribution, and is neither familiar to our people nor intimately associated with our life and legends. Actually, it is the highly Greek lions of Asoka's capital that have achieved emblematic status among our wild beasts; never did the lion enjoy an all-India range, and today it is even more restricted in its distribution, being more or less confined to the Gir sanctuary. But all the same its choice as a national emblem can be defended on the grounds that it was not uncommon in the north and west of India 150 years ago, that the Asiatic strain of the lion, *Panthera leo persica*, is now to be found only in India, and that in our country (as in some others) it has been the symbol of sovereignty from ancient times, and that in legend and sculpture it is a beast familiar to everyone, even in South India.

That is why I say that, provided it has a wide range in our country, and is familiar and representative, and well known to the legend and culture of the country, the bird chosen need not be exclusively Indian. Having the power of flight, it is only natural that many birds should enjoy a wider distribution than beasts, and therefore insistence on exclusive restriction to a country as a condition precedent to choice as national emblem would be unrealistic.

There are two other important criteria that have nothing to do with natural history. First, any bird chosen as a national emblem should lend itself to formal depiction, and when I say formal, I use the word not to connote orthodox conformity to some accepted standard, but as something concerning physical form—an emblematic bird's contours should lend themselves to abstracted or stylized depiction, its shape should convey its entity unmistakably, even in formalized representation. It follows that a bird whose identity is dependent mainly on the patterns of its plumage would not suit, unless its plumage can be simply and effectively stylized. All that sounds like a lot of words, but here is an acid test. If a bird can be depicted in a spontaneous one-line drawing (in a quick drawing where the pen never leaves the paper) it passes the test.

Second, the chosen bird must not be susceptible of confusion with the bird emblem of some other country.

Judged by these considerations the Great Indian Bustard is eliminated straightaway. It is not a familiar fowl, and is not distributed sufficiently widely, and today it is rarer than ever before, having been snared and shot almost to the point of extinction. Remember the story of the Baboo examinee who, asked to annotate the lines from Keats's ode,

Thou wert not born for death, immortal bird,
No hungry generations tread thee down

answered, succinctly, that the poet felt assured of its survival because 'the nightingale is not an edible bird'? Well, the bustard, in addition to being one of our largest birds (the heaviest, anyway), is also highly edible, and is much sought after by our epicures. It is practically on its last legs today. And I defy even Picasso (a master of the complicated one-line drawing) to draw a recognizable Great Indian Bustard without lifting nib from paper. Altogether an unhappy choice it would be as the bird emblem of our country.

The Sarus Crane, too, is not a bird familiar all over India, having a decidedly northern and localized distribution. True that where it occurs it is a well-known bird, and that its looks are distinctive and capable of being stylized, but still it is not a good choice. Once I wrote a note in these columns proving, or attempting to prove, that the 'Crowncha Pakshi' of our Puranas was none other than the Sarus, but though it is no stranger to our legends (as the bustard is) it is a bird which the majority of Indians do not know, either in the field or in legend, and I think that disposes of the Sarus's claims.

The swan is quickly disposed of. It is not an Indian bird—it is simply not to be found breeding anywhere in India (the test of a bird's indigene), and even as a straggler is not known in 90 per cent of India. Surely we cannot have a bird that does not belong to the country as a national emblem even if it is known to our art and poetry.

The Brahminy Kite (the 'garuda'—though 'garuda' applies to other birds in places, it is the Brahminy Kite that is generally meant by the term) is, I think, eliminated on a criterion so far not invoked. Yes, it is Indian—familiar, widely distributed and easily formalized, but though in the flesh the two birds are so dissimilar in size and looks, in an emblem the Brahminy Kite is bound to look remarkably like the emblematic Bald Eagle of America, in spite of the latter's white tail.

The peacock remains among the birds listed, and it is difficult to think of a bird that more admirably satisfies all the tests. Everyone knows it and has seen it, it is to be found all over India, and it is intimately and anciently associated with our religious and countryside legends and culture. And it is so distinctive in its arresting beauty that it lends itself to unmistakable formalized depiction—in fact it has been so depicted both in our folk and classical art. I shall be greatly surprised, why, I shall be astonished if any other bird is ultimately preferred for the honour.

However, if for some reason that I can't think of now another bird is preferred, I would press the claims of the Common Mynah. Though sacred to no god, it is well known to our legends and folksongs, and is one of the most familiar birds in the country, being specially common in and around human settlements, both in the plains and lower hills. And in spite of being so common few birds have a richer plumage as Eha pointed out long ago. The contrast of the cadmium yellow of its legs and beak and facial patches with the Vandyke brown of its plumage and the black of its head and the blaze of white on each wing that lends its flight such vividness, are not only distinguished but also contrasts that can be most effectively formalized in an emblem. It has an additional claim. It is frequently caged and trained to talk and in our folksongs it is often entrusted with the delivery of messages to loved ones far away, a kind of ambassadorial responsibility that is surely an asset in any National Bird.

1961

E

Eland: Large heavily built ox-like African antelope, ... with spirally twisted horns.
—The Reader's Digest Great Encyclopaedic Dictionary.
(Actually, the largest of all antelopes: the second largest being our own Nilgai.)

ELAND

The eland is an antelope
though looking like a cow,
its horns are twisted like a rope
and serve, beyond all doubt, to show
it is an antelope, with not
of bovine blood a jot.

If trekking through the veldt you see
an eland browsing at a bough,
subject its horns to scrutiny
lest it turn out a cow.

For eland-hunters have been known
After a long and patient stalk,
long hours spent half-erect, half-prone,
in creeping through the predawn dark
through bush and grass and thorny bough
to shoot — the common cow!

Nature's Marvels

8

Tiger Talk

TIGERS ROAR. They also moan, and both sounds have been much described in Indian shikar literature. The short, coughing roar of a charging tiger, the terrifying accompaniment to an all-out attack, and the growls, snarls, hissing and spitting indulged in during intraspecific communications of threat or hostile intent, have all been carefully observed and recorded: these sounds may also be used to express anger and hostile intent towards other animals and men intruding on a tiger, or encountered accidentally by a tiger. The 'whoof!' of surprise has been mentioned by a few, but not in specific detail.

The rarely sounded 'pook', closely resembling the bell of a sambar, has provoked much inconclusive speculation and argument, and tigrine yowls and miaows have also been reported. The most complete collation of the voice of the tiger that I know of along with closely studied personal descriptions of tiger vocalizations heard at Kanha and elsewhere, is to be found in G.B. Schaller's 'The Deer and the Tiger'. In this he also writes of an aspirated and somewhat equine sound used by tigers approaching one another in a friendly way.

Other tigrine sounds are only variations of these calls. It is not settled whether or not tigers, at some stage of their life or other, can purr—I have no personal knowledge of this question.

But in May last I realized that tigers or at least some of them, are also given to other and stranger sounds. I was staying at the Anantpura rest-house of the Ranthambhore Tiger Reserve, and tired with the day's work and with the need to conserve the kerosene lanterns went to bed early, about 9 o'clock. My cot was in an open verandah, and by 7 p.m. the afterglow would turn to an inky blackness and suddenly it was no longer scorching—the nights were delightfully cool. I would be wide awake by half past three in the morning, and sit listening to the dark forest till dawn, when my pot of tea was due.

One morning, as I sat in the dark, I heard a distant musical sound, a vibrant and somewhat nasal long-drawn twang, like a taut length of steel wire sharply plucked. It was repeated several times, and then followed by the unmistakable 'aaoonh!' of a tiger. Evidently the tiger was in a gorge half a kilometre away, and both the moan and the plucked-wire call were repeated several times: they grew faint as the tiger moved off, and then there were no further sounds till the dawn chorus of the birds.

With the first light, I was at the gorge. There, in the moist earth around a tiny pool were the fresh pug-marks of an adult male tiger—there were less clear but still fresh prints in the dry soil around, and with the help of a local tracker I followed them till they finally petered out in an ascending, stony nullah up which he had gone. For days in succession, this experience was repeated.

The nullah, I found the hard way, went right up the hill and intersected a hilltop road at a point 11 km from our rest-house. I decided to take that road home in the evenings, and to stop at the point where the road crossed the nullah—the nullah went on down the other side of the hill.

Nothing happened for a few days, and then, one evening when we had been delayed and reached the junction of the nullah and the road only after sunset, we saw the tiger on the road right ahead of the jeep. He heard us, and without turning his head accelerated his pace to a trot, and then disappeared into a patch of dry tall grass flanking the road. We too halted, and moved on only when the crunch-crunch of grass being trodden down told us of the tiger's exit from that patch, and there, right out in the open, was the tiger—dark, indistinct and magnificent in the failing light. Then somehow our jeep slid into a ditch and came to a crashing halt, with the front wheels in the ditch and the rear wheels on the road, at a cant of 30 degrees. The tiger gave a bound forward, and vanished into the nullah down the hill.

There was another rest-house about 4 km away, and I sent the man with us to it to get help, while the driver and I stayed perched uncomfortably on our seats. In a few minutes it was pitch dark and the shrill alarms of chital and the explosive 'dhank!' of sambar proclaimed the passage of

the great cat down the nullah. Then all at once there was total silence,
unrelieved even by the rustling of grass or insect sounds, and it was cold.

We speculated on the chances of our getting a rescue jeep, and then
slumped into silence. After a while, I heard some animal breathing softly
as it moved around, and a low moan informed us of its identity. 'Tiger',
whispered the driver to me, and jerked himself bold upright on his slanting seat. For fully half an hour that tiger circled us, never approaching
close but never too far away either, coming out with musical, vibrant
twangings and low moans, obviously intrigued by our presence there. I
noticed that his twangings were now pitched much lower than when I
heard him from far away.

Suddenly, there was silence again. Risking my reputation as a naturalist, I informed the apprehensive driver that the rescue jeep was on its
way, and that was why the tiger, with his infinitely sharper hearing, had
moved off. In another minute we too could hear the purr of the approaching jeep, and then see the road behind us being lit up by its headlights.

1980

9

When Elephants Die

LAST WEEK, I had a letter from an Argentinian palaeontologist. Professor Ruben Martinez of the National University of Patagonia, heading a research team, had unearthed the fossilized remains of a new kind of dinosaur, and it was computed that millions of years ago, when it was alive, it must have stood three metres tall and seven metres long, larger than an elephant. What intrigued the professor and made him write to me was this: it was usual for dinosaurs to die, and their remains to be found, lying on a side, whereas this specimen was found lying flat on its belly, 'in the prone decubitus position' as he put it. He had heard of me as a naturalist specializing in the larger mammals of India, in particular elephants, and wanted to know if I could give him instances from personal knowledge of heavy animals like rhinos and elephants that had died in the prone decubitus position.

I wrote back promptly and at length to Professor Martinez, but could not be of much use to him. I have never seen the carcass of a rhinoceros that had died a natural death. One that had been shot by poachers in the Kaziranga area, had been subject to some handling in the course of the removal of its tusk, but had fallen flat on its stomach. I have no hearsay knowledge even of the natural death of rhinos, but have heard romantic legends about the way elephants die, of illness or old age. It is about this that I am writing.

In 1960, in a narrow, tortuous limb of the many-armed Periyar lake of Kerala, I came upon the remains of a big tusker that had died a natural death. But it had died almost a year previously, and all that remained was its disjointed skeleton scattered by scavenging animals. However, the skull lying on a bank still had the tusks, though these were mere stumps, much gnawed by porcupines and other bone eaters. Obviously, this tusker had not been shot by poachers.

Twice I have seen carcasses of bull elephants shot by men. The first was in the Nagarhole preserve of Karnataka, days after the animal had been killed, when its carcass was in an advanced stage of putrefaction, and could hardly be approached because of the stench. But it was necessary to take the officer in charge of the sanctuary close to the remains, to prove to him that it was a bull whose tusks had been extracted, and not a cow as he said it was. I proved my point all right, though both of us were violently sick in the course of the proof. That elephant had collapsed on its belly.

In 1980, it was unfortunately necessary to shoot a big, massive, light-coloured tusker in the Corbett Tiger Reserve, because it had taken to killing men, and I witnessed its execution. In fact, I identified the animal to the execution squad. It fell to a regular salvo of rifle bullets, and fell flat on its stomach, with its limbs folded beneath it.

To return to beliefs about the natural death of elephants, readers may have heard the legend of their graveyard. Dying elephants, it is said, take themselves to a particular remote location and expire there. The remains of many are to be found in such graveyards. Over decades of diligent inquiry, I have not been able to find anyone who has actually seen such a cemetery, and the legend has no basis in elephantine behaviour. Elephants range far in their feeding, trekking along routes well known to them from one forest to another, covering several hundred kilometres in the course of a year. How then would different members of different herds, when dying at long intervals in the course of their peregrinations, go to the same spot to die in? Even if someone claims that he has actually found the remains of several elephants in one place, that only goes to show that a herd, killed by some natural catastrophe (what the impious term an Act of God) must have perished there. Further, hypothetically conceding that several such graveyards may be there along the immemorial trek routes of elephants, in the course of the past four decades of the ramified and intensive penetration of all elephant forests by human enterprise, all or most of these graveyards must have been exposed—as not one has been.

But if the specification of a particular location for death is given up, and it is said that, when they feel their vitality ebbing, the great beasts betake themselves not to any one spot but to a particular kind of place and die there, the theory is acceptable, even likely, though still to be established by actual observation. Tribals in elephant forests far apart and belonging to different tribes share the belief that, when its end is near, an elephant is liable to go quietly away by itself to some secluded pool or creek, to enter the water and die. This seems not unlikely to me. An elephant's limbs have to support the great mass of its body, three or four tons, and enfeebled by its failing vital resources it may be hard put to carry this weight. Being much given to baths in forest pools and to swimming across rivers and lakes, it knows by experience (and not by intelligence) that water will instantly lift the weight of its body off its limbs.

My illustration* shows a truly magnificent old tusker of the authentic 'koomeriah' type, deep in the barrel and stout in the limb, with its back sloping in a straight line from its proudly carried head down to its tail, that I saw half-a-dozen years ago in the Bandipur Tiger Reserve. An old Kuruba tracker of the reserve, recently retired from service, was with me and, if he is still there, Mara can bear me out over this. We were on foot and right across an expansive lake we saw this tusker, and watched him. His behaviour puzzled me. He was walking deliberately along the farther bank, making steadily for some destination but at a slow pace, halting every now and again but not to feed or drink, only to stand at ease, not even flapping his ears.

Mara said he was going to some pool he knew, maybe far away, to die in. Asked how he could be sure of this, he replied that he could not tell me how, logically, but knew it was true all right. When he was a boy, his uncle (who had a great store of knowledge and who had taught him all he knew about wild animals) had once pointed out just such a bull to him and told him it was seeking a quiet piece of water to die in. Well, they had followed that old tusker the entire day, keeping their distance, and in the evening he had found the pool he had been headed for, entered it, and with obvious relief closed his eyes and died in it. Mara and I could not follow the tusker we saw for long, we gave it up after an hour, because both of us had urgent business at the camps, but certainly the way that great bull behaved was strange and totally unlike normal behaviour.

1990

*Not reproduced here.

10

Python at Home

THE WRETCHED THING about being a naturalist is that one is so handicapped in one's expression. A big-game hunter now; or an explorer, can afford a sense of style. He doesn't have to use pompous-sounding words like 'dorsal' for 'back' or 'dormant' for 'resting'—and when he has a photograph to illustrate his experience, he can choose his mode of retailing it.

And it is not as if I do not know that mode, after having been an avid reader of shikar literature from boyhood. This is how I should tell you about my python.

'There was an ineffable assurance of peace in that sylvan retreat. The morning sun, filtered by the green canopy high overhead, illumined the scene with a soft, clear effulgence. The young grass underfoot cushioned each footfall like a carpet, and was as innocent of guile, the still vistas, flanked by the great gnarled boles, seemed inviolable in their ancient calm, and somewhere at hand an iora was calling flutily to its mate.

'But that sixth sense that we, who wander through the jungles, learn to know and trust, warned me just in time. Suddenly I felt a prickling sensation along the nape of my neck, as a feeling of imminent danger overwhelmed me. I looked up hastily, and saw the python lying in wait on the outflung limb of a giant mango, right above my head. Still as a log it lay, the thick, pale-bellied body stretched along the branch, the very tip of its tail curled securely around the trunk to lend anchorage to the monster's weight when it threw itself in coils on the unsuspecting victim passing beneath. I stopped dead, and frustrated in its hopes the reptile lay unmoving on its branch glaring balefully at me from its cold-blooded, evil eyes. Quickly snatching up my trusty old 105 mm . . .'

On second thoughts, I withdraw my regrets. Just as well that I am a naturalist and no shikari. However, I did have an adventure of sorts with this python, and the man who owned it and brought it to me. It was no monster being only about 10-foot long, but the man assured me that it was quite grown-up; he himself had had it only for two years, but by certain tokens, known only to an expert of his maturity, he estimated that python was as old as he was—and he looked a hard-lived 50. What he said could be true, for in many reptiles growth is not mainly dependent on age, as it is in the higher animals, but mainly on food supply—if systematically starved a reptile may remain dwarfed like a Japanese pot-tree. However when I questioned that man about his pet his replies were so evasive and patently false that I felt sure the snake was only 10-foot-old, by the normal growth-rate of pythons.

That man knew a thing or two about snakes, though. The trouble with him was not that he was a charlatan, but that he looked so obviously a character, and felt he had to live up to his looks. Having concluded a contract with me to allow me to photograph his python, he felt he could not part with any piece of information about the snake, however trivial, without further fee—and for my part, having agreed to an exorbitant photographing fee, I was unwilling to part with so much as one extra paisa.

He wanted to know if my weak flash radiated heat, along with light, and would allow me to use it on his python only after I had demonstrated its lack of warmth to him. That showed a real understanding of snakes, which are quickly killed by an over-all thermal shock. When I had taken two of the four pictures allowed me by the bargain, I wanted the snake up a tree—and my mango was conveniently handy.

The python had cast its skin recently—its skin was smooth and glistening, but about the head and neck bits of the old skin still clung to it. The man said that in its tender, new skin the snake would not climb a tree of its own accord, and that it would have to be hoisted bodily on to the lowest branch. This might involve some risk of abrasion or other injury, and in the circumstances he felt the compensation of a tattered old shirt, that I wanted no longer, was indicated, in addition to the stipulated cash. I did not like the prospective look he gave my shirt, which was only frayed at the collar. Meanwhile the snake resolved the argument by flowing up the tree.

I have seen many other snakes climb trees, easily and speedily, but none with the sheer fluency of that thick-bodied python. It just flowed

up the trunk, unhurried but swift, and ignoring the lowest branch, elected
to stretch itself along a higher, horizontal limb of the tree. By the time
I had taken my quick snaps, its furious owner was at the tree, and climbing it after his property. Thereupon the python swayed its head, and the
front third of its body, outwards and upwards, established contact with
a bough higher up, and swarmed on to it.

No doubt the man could have climbed on to that branch, too, but he
was too canny to do so. He saw no point in panicking his snake which
might result in its precipitating itself on to the kitchen roof and in a frantic chase over the tiles, only providing me with more pictures—especially
in view of my determination to hang on to my shirt. So he asked for a
stout bamboo pole, and padding one end of it with his turban, pushed
steadily with the padded end against the side of the snake, a yard above
its tail: he threw this length of the python off the bough, and then it could
not go forward but had to turn back—evidently the forward urge begins
at the tail end, or else it has to be sustained by stability at that end; with
this basic stability upset, the snake had to seek a fresh hold, lower down.
By repeating the manoeuvre, he had the snake climbing down the tree,
and in another minute it was round his neck in a mottled garland once
more.

A python can swim with the same effortlessness with which it climbs—
only those who have seen this great, heavy snake in a pool or river can
know how graceful and quick it can be in the water. We have many swift-
er snakes in our country and many that are much more dangerous, but
few that are as impressive or beautifully marked as the forest-loving
python.

I don't think the python is dangerous to man. That it can attack and
overcome prey the size of langurs, pig and deer is a fact—there are reliable
records of big pythons having seized and swallowed such large creatures.
There have also been rare, quite rare, instances of a python attacking a
child—the circumstances, in such instances, were probably exceptional
in the extreme. In areas where pythons occur, and have occurred for generations, I have not been able to elicit a single record of a man having had
anything worse than a bad fright from a chance-met python. Of course,
in weighing such evidence, one has to take note of the fact that men stum-
bling on a python in a jungle, usually run away—though some tribes,

which fancy python meat, hunt the snake. Anyway, pythons do not, without provocation, attack or chase men trespassing on their territory as some poisonous snakes do. It is said that they strike out in self-defence with the heavy, blunt tip of their noses, with their body weight behind the lunging movement: such a blow can knock out a grown man.

Once I was asked to comment on a newspaper report of a python that had entwined itself around a young elephant: the report said that after a titanic struggle, the snake had succeeded in asphyxiating the elephant— and did it go on to add that, spent by the effort the python, in turn, gave up the ghost? I do not remember if it did, but I do recall that wisely I refused to comment on the report. The point of the story does not concern the crushing or swallowing capacity of the python, but only the swallowing capacity of the reader.

1958

11

The Disappearing Cheetah

IT IS YEARS since anyone came across a Cheetah (or Hunting Leopard) in our jungles, and I am afraid it must now be presumed that within the past 15 years or so it has become extinct in India. Some time in the forties, a nobleman shot three young cheetahs in the course of a nocturnal motor drive, and published the photograph of his victims to prove their identities—and naturally got no kudos for what he had done. Later, another nocturnal motorist reported having seen a cheetah in the glare of his headlights, somewhere near Chittoor, I think. The last claim of a sight-record that I heard was at Muggumpi, on the Hyderabad side of the Tungabhadra area, in July 1951.

Here, some local shikaris said that one of them had seen a Sivungi (the cheetah, which is the Sivingi in Tamil, is the Sivungi in Kannada). When I questioned him, the man who was said to have seen the beast said that it was a fact that he had seen a Sivungi. Asked to describe it, he said it was a Sivungi. Asked if he was sure that it was not a leopard he had seen, he was quite sure it was not. Questioned about the specific differences between a leopard and the creature he had seen, he said he knew it was a Sivungi and no leopard because, didn't I see, it looked like a Sivungi. He had seen it from over a 150 yards away, squatting on its haunches like a dog (or a leopard!) in the shade of a bush. I explained the difference between the solid spots of a cheetah and the rosettes of a leopard and asked if he had observed this difference, and he said yes, that was it, now that he had been reminded of it, he could distinctly remember that the creature he had seen had solid spots and not rosettes—I thought that conclusively established the uselessness of his report, because he who can tell the solid spots of a cheetah squatting in the shade of a bush from the rosettes of a leopard, from a 150 yards away, is not gifted with keen sight, but only with a keen imagination—both animals look a warm, murky, indistinct grey from that distance.

However, I persisted with my cross-examination, for the area was one of the likeliest to hold cheetahs if they were still to be found in India, but only succeeded in provoking that shikari into defiant and positive statements. He had not seen the animal in movement, but twice, or may be it was four times, he had seen a Sivungi squatting in the shade of a bush, which, he assured me, was its favourite method of spending its time. So I dismissed the man's claim from my mind—till last year.

Last year I met someone who had travelled miles to a place not far from Muggumpi to see the imported African cheetahs of a Maharaja run down blackbuck. Never having witnessed the sport and spectacle, I asked for a detailed account of the hunt, and got it. Following the traditional mode, the hooded cheetahs had been taken in a cart (or perhaps it was a jeep—I cannot recall this detail) to near where a herd of buck was grazing, then unhooded and released. Thereupon the cheetahs promptly made for the nearest bush, and sat in its shade. Egged on by their handlers to chase the fleeing quarry, they had retreated to a more sheltered bush, under which they sat solidly on. Well, well!

The cheetah is the fastest animal on earth for the first furlong or two—it is the only hunter that can give blackbuck a start of some 50 yards, and overhaul them within two furlongs. It has the ability of the cat family (to which it belongs, in spite of its claws being only partially retractile, and its greyhound-like build, and its classification apart from the true cats) to reach top speed almost at once from a crouching start. This, and the way it takes advantage of every bush and dip in the ground to get as close as it can to the grazing herd before launching its headlong attack, no doubt help substantially in the effectiveness of its hunting, but though blackbuck take some time to reach their best speed (the first few bounds are rather high, even when they do not indulge in their characteristic 'high jinks' but scatter at once in panic flight), no other animal can overtake them as the cheetah does—greyhounds are left far behind by the buck. Many estimates of the cheetah's speed have been made, some with stop-watches, timing the animal over a known distance, and when going all out its speed is over 70 m.p.h.

If it does not catch up with its quarry within a quarter of a mile or so, it gives up the chase, for it does not have the buck's capacity for sustained speed over long distances. But of course, blackbuck were not (the past tense, unfortunately, is necessary) the only prey of the cheetah here—chinkara, hares, and the other small animals of the hill-dotted scrub-jungles it liked, all helped to keep it going. I believe I am correct in saying that no wild cheetah has ever been known to attack a man, but occasionally it took a goat from a nearby village.

Blackbuck hunting with cheetahs was a sport much in vogue in the old days. Some of the Moghul emperors maintained regular armies of cheetahs for the purpose, some hundreds of them, and the pastime was popular even with the lesser kings and chieftains. Some of these hunting leopards were imported from Asia north of India, and some perhaps even from Africa, but the majority were indigenous—the Deccan was the stronghold of cheetahs in India for centuries. And although the cheetah was known elsewhere in Asia, and in Africa (where it is still to be found), it was here, in India, that the art of catching and training the animal for the sport was developed.

Only fully adult animals, already experienced in running down fleet-footed prey, were caught for training—as in falconry, it was held that only a hunter that had learnt its hunting skills in the hard school of nature would be fitted for the sport. The animals were snared and netted, and then tamed by a curious process of attrition, not dissimilar to modern methods of treating prisoners of war. The captive was securely tied up, and given no food or peace; shrill-voiced men and women sat around it in relays, scolding it continually, night and day, till it gave in and its resistance was broken down by sheer puzzlement and exhaustion. Then its handler would feed it and make much of it, and very soon it was quite tame and obedient. It was unnecessary to teach it to run down buck, for that it already knew to do, but naturally a measure of obedience to the keeper's call was highly desirable in a pet whose speed, when liberated, was superior to the buck's!

Since there is no real difference between the African and Indian cheetah, and since the animal is still to be found in Africa, people have suggested the revival of the cheetah, the so-recently lost pride of our fauna, by reintroduction of imported stock into suitable areas. But where are the suitable areas? Till we have established a sanctuary for the animals of the plains sufficiently spacious and sufficiently stocked with the fauna anciently native to it, and, as far as possible, free of exotic plants, I do not think the trouble and expense of getting a few cheetahs from Africa for liberation into an Indian sanctuary is justified—such an experiment, without such an established territory, can only fail. I have not seen any sanctuary or national park in India meant exclusively for the animals of the open country, and which is wide enough to hold a pair or two of cheetahs—nor have I heard of it. Perhaps Madras State, which has in recent years done such excellent work in the cause of our wildlife, can take the lead in this.

1960

12

An Afternoon Idyll

R ETURNING HOME ON the evening of the third day, I was full of black thoughts. The first day, the all-important cable release of my most valued camera had been broken to pieces—I had already been assured that this release (without which the camera would not function) was not available anywhere in India, and could not be imported. The second day a roll-film holder, containing eight painstakingly obtained records of gaur indulging in their midday siesta, had gone phut. And the third day the mahout had steered us straight into seven-foot-high grass; asked to get us out of that tall grass, where no photography was possible even in the unlikely event of an animal being seen, he had done so promptly and taken us into a sea of 12-foot high grass. Apparently, the man had lost his bearings.

When we got down from the pad, I remembered to offer Vikram, the lusty young tusker that had transported us through that ocean of grass, the customary bananas. Prompted by a belated wish to please me, the mahout asked his charge to salute me, which the greedy beast did readily. As we were walking towards the camp, my wife called my attention to the remarkable behaviour of our late ship.

There was a lush growth of grass atop the embankment by which the elephant stood, and the mahout was busy attending to some ropes. Left to himself, Vikram was going through a curious ritual. He would fling up his trunk in a faultless salute, then, by a deft lateral shift of the upflung tip, coil it around the young grass and tear up a bunch, which he would convey swiftly and furtively to his mouth; again he would salute the air, and again grab a mouthful of tender grass. Apparently he had been taught to salute with toothsome inducements, and in some vague elephantine manner associated the gesture with legitimized food. It was the most risibly cynical interpretation of Grace before Meal I had ever come across, and it amused me so much I clean forgot my failures!

However, I decided to take complete charge next day. I could not say I had contributed nothing to my poor luck so far, but others had contributed much more. Twice we had seen a herd of gaur on approachable terrain, and both times the beasts had been alarmed and then stampeded by the insistence of the mahout on the wrong tactics. I am a man who is content with doing his own bungling, and need no outside help. Assured by a morning reconnaissance, that a herd was resting in a jungle nearby, I arranged to have entire charge of operations.

This is not a photographic note, but I should explain that already I had some passably good pictures of gaur, and wished to get to within 20 yards of a dark, fully adult specimen, standing more or less in the open, to secure the kind of intimate photographs I wanted. At Mudumalai, where I was, the gaur are not accustomed to such a close approach, even when they are in a herd and the observers on elephant-back. They were in September, very much on the *qui vive*—I believe they are easier to approach in summer. My plan, which depended on my interpretation of their instinctive responses, was to let the beasts see us before they could smell us, and stop a fair distance away in sight of the herd, without panicking them unduly. Then, by a circuitous approach, which would certainly involve their scenting us on occasion, and taking care to keep within their sight all the time, I hoped, by slow advance on opportunity, to get close to them.

The herd was in the lantana, close to a field of comparatively short grass, when we sighted them at 3 o'clock. There were eight of them, five adult cows, three heifers, and no bull. We stopped some 60 yards away, and promptly our elephant began to feed.

They looked up at us, heads high, noses in the air, ears forward, ready to bolt. Apparently our immobility reassured them, but they moved deeper into the lantana, and kept looking back at us over the tops of the twigs. After ten minutes of this uneasy scrutiny, during which we took good care not to stare back at them, they seemed still undecided. Then, suddenly they lay down in the heavy cover.

We zigzagged in with frequent halts, ever so gradually, but even when we were quite near they would not get up. Knowing the futility of attempting against-the-light pictures of gaur lying down in dense bush-shade, I decided to withdraw, and then circle around the bushes into the field. Once we were in the field we could not see them, and they too lost sight of us, but we were exposed to their more acute and apprehensive senses of hearing and smell. After moving close in from this blind side, we circled back to see where they were. They were still in the lantana, lying down and placidly chewing the cud!

I will not tire you with the many approaches and withdrawals we made. Finally we had them where we wanted them, in the field, grazing more or less alongside our halted elephant, which was also sampling the grass. They were over 40 yards away, but were grazing towards us, so that all that we had to do was to wait for them to move closer. They seemed completely indifferent to our presence, but I am sure there was no conscious or deliberate evaluation of our harmlessness behind that indifference, it was just that gaur are sociable creatures and used to elephants in their forest haunts, and that our approach had been so very casual, gradual and seemingly haphazard that they were accepting us for the time being till some betraying sound or scent alarmed them.

The cloud-filtered sun lit up the field softly, but with wonderful clarity. Slowly the gaur grazed their way towards us, the great dorsal ridges clear of the grass-tops, heads low and hidden, seeking out and cropping the young shoots with unhurried relish, the short tails flicking busily from side to side. It was a scene charged with a serene pastoral beauty which, for many minutes, made me forget my mission. Then, with my camera held ready I waited, thinking of a bit of verse I had read as a boy:

> The cattle are grazing.
> Their heads never raising.
> There are forty feeding like one!

There were eight, not forty, here, but they were feeding like one all right, their heads never raising. I whistled sharply and instantly every head was up, broad ears switched forward, gazing up at me in mild surprise. I took a snapshot of the nearest cow (the largest in the herd), but realized at once that that picture, with the head thrown back and a mouthful of grass clamped between closed jaws, so that the stalks projected stiffly on either side like whiskers, could never have any naturalness or convey the idyllic charm of the setting though it might be morphologically sharp. However, by waiting and moving a little in or away, by 5 o'clock I had all the pictures I wanted, and thereafter we turned homeward, taking care not to alarm the grazing animals with too hurried a departure.

Financially, and in damage to equipment, this trip has been unfortunate, but long after I have recovered from such setbacks the memory of that afternoon will stay with me.

1958

13

Onti, or a Lone Champion

THERE WAS A regular wall of screw-pine, 10 feet high and grown in a thick tangle, bordering the shallow streamlet on either side, and as we approached a gap in it some heavy animal rose from the nullah and crashed its way through the farther wall of screw-pine. From the sound of its passage, we knew it was something really large and massive, and for a moment my mahout turned as near grey as his dark complexion would allow.

'Onti!' he whispered.

There was a singularly aggressive lone tusker in that area, whose movements we had to study each day in order to avoid a possible brush with him in the jungles, and that morning we had taken the usual precautions. 'Onti' in Kannada means 'singleton', i.e., a lone bull—and knowing the likely reactions of this notorious tusker to men on elephant-back, we had every reason to feel apprehensive, but a second later we could see for ourselves that it was no tusker that we had flushed from the cool retreat of that fenced-in watercourse. It was a gaunt old gaur bull, black as night and huge, with thick, blunt horns that swept out in a wide curve—the lack of fodder of dry March was reflected in the way his great ribs stood out on his sides.

He stood there, on the open ground beyond the nullah, nose high in the air, staring at us. I had our elephant stopped at once, and after a long, level look he walked casually away. Then he lowered his muzzle to the charred earth, black with the recent forest fires, and began to nibble at the tiny sprouts of grass, just coming up.

Knowing from experience just what that meant, I looked away and kept still. Suddenly he threw up his head and stared at us again, then moved a few steps to one side and again began to nibble at the young grass. Ten seconds later he would raise his head quickly and look at us again, and if, in the meanwhile, we shifted our stance ever so slightly, or stared back at him, he would bolt—and in hilly country, when a gaur decides to be elsewhere, an elephant has no chance of catching up with him.

After a while he gave up his desultory grazing, and turned to face us squarely. Then I had our mount moved slowly forward under his direct scrutiny, steering a zigzag course and halting at every third step. Such wind as was there was in our favour, which was due to no lucky accident.

Here I may go into a pet theory of mine. Since it concerns wild creatures, it is conditioned by many factors, the most important of which is that it has the best chances of success in places where the fauna has not been disturbed or harassed by men—and even in such places, success is never sure. I believe that it is possible, when on elephant-back, to get fairly close to true forest-loving animals (which habitually depend less on sight than on hearing and scent) by studiously keeping the wind in one's face, and making the approach only when the quarry is using its secondary sense, i.e., sight, and looking at one. A seemingly aimless approach, made very casually, is then possible, if one can prevail on the mahout and oneself never to look directly at the animal—when one is near enough, the wind does not matter, for the height of the elephant helps to carry the human scent above the head of the animal. Till one is really close, however, the wind must be studied, irrespective of obstacles in the path; one whiff of humanity, and the gaur that has been placidly watching the men on the elephant's back is away at a gallop—in Mudumalai, and many other sanctuaries, the animals certainly do look up at people atop the elephant.

Finally, the big bull sauntered off, and we crossed the nullah and followed him, keeping to one side of him and keeping our distance. We were about a hundred yards from him, on ground sloping gently upward, and bare of undershrub. Half a mile away, as I knew, there were some patches of coarse, waist-high grass that had somehow escaped the fires. If we could head him towards those patches (no great feat), I thought I had a fair chance of getting a picture of the bull lying down.

Again no hard and fast rules can be laid down, but in forests where the undershrub has been burnt down, and in the daytime when there is a hot sun, gaur (or sambar, for that matter) are apt to lie down in any patch of grass or other cover, when not alarmed and when being followed. Since this move is instinctive the fact that the grass fails to hide them does not seem to lessen the sense of security that the animals feel in the cover.

I got my picture, and then I had time to have a really close look at the great beast. The wide sweep of the horns and their blunted tips gave no idea of their real size except in a front view, and the size of the body made the head seem small—even the ridges at the base of each horn were so worn that they did not show up except in certain lights. A very old bull, obviously, and quite enormous. By the sheerest accident while following him we had to pass a big herd of gaur, and I had the opportunity to compare the herd-bull (a very big bull which I knew well) with this lone bull. Only then was his great size and spread of horn apparent—that herd-bull, which was definitely no farther away looked positively subadult by comparison!

Twice again, during my stay at Mudumalai, I came across this lone bull, much the biggest gaur I have ever seen (incidentally, he was mistaken for an elephant by a Forest Officer who saw only his black-looking mass behind a bush). The second time was a week later, when he already seemed less gaunt—the grass was coming up rapidly. That was at sunset, and right on top of a hill, and I tried for a picture against the light, and naturally failed. . .

The third time was three weeks later, the day before I left those forests. I was out in the afternoon, looking for flying lizards, and he was lying down on a bank, chewing the cud. His ribs were no longer visible, and his hide had taken on a dull sheen. He jumped to his feet with a quickness that surprised me, and took a course more or less parallel to ours. My camera, intended for close-ups of a small reptile, was equipped with a short lens, and I would have to get quite close to the gaur for any worthwhile picture. Repeatedly I urged the mahout to go slow, but familiarity breeds contempt, in mahouts as among other men. Ignoring the pressure of my hand on his back, the mahout made straight for our quarry. The big bull stopped dead in his tracks, spun around to face us, threw up his head and snorted—then he came straight for our elephant, without lowering his head.

He pulled up a mere yard from us, and shook his horns in the elephant's face, with quick, fierce, sideway tosses of his head—I know this sounds fantastic, but that was just what he did, a rattling of sabres that was most impressive.

I felt so taken aback that I failed to take a single picture, and our peace-loving Tara promptly turned tail and bolted. Thereafter our only concern was to stop our frightened mount somehow, before she charged through a clump of bamboos.

Some day, perhaps, I will revisit Mudumalai, and meet the old champion again, but if I do I shall make no attempt to get close to him for a picture. Not that I feel apprehensive, but I have by now a sincere respect for his desire for freedom and privacy.

1959

14

Five Encounters

OR OVER SIX decades, right from my college days, I have been wandering over the forests and scrublands of India, investigating their wildlife. And in all that time, and in spite of dangerous risks run in ignorance of animal ways, only on four occasions have I been in the shadow of imminent death, once when I almost walked into an enormous sloth bear while looking up at the fruits on a tree, and thrice when following wild elephants on foot by myself—it is best to go alone, for a companion doubles the chances of being detected. There was no time to feel frightened then: one is wholly preoccupied with escape, and it is only after escaping that one's liver turns to water and belated fright-reaction sets in. Strangely, it is not these crises that I remember most vividly, but comparatively minor encounters with wild animals that excited me, and filled me with wonder. I recount some here.

Long ago, I was in service in a small princely state in the Deccan, in a narrow, green valley girt round with a double ring of hills. The flora was distinctive (as noted nearly a century ago by J.S. Gamble in his monumental *Flora of the Presidency of Madras*), the bird life was rich, and the mammalian fauna varied, featuring sambar, wild pigs and leopards among the larger animals. My official duties were heavy and laborious, but compensated by unspoilt nature all around.

I do not shoot, and disapprove of all hunting, but my best opportunities for seeing animals lay in joining the occasional shikar parties organized, usually just outside our state. If there was to be a beat, I liked to stay with the beaters: that way one could see many birds and small animals usually missed, hares, mongooses, monitors, snakes and the like. A hillside was being beaten towards the guns on top by a dozen men, and I had been posted as a stop—that is, to turn what came along a game patch back into the beat. It was almost evening, and I was standing where the path ran through a line of tall bushes, blocking the gap. In those days I used to supplement my olive-green clothes with a cap having a deep peak and side-flaps to prevent incident light causing my spectacles to glint. I stood some distance from a bend in the path, and nothing came towards me. Then, as the beat was nearing its end, a pair of fourhorned antelopes came tripping round the bend.

The chowsingha, or fourhorned antelope, is the only wild animal which, in the buck, has an additional pair of little knob-horns above the eyes and below the regular spike-horns on top of the head—the doe is hornless. Even otherwise it is unique—exclusively Indian, without any close relative anywhere, capriciously distributed across the country on low hilltops, given to drinking every day during the hottest hours, and unlike most antelopes, not gregarious but going about by itself or in a pair. It is small and compactly built, just two-foot high, a greyish brown on top and furry white below, and has a dainty gait.

I stood stock-still and the pair came tripping along in no hurry, almost side by side. They did not see me till they were quite near, only some ten feet away, and then froze instantly, and half-squatted. Then they rose in a brace in the air and flew right overhead, to my incredulous surprise. The most athletic of our animals, the leopard, could not have jumped so high from a standing start—in my thick-soled boots and cap I stood six-foot tall, and they cleared my head with a cubit to spare! By the time I could turn around, they had disappeared into the bush cover behind me, and I just stood there, almost unable to believe my eyes. Then slowly my amazement turned to a feeling of relief and gladness, that they had escaped the beat so comprehensively.

The road from Masinagudi to the Moyar hydel project is over a dozen kilometres long. On one side of it is the concrete-flanked Maravakandi canal, carrying the waters of the project, and on the other the north-eastern border of the Mudumalai sanctuary. This part of the preserve features alternating stretches of dense forests and clearings, and wild elephants frequent it after the rains. The rainwater collects in shallow, linear pools in some of the clearings, and elephants like to drink at them, standing five or six in a row. I had long wanted to photograph them drinking here, and that forenoon offered the opportunity.

A herd was approaching a clearing through the forest, a large and bois-terous herd to judge by its many voices. Old Mara and I stood on the road, facing the clearing. He knew the area well, and I did not, and he said the herd would cross the clearing, enter the belt of forest beyond, and proceed through it to a sandy clearing still further off where there was a chain of pools: we should give them time to get to the water, and then take the path they had taken through the trees, the only path there was to those pools. I do not like having anyone with me on such occasions, but needed Mara's guidance, for it is easy to lose one's way in dense cover.

We did not have long to wait. The elephants came on to the clearing in small groups, 20 of them, and entered the belt of trees beyond. We waited 10 minutes for any lagging behind to come out, and none came. We had to go quite some distance into the clearing to reach the point of entry into the tree cover, and overshot it. And as we were retracing our steps, we saw that two cow elephants had entered the clearing just behind us, and were crossing it towards the trees. They were to our left, between us and the road.

There was no bush to hide us, to try running away would most prob-ably provoke a charge, and standing still we were conspicuous. We sank to the ground and crouched low. 'Take off your clothes,' whispered Mara urgently. For a moment I did not understand him, then did. He had already stripped, and gathering the fresh elephant dung in front of him in his hands, was smearing it all over himself. Quickly getting out of my clothes, I followed suit. It was nauseating, but necessary. The ground breeze was blowing directly from us towards the elephants—the over-powering stench of the still-warm dung would mask our man-smell.

The two cows sauntered to the trees ahead of them and went in. To our consternation, we noticed that a cow with a young calf, and behind them a big tusker, had now come on to the clearing from behind us. We continued to crouch and stay still. Slowly the cow and calf crossed to the trees in front, but the tusker stopped directly in a line with us, and very near: he was less than the length of a cricket pitch to my left. I dared not turn to look, but after what seemed an unbearable 10 minutes, and was probably two, I glanced sideways. He was standing at ease, flapping his ears (always a sign of contentment), with his trunk lowered right to the ground—and he had sharp, curved, murderous-looking tusks! After an age, I stole another sideway look, and he was still there, flapping his ears.

The most remarkable thing in existence is not the behaviour of wild elephants but of the human mind. By now my curiosity had overcome my dreadful apprehensions, and inch by inch I turned a little to my left, to watch. The tusker was standing at a patch of *Mimosa pudica* (the sensitive plant, the ground herb whose tiny, feathery leaves shrink and close when touched) covering the ground in a flat, dark-green spread. The spread was in bloom, with a great many tiny flower heads, like minute, pink badminton balls, dotting it all over. Laboriously the great beast was gathering the flowers in the crook of his trunk-tip and conveying them carefully to his mouth!

After a while he too crossed over and disappeared into the tree cover, and getting to our feet, we raced to the road, crossed it, and plunged into the Maravakandi canal. The water here is never clean and clear, but there was a distinct current, and in no time at all it had washed our skin free of every trace of elephant dung. In my hurry, I had left my clothes behind in the clearing and sent Mara to get them, while I climbed out and let the sun and air dry me.

(*PS* I can find no reference to elephants fancying *Mimosa pudica* flowers in the literature on the animal, but can vouch for this authoritatively. Incidentally, the flowers have a faintly acid taste in the human mouth.)

I have seldom photographed animals from a hide. I have often used treetop hides overlooking a forest pool or path to observe wild elephants in safety, unknown to them, but taken very few pictures of them then. And at the Guindy national park around the Madras Raj Bhavan, I felt the need for a ground-hide to study the native blackbuck and the introduced chital closer than I could otherwise.

I need not explain why I felt this need, except to say it was for evidence to substantiate my reasons for chital thriving in places into which they had been newly introduced, to the detriment of the native herbivores. Preliminary reconnaissance disclosed a further problem. It was no use

setting up a ground-hide at a selected spot. At Guindy, men are cons-
tantly moving about and the animals, while used to human proximity,
keep their distance and shift ground frequently. I needed a portable hide.

It then occurred to me that with a modification of what I wore in the
field, no hide was necessary. Over the years I have acquired the ability to
stay still and to move, if I must, in slow-motion. My stained and patched
brownish green trousers and bush-shirt were inconspicuous, and if I had
a light, wide-brimmed hat from which a veil could be hung, to mask my
face, that should do. A khaki soft hat, such as some policemen wear,
seemed best, and I bought one at a second-hand clothes shop. Then I
consulted an acquaintance who had worked as a sempstress, for the veil,
and she advised not a fixed veil, but a number of slip-knot nooses around
the brim from which thin green twigs could be hung, for better camou-
flage and to enable me to see through readily. This she was kind enough
to stitch on herself, and armed with my new headgear, I set out for
Guindy after lunch.

By 3 o'clock I found a promising spot, with no men near and a flat
stone at the foot of a woodapple tree to sit on. The ground in front was
bare and brown with sparse patches of low herbage, but there were some
tall bushes. A soft-haired, leafy twiner with a sticky white juice festooned
two of the bushes: it was in fruit, hung with long, green, paired follicles
along its pliant coils—obviously, a plant of the Aclepiadaceae (*Pergularia
daemia*, as identified later). Taking the hat out of my handbag, I collected
lengths of the twiner complete with follicles, so that the twin fruits would
stabilize the pendent veil of their lengths. Securing them in place, I put
on the hat and ensconced myself on the stone slab.

Soon it was apparent that I had overdone things a bit. The hanging
greenery in front of my face was too closely spaced and in the way of clear
vision, even of easy breathing, and the twiner had a strong, foul smell.
Thanks to the slipknots, this could be easily remedied, but as I raised my
hand to do so, five chital came into view, feeding steadily towards me—
three adult hinds, a young stag in velvet, and a half-grown fawn. I froze,
and watched.

They were both grazing and browsing, cropping such ground vegetation as there was, and feeding on the foliage of some bushes: they were
partial to the follicles I had left behind on top of the bushes, standing up
on their hind legs to get at them. By now they were very close, and I wondered when they would spot me. Then the hind in the lead trotted right

up and snipped a follicle off my hat, and at once the rest joined in, tugging at the fruits from all around so that the hat stayed miraculously wobbling on my head. Then it fell away, and at once they scattered and bolted.

Chital are short-scented. How was it, then, that from so near they had failed to notice my sweaty man-smell? Had the stronger smell of the fresh-cut twiner masked it? I do not know the answer to these questions. I never tried the experiment again.

I made an early start on elephant-back, so as to be at the expanse of up-and-coming grass in time to see what was feeding there, but on the way we chanced on a huge lone bull gaur and followed him for almost two hours. It was nearing noon when we reached the slope lush with fresh-grown tall grass. There was no animal to be seen, but something had fed there quite recently. There was a darkish furrow in places going up the sea of bright green grass tips. It was Maasthi, my mahout and companion, who noticed this first and pointed it out to me.

We went a little way up, for a closer look. It had rained in the night, and the ground was moist and impressionable. The unmistakable, so-human footprints of a large sloth bear zigzagged up the rise, and alongside the track the grass had been bitten off in sheaves. I remarked to Maasthi that the bear must have had quite a feast here. He shook his head.

'Bears do not eat grass,' he said.

I assured him they did, and that I had seen them feeding on fresh grass with gusto. Maasthi had great faith in my knowledge of animals, and had often consulted me when in doubt—he had also told me things I did not know, which I subsequently found to be factual. He knew perfectly well that I would not make a positive assertion unless it was true, but this once he was unable to accept my authority. He said that I must have seen what I had seen elsewhere, not here—here, bears did not eat grass.

I asked what animal, then, had guzzled the tall grass here so zestfully—there were no other tracks on the ground, not a single hoof-print. However, I did not argue the point further. I was already feeling peckish, and it would take us an hour and a half to get back to the resthouse and lunch. We decided to be at this pasture early next day.

And when we were there next morning, the bear was also there, busy

with his breakfast. For a while we watched from behind a thick-boled
tree. He was facing away from us, but we could see him quite clearly. He
fed choosily, taking his time, selecting a tussock of tender grass and bending its top to his mouth with a paw to munch it up. I was keen on a photograph if I could get one, but had to get closer—he was already halfway
up the rise. Not following in his wake, but keeping to one side of it, we
moved the elephant up, and at once he began to hurry. He had his back
to us still, but had somehow sensed our presence. I called a halt so as not
to panic him, and he went right up to the bare, stony top of the rise and
stopped. He still faced away from us, and did not turn round to look, but
bending his head low down so that the crown almost touched the ground,
looked at us from between his legs! For nearly a minute he stared at us
like this, and then went down the other side of the rise at a bobbing run
to vanish into the forest.

Maasthi turned to me in utter puzzlement.

'Would we have seemed upside down to the bear?' he asked.

Late in the year, when cyclones hit the south-eastern coast, I was at Point
Calimere in a tiny cottage on the beach. Very late one afternoon, it grew
suddenly dark, black rainclouds blotted out the sun, and a high wind
sprang up. By the time I could close and bolt the door and the two small
windows, the storm was upon me.

Torrential rain beat down on the steep tiles, thunderclaps crashed
overhead and the wind's voice rose to a banshee shriek. Not a drop of
water penetrated my retreat, built to withstand the elements. My food
was being brought from outside, and I could not hope for dinner, but I
thought this primeval fury could not last all night, and sat down stoically
to wait. There was no let-up, and by four in the morning I fell asleep to
the strident lullaby of the cyclone.

A hammering on my door awoke me, and when I opened it, it was
bright outside and 7 o'clock already. The Forester was there with a flask
of hot coffee and a substantial pack-breakfast. I was feeling famished, but
ate sparingly, for it was important to go out at once to see what damage
the vegetation and animal life had suffered. The Forester vetoed the out-
ing: there was an almost overpowering wind blowing just above the
ground, and he had experienced considerable difficulty getting to me.

He was lath-thin and insubstantial: I was almost twice his weight and in hard condition. Picking up a light 35 mm camera, I ploughed my way to the sea.

I have never known anything like that two-level groundwind. Up to knee height there was no stir of air, and then till well above one's head there was an almost solid blast of faintly sibilant wind, repulsing one. I had to lean into it to force my way through. The sea, flat and placid at Point Calimere, was calm again, but it had run amok in the night. The wreck lay scattered high up the shore, shellfish, squishy molluscs, broken-up crustaceans, bits and pieces of long-drowned wood, and small fishes—nothing large and, surprisingly, no seaweed.

I was astonished at the way the vegetation had survived the cyclone's violence. Trees and bushes here are tough and flat-topped: they had bowed their crowns to the raging wind, and except for twigs and branchlets torn off and flung around, had escaped unscathed. The ground vegetation was unaffected: in places, ephemeral little pools had drowned it, but the sand would suck in the water by nightfall.

Round a bend, I came upon a pair of jackals scavenging on what the sea had thrown up, and seeing me they decamped into the bushes. A little beyond some two hundred brownheaded gulls were sitting tight on the wet sand in a long row, all facing the air current, waiting for the wind to die down. They ignored me as I passed very close by them and took some pictures. Further still, I came to what had been a little bay the previous day, now scooped by the storm into a miniature lagoon extending far up the shore and about seventy yards across. The opposite bank was topped by ground vegetation and through its tangle I could just glimpse what looked like the heads of some large sea-birds.

The sea at Point Calimere is quite shallow for quite some distance from the shore. A few days earlier, I had spent an hour standing waist-deep in the sea, photographing the assorted crowd of gulls flying around the incoming boats for the guts of the catch being tossed out. I had been sternly warned by the fishermen not to be so foolish—there might be sting-rays in the shallows that could inflict a fearful injury.

Far out to sea, I could see dolphins circling and occasionally leaping up into the air. I had seen them here in the sea many times, always too far away to be clearly watched. There was nothing else in sight, and I wanted to have a look at the birds on the further bank before turning back.

To go all the way round would be progress through the buffeting wind, but I could easily wade across. I walked into the water, which came only up to my knees, and then to my waist, and was half-way through when I was suddenly almost shoulder-deep in it. Evidently the storm-tossed sea had dug into the sandy bottom here, and it was best to get out of the trough: holding my camera at head height, I turned round. Something long and live and heavy brushed gently against me in the water, and I stopped dead. Again something long and thick brushed my back, hardly touching me. Then the dolphins were swirling around me, in a whirligig of *joie de vivre*.

There were half-a-dozen of them, circling at high speed and skimming the surface now and again to throw up an impetuous spray. I just stood there, holding the camera pressed to my head, utterly spellbound. These were common dolphins, eight-foot long and sleekly streamlined, steel-grey on top and white below with a yellowish streak along the flanks, and the jaws in a beak armed with teeth that could probably bite through one's arm. I felt no fear—only amazement and wonder. Then, as suddenly as they had come, they raced away, far into the sea. I have seldom felt so thrilled.

These dolphins are the only wild animals that have a strange affinity to humanity. Right from Greek mythology to Mediterranean tales there are accounts of their friendliness towards men. I had read these accounts, and thought them only charming legends.

1997

G

Gnu or wildebeest: Large antelope of
East and South Africa with buffalo-like head,
hairy mane and tail. Genus: *Connochaetes*

GNU

The gnu is sullen and morose,
his horns are like a buffalo's,
his tail is like a mare's:
he fiercely roams his native leas
and charges everything he sees
from hills to harmless hares.

And woe betide the hunter who,
with careless aim, has shot his gnu
not in a vital place!
The only way the charge to flee
is swarming up the tallest tree
within the nearest space.

Nature's Miniatures

15

A City's Bird Life

THIRTY YEARS AGO, we moved out of a crowded part of Madras to the house that my father had built in Mylapore. No one consulted me over the move, for I was the youngest of the family, but I remember the occasion and the sense of pioneer adventure it gave me. My father had chosen this spot after much cogitation, as the likeliest to offer peace and space to his retirement.

There were a few bungalows around, and many groves and fields in between. Our road, or rather the section of it that held our house, was the northern boundary of an oblongish area, the other three sides of which were also closed in by roads. I am tempted to draw a map, but words will do. The tramline and a row of houses formed the eastern edge. The southern edge was more or less lined with residences, and a new colony (to which we belonged) was coming up on the north—but the west was still wild.

The triangular, south-western half of the oblong was a series of paddy-fields, coconut groves and pastures, with only two small churches and a 'mutt' to break their continuity. I use the past tense from a regard for accuracy. I live in the house that my father built, and the locality still retains its oblongish shape, but it is chock-full of construction now, built up ruthlessly with just sufficient space between for secondary roads.

In those days I used to wander around with a catapult in my hand and a jack-knife in my hip-pocket, feeling every inch a settler in a new land. There was a pond on either side of our house and a much larger one on the southern periphery—all these are filled up and built over.

My neighbour's compound was a miniature jungle. In it there were mongooses, palm-civets, snakes, tortoises in the pond, even a starry-eyed blackbuck, though I must confess that it wore a collar. Beyond, further west, were the paddy-fields, coconut plantations and scrub, which jackals visited after sunset and where quail were not uncommon after the rains: once, I saw a hare here. It is all concrete and metalled byroads now, and squirrels and rats are about the only wild beasts one can find in it.

It is of the bird life of this restricted, oblongish area that I write. The title, with its wide scope, is misleading, but perhaps I may justify it by a brief, necessary mention of the rich avifauna of Madras. It is curious but true that Indian bird lore has grown up around the cities—'Eha' in Bombay, Cunningham in Calcutta and Dewar in Madras have contributed much to its literature.

It is a mistake to think that cities hold few birds, and that these are mainly dark and metaphorical in character. From a varied knowledge of the countryside, I can say that parts of Madras are quite as bird-filled as the country can be, even today. Adyar is still an ornithologist's paradise; one could name other localities in the city's purlieus, but what I should stress is the fact that the part of Mylapore I live in was not less plentifully favoured with birds, and that even now there are birds here.

Birds, with their wonderful powers of adaptation and air-borne freedom, are less immediately affected by colonization than terrestrial fauna. As a boy, I got to know the birds of this area the hard way, with little help, and my recollections of them are trustworthy.

What changes do I notice? With the disappearance of extensive woodland (provided by contiguous, tree-stocked compounds), meadows and inundated fields, certain birds have also gone. Spotted doves, ioras, magpie-robins, fantail-flycatchers, the Brahminy mynah, hoopoes, king-crows and the grey shrike (the thorn fences and pastures are no more), cattle egrets, pond herons, the common kingfisher (the smallest of the tribe) that used to frequent the ponds—these once common birds have left the place, and few of them come in again, even as stragglers.

Other birds are in the last stages of departure. Orioles and bulbuls, somehow never plentiful even in the old days, and bee-eaters and rollers, belong to this class. For the rest, the birds that were here are here, but in much reduced numbers. I think it would be best to group them in some manner before telling you of them: classification is tedious, but unclassified, profuse listing can be worse.

First, the stray visitors, the birds that come in by chance or mischance. Naturally, it is not possible to be specific about them. Night herons visit my area occasionally, though they have no roosting tree near here, as they used to have. On moonlit nights I have heard lapwings, but I have never seen them.

A few years ago my son found and captured a pitta in a recess under the ancient wood-apple tree in my little garden. This was late in April, but obviously the bird was a migrant, for it was in an exhausted condition. Pittas visit Madras during the winter, and have been known to stray into outhouses, but I had never before seen the bird in this locality. We felt quite touched that this beautiful wanderer should have crossed so much outlying construction to find sanctuary in our modest little garden.

Another vague group belongs to the skies. In spite of the law, the skies do not belong to anyone, and have been little affected by our congested architecture. But it seems reasonable to conclude that birds sailing and soaring day after day over a particular locality find the pastime worth their while, that the lesser fauna of the place and its isolated bits of waste provide them with prey.

Except for swifts, and occasional intruders, these sky-birds are all birds of prey, that is, birds that live on anything from vegetable refuse to insects, lizards, squirrels and small birds. In this reckoning of aerial fauna, I leave out the early morning and late evening skies, through which many flighting birds pass.

There is surprising variety in the birds of our diurnal sky—besides the ubiquitous pariah kite, there are Brahminy Kites and eagles whose flight suggests power in reserve, scavenger vultures on dazzling, graceful wings, hawks, even an occasional peregrine.

About a furlong from my house there is the last patch of nature in these parts, a small, grassy field, fringed with a wide border of thin scrub, with a strange grove of dead and decapitated coconuts at one end. This is the beat of a kestrel, scanning the mean scrub for insects and small fry, from its hovering stance in the air.

Then there are the garden birds, though the gardens today are few and nominal in this place, and mostly limited to the roadside trees. However, a number of birds find the vegetation adequate. There are honeysuckers where there are flowers, tailor-birds, coppersmiths (there are banyans along the outer roads), flaming golden-backed woodpeckers, looking strangely out of place in this drab setting (building in coconut groves, householders have retained a few marginal trees with thrifty forethought), shikras (they have been included among the skybirds, already), spotted owlets where there are old trees, and koels and white-headed babblers. The last two are especially plentiful.

Dewar, writing some half-a-century ago, remarks on the abundance of koels in Madras. The babblers are a triumph for the axiom that unity is strength. Most babblers babble, and stick together, but each sect has its own distinctive voice and demeanour. White-headed babblers are characterized by pale, watery eyes, weak, tremulous voices that grow suddenly shrill in excitement, a certain laxity of plumage and purpose. They go hopping along to some corner, and one bird turns a dead leaf over while its fellows look on with a critical slant of their white heads—then, suddenly the party dissolves in hysterical squeaks, and whirrs across on weak wings to another corner of the compound, where they proceed at once to turn over dead leaves again.

Clearly, the birds are daft, but they are a feature of Madras gardens (however nominal the garden) and will always be. By sheer *esprit de corps* and an inability to take life too seriously they have prevailed where their betters have given up.

I must devote a separate paragraph to the Common Mynah. It is a highly cosmopolitan bird, and is at home in the bustle of cities, as those who have seen the bazaars of Bombay and Mysore will know. But in this locality it keeps more or less to the roadsides and open spaces, entering dwellings after the rains, when grass sprouts up in the yards and grasshoppers abound.

Two very dissimilar birds, the white-breasted kingfisher and the rose-ringed parakeet, must go into one group, the garden-cum-house group. Thanks to the undependable water supply of the city, many householders here have retained the wells in their backyards, a conservatism that the kingfisher appreciates. This most interesting bird has largely given up fishing as a profession, and prefers to sit up over puddles, water-drains and other places (often far from water), hunting tadpoles, insects, lizards, anything that it can pounce upon and gobble up.

The posts of clothes-lines are favourite perches with these birds—these posts are usually just the right height for them, for they like to sit up not too high above ground, being less expert on the wing than other birds that hunt from look-out posts, king-crows, for example.

The parakeets are loud and numerous. They perch on coconut leaves and promenade the parapets and mouldings of the houses. What do they find to eat here? There are still a few fruit trees that no one cares for in our gardens—mine has three mangoes and a custard-apple tree, the fruits of which I do not dispute with parakeets and squirrels. But, apparently, these versatile birds are much less dependent on cultivated fruits and grain than I had thought.

Elsewhere, I have seen parakeets taking up permanent residence in terraces and turrets, but here they are not yet our co-tenants. Most of them nest and roost in the grove of dead coconuts; the charred, black, columnar trunks there are riddled with holes, occupied by the para-keets—the birds lend a fresh, verdant touch to that desolation.

On ledges and parapets, these parakeets assume curious attitudes, which they rarely do when on trees. As they walk clumsily across the flat, hard cement, their backs are humped and their tails trail behind them— sometimes, on a narrow ledge, the tail is thrown up spread against the wall by the force of friction, as the bird turns. Parakeets in classical sculpture are often shown in these very attitudes—I have heard art cri-tics, with no eye except for the stone, go into raptures over the rhythmic formalism of such carvings. It so happens that I have a quick sketch of a parakeet on my neighbour's terrace, in this same pose, with tail spread against the parapet wall. May be 2,000 years ago, another artist was so struck by a parakeet in this pose that he depicted it, more lastingly than I can, in stone. Parakeets have frequented towns and parapeted buildings from time immemorial, and our artists have taken their models from these birds on ledges.

Lastly, co-tenants. One of these, the domestic sparrow, can be ig-nored—for some reason that is beyond me, it has always been a *rara avis* here. The others are very much with us, both the grey-necked house-crow and the all-black jungle-crow. Crows are such sapient birds, their ways are so curiously dark and daring, that one could write pages about them—(Dewar has, in fact, devoted a whole book to the grey-neck)— and I dare not add another paragraph! But I will say this. I have watched civilization overtake the jungle-crow, in my own backyard.

It was a rude, uncouth, apprehensive bird in my boyhood, lacking poise, shy and sidling in its approach to the tap for a drink, clumsy and precipitate in its get-away. Today it sits on top of the bucket with easy self-assurance, and wears a sophisticated look. The amused, tolerant glint in its eye suggests that it is reflecting impersonally over something ludicrous.

It is possible that it is thinking, in its black mind, that in the past 30 years it has witnessed the gradual taming and civilization of one who was a robust young barbarian?

1953

16

Rescuing a Fledgeling

AFTER A SOLID breakfast I smoked my favourite pipe and, while my table was being cleared and dusted, had a nice, cold wash. Then I had a cup of strong, hot coffee. I was preparing to work.

By two o'clock I had decided on the plan of work—before tackling hard jobs it is wise to spend a moment in planning the attack. And as I sat down at last to the hateful, necessary thing, a commotion broke out in my backyard, a series of high, thin squeaks and quivers, like the 'ghosts that did squeak and gibber in the Roman streets'. White-headed Babblers are excitable creatures, and there is a clan of them living in and around my compound, sounding the alarm at each passing cat and human. However, there was a sustained hysteria in their alarm now, something in the way their *chee-chee-chees* and tremulous *chrrrrrrs* rose in outraged pitch till they were choked altogether, that called for immediate investigation, and I stepped out to the corner of my backyard.

On the clean-swept ground beneath the mango tree was a fledgeling babbler, just out of the nest, fluttering weakly against the corner of the compound wall and the bathroom, falling to the ground after each futile attempt to gain the top of the wall. Two adult babblers were on the ground beside it and three more in the boughs above, all encouraging the premature adventurer with frantic voices and quick flirts of their round, half-spread wings and loose-feathered tails. And strolling along the top of the wall towards this domestic group was a small, grey cat.

The cat was the first to see me. It froze in its tracks, gave me one intense, green-eyed look, and disappeared down the other side of the wall into my neighbour's territory. The birds flew into the tree at my approach, but when I was right under the tree and just a step from the fledgeling, they flew away in a loud body to a drumstick tree some twenty yards away, and there continued their alarm even more agitatedly than before—I noticed that not one of them was facing me and that some hopped down to the grass beneath the drumstick tree, as if what excited them lay there.

The moment its elders left, the infant babbler crouched low and was instantly turned into a small, grey, shapeless, immobile lump; it did not move or bat an eyelid even when I touched it. Here was an intriguing situation! The fledgeling on the bare ground was exposed to every passing enemy, and the older birds would not come to its rescue so long as I was near; they would persist with their instinctive demonstration at the grass beneath the drumstick tree. Should I move the youngster beyond the drumstick tree, where it would be safe in the innumerable bolt-holes offered by a pile of broken brick and scrap, or should I leave it where it was, keeping an eye on it from a distance and watching further proceedings? Finally I retreated to a point equidistant from both trees, after taking a photograph of the fledgeling, and sat down to watch.

Till five o'clock I sat stolidly on, observing happenings. First all except two of the babblers (the parents of the grounded youngster?) left ostentatiously, whirring and skimming on weak, blunt wings over and beyond my roof. The birds that stayed behind stuck to the drumstick tree, twittering feebly from time to time. Next, a pair of ill-assorted baby-snatchers arrived on the scene, a jungle-crow and a house-crow; they perched on the compound wall and cocked their heads from side to side, looking at me and at the ground beneath them with sly, sidelong glances. After a while they hopped towards the mango tree.

This was the signal for the waiting pair of babblers to fly headlong into the mango tree, yelling blue murder and the rest of the clan was there at once, as if by magic. Routed by the pack of yelling, gibbering babblers, the crows fled to a coconut top some distance away. This performance was repeated several times, the babblers leaving the mango tree and even my compound, the crows approaching furtively, the babblers returning in screaming force at once to mob and drive away the enemy. The grey cat, which appeared on the wall again, was also mobbed and chased away, but the passage of a shikra low overhead was marked by silence.

All the time the little one stayed put. I doubt if it as much as lowered its bill by a fraction of an inch in all those three hours. But it closed its eyes and did not open them except when the crows, whose proximity was proclaimed by the furious babblers, were near. It was evident that no attempt to induce the youngster to move to safer quarters would be made so long as I was there. The sky was darkening, and rain imminent. I decided I had watched long enough, and taking the fledgeling gently in my hand, deposited it on the scrap heap, and it promptly disappeared into a crevice.

In a moment the adult babblers had joined it and, the new ground being sufficiently far from me, vociferously encouraged the fledgeling to essay flight. However, in the further fifteen minutes that I watched, it did not succeed in getting out of my compound—the babblers have no nest here, but probably have one in my neighbour's compound. Next morning they were more successful, and the youngster cleared the wall after a few tries. Apparently, a day and a night make all the difference in development to a fledgeling learning to fly.

1956

17

The Anril

TWO YEARS AGO, there was a protracted controversy in the 'Letters' column of a newspaper on the identity of the bird known in classical Tamil as the 'anril'. According to early Tamil poetry and to subsequent literary traditions these are the characteristics of the bird: it is specially noted for the constancy of its attachment to its mate, and is the embodiment of marital affection and fidelity: the top of its head is red: one reference speaks of its curved beak and its assembly in a palmyra top in the evening with loud calls.

According to one school of letter-writers the 'anril' is the Sarus, no less, celebrated for its constancy to its mate, and definitely with a red, papillose patch of skin on the head. I quote from Hume with regard to its attachment to its mate; writing of the Sarus, our only indigenous crane, he says: 'Whether in large or small numbers, they are always in pairs, each pair acting independently of the other pairs . . . they certainly pair for life, and palpably exhibit great grief for the loss of their mate . . . on two occasions I have actually known the widowed bird to pine away and die.'

That seems fairly close to the classical Tamil account, but the Sarus was never known in the Tamil country. The protagonists of its identity with the 'anril', however, argue that the literary account is in the nature of a transferred epithet, and that, therefore, the non-existence of the Sarus in the Tamil country means nothing. The lion, for instance, was also never there in the Tamil country, but there are certainly many references to it in classical Tamil. But whoever heard of a Sarus atop a palmyra.

The other school favours the black ibis. Unlike the Sarus (whose neck, on top, also shows a patch of red skin) only its crown is covered with red, papillose skin, and its beak is definitely curved like a sabre, whereas the Sarus is straight-beaked. Moreover, it certainly does resort to palmyra

tops in the coastal inland plains of Tamil Nadu, in the evenings, and it
does come out with a strident, long-drawn call then. I can never forget
my first evening in the Kanha National Park. The Wildlife Warden of
MP was with me, and some half-a-dozen black ibises came in at evening
to roost in a tree close to the lodges, and came out with their grating,
carrying calls. 'Say, what is that dreadful sound?' the Wildlife Warden
asked me: 'Is it not a barasingha being killed by a tiger?'

Oddly enough, those who deny the black ibis the distinction of being
the 'anril', rely on its being not a Tamil country bird exclusively but one
with a practically all-India range—the closest look I have had at these
birds, actually, was in the Thar desert, where five of them flew up to perch
in a stunted tree very near me. One of the Sarus-fanciers wrote to me (not
that I ever entered this controversy) pointing out that a distribution
south of Madras was not mentioned in Dillon Ripley's Synopsis, and
that the black ibis did not occur in Sri Lanka—so how could it be called
any more a bird of the Tamil country than the Sarus? He must have
looked into the first (1961) edition of the book when 'Madras' meant a
wider area than Tamil Nadu today. Anyway, the black ibis is quite a common bird in the dry flat country of the south—I have seen it dozens of
times in the southern reaches of Tamil Nadu (where it is much commoner, actually, than in the northern parts of the State) and scrutinized
it through binoculars to make quite sure it was not the glossy ibis.

At this juncture, a literal translation of line 219 of one of the oldest
extant classics of Tamil, *Kurinji-p-pattu* (some 18 centuries old), may be
provided. Writing of the approach of evening the poet specified, among
other things typical of the day's end, that 'curve-beaked anril arrive at the
broad-leaved tops of tall palmyras, and sound their calls'. My picture*
taken quite recently in the scrub around Tirunelveli, shows the black ibis
atop a palmyra, to which the birds do resort at sunset in these parts, there
being few other suitable roosting trees in it. I may add that the light shade
of the neck in the picture is due to the slanting evening light, and that
the neck was dark all right, and the scarlet patch of pimpled skin on the
crown is clear in the live bird.

Last year, during a long motor drive along country roads from Ramanathapuram to Kanya Kumari, I saw many black ibises, and took pains
to point them out to seven chance-met rustics and ask them the name of
the bird. Four said they did not know its name specifically, it was just

*Not reproduced here.

another wasteland bird, but described its habits accurately: the other three called it 'anril'!

That is pretty clinching. However, the problem of the anril's identity still remains, in spite of all this evidence, for I am unable to find any mention in ornithological literature of the black ibis mating for life, or always going about in a pair. I have seen it singly, and in small parties of three to nine, most often in odd numbers which do not suggest pairs, and watching them, have never seen them moving in unison in pairs, only very much by each bird, individually. Perhaps some specialist on this bird can tell whether or not it pairs for life.

1986

18

A Flight of Danaids

LATE IN THE afternoon of 27 June I was watching wading egrets from the bank of an estuary, and thinking pensively of tea. A wind sprang up across the water and blew gustily towards me, dispelling the muggy stillness around, bringing the smell of rain with it. I looked up at the sky—black, billowing clouds had already obscured the horizon and were rapidly mounting the sky. Then they were over the water and I could see that they were no rain clouds, but a great swarm of butterflies, thousands upon thousands of them, floating down on the breeze.

They went past overhead on a loose pile, perhaps a hundred feet in depth. In the lower layers they were using their wings to flutter, but higher up they just rode along on outspread wings, like dry leaves caught up in an air current: only they did not flurry and twirl about like dry leaves, but sailed smoothly past on taut wings, steering their airborne course. Most of them sailed on out of sight, and the next day they were to be seen in every garden within a ten-mile radius, but a few thousands from the lower layers circled my bank and settled on trees.

There were two kinds of them more or less in equal numbers and mixed: one with brownish-black wings laced along their edges with white dots and the other marked with an elongated network of black on a pale cerulean ground that blanched to white dots at the edges of the wings. I had seen numbers of these same butterflies the previous day (26 June) in small flights, but that was a casual incursion, a few hundreds, nothing at all like this. By 5-45 p.m. the swarm had passed, and those that had settled on my bank were clustered thickly on twig and leaf, most of them on a jamoon tree in full flower.

What amazed me even more than the sight of these countless beautiful wings, was the indifference of the birds around. There were four spotted owlets sitting in lumpy pairs on a tree, three or four crows, half-a-dozen kites in the air, a pair of king-crows perched on electric-supply wires, a pair of common mynahs and a party of white-headed babblers, all birds that would normally gorge themselves when such a swarm of insects came their way.

But none of them took the least interest in the swarm, except that the kites circled higher to avoid it. I noticed that two of the owlets were just out of their babyhood and still very juvenile—they were as indifferent to the butterflies as the older, more experienced pair.

Obviously these lovely insects were highly disagreeable as prey, and advertised this quality unmistakably. Both kinds seemed familiar to me but being innocent of butterfly lore I could not place them. However, having collected butterflies occasionally for an enthusiast, I knew how to kill them when one had no cyanide bottle—one holds them by the thorax between thumb and forefinger and a firm, quick pinch kills them instantly. I collected two specimens of each kind by this method, but had to pinch hard to still them. I put them into an old envelope and turned home.

When I took them out to sketch, they were patently alive still, to my surprise and pain. One of the dark ones got clean away, flying strongly, and one of the blue-white-and-black spangled ones fluttered up and was promptly caught by the ogrish gecko that shares my den with me. Quickly I tried to kill the remaining two again by pinching their thorax, and failing in this, painted them over their bodies with a powerful insecticide, containing 5 per cent DDT. Still they died slowly, to my mortification—evidently they were much tougher than the kinds I had collected for my friend.

An obliging entomologist identified these butterflies for me and told me that they both belonged to the same Danaid family, and were very common—also that they were highly disagreeable to birds and lizards, probably on account of odour or taste or both (I think it must be some quality like odour or roughness that is perceptible even to inexperienced birds, though of course they may also taste nasty). I was told that both kinds are strong fliers and that their migratory flight was probably seasonal and influenced by atmospheric conditions.

The dark kind is *Euploea core core*, and the blue-white-and-black kind is *Danais melissa dravidarum.*

In a book kindly lent to me, I find that Aitken, writing with reference to Ratnagiri says, of *Euploea core*: 'For the last ten years I have kept notes of the dates on which I observed the migration, and I find it ranges from the 1st to the 10th of June, and is always connected with the coming of the regular rain'; also 'The natives say the rain will come three days after the butterflies.'

I am happy to confirm those natives of Ratnagiri. I write this two days after the migration I watched, and the rains have just arrived here.

1953

19

Argemone Mexicana

MR THOMPSON, THE systematic botanist, stood beneath an enormous tree on the crest of the hill, panting and stiff from the climb. A withered brown flower fell at his feet, and he stared dully at it while he eased the rucksack off his back, for he was thinking of tea. Then, suddenly, Mr Thompson swooped down on the flower and held it up in trembling hands. 'Malvaceae,' he murmured gazing at the great boughs above him. 'Yes, Malvaceae without a doubt. Some near relative of the Baobab, perhaps. But surely this glabrous calyx and these pentadelphous stamens—is it possible that this is—*new genus*!' Suspense was insufferable. He raced down towards the solitary figure coming up the shoulder of the hill, fatigue and tea forgotten. 'Say, tell me, my good man,' said Mr Thompson, 'what is that noble tree on top?' The native shook his head and climbed on. 'Yonder,' shouted the urgent botanist, pointing, 'on top of the hill.' '*Theriyathunga*,' replied the man (which is just polite Tamil for ignorance), and continued his way. And that was the origin of *Theriyathunga Thompsoni*, a tree which does not exist, but there are hundreds of herbs and shrubs and trees with names no less ludicrous or grotesque.

If the Latin names of our plants are often far-fetched and allusive, their common or garden names are equally misleading. The American Aloe is no aloe, the beautiful Eucharis Lily is not a lily at all, and neither Thorn, nor Wood, nor Custard-apple is an apple. It is refreshing to find a simple, straightforward name in the midst of all this whimsicality. *Argemone mexicana*, the Mexican Poppy, is one of these rare plants. It does come all the way from Mexico, and it is a poppy. Not that there is anything 'sleep-flowerish' about it. It is a businesslike, prickly weed, with shallow yellow flowers and whitish leaf-veins, and the leaves and the stem and even the fruits are covered with small, sharp spines. The Mexican

Poppy is one of the commonest plants of our wastes, where it flourishes in company with other exotic weeds. Often it is found in sole possession of a plot of barren, limey clay where even the Lantana has failed.

> Come rain come sun it flowers
> Blow east blow west it springs,
> It peoples towns and towers
> Above the courts of kings,
> And touch it and it stings.

I am quoting a fastidious poet from memory, which is always a bad thing to do, and anyway he wrote of the Nettle: but that was only because he never knew the Mexican Poppy.

'The Mexican Poppy,' says the industrious Pfleiderer, 'is a well-known weed with prickly leaves and a yellow juice in all its parts. Oil for lamps is extracted from the seeds. The seeds are also used as a purgative.' What he does not say is that these seeds are black and angular and very tiny, much smaller than mustard, and also very numerous. They are inside the dry, capsular fruit, and when the capsule is ripe it opens along predestined lines at the top, as in other poppies, and the microscopic seed is broadcast by the wind. No doubt these seeds contain an oil, which has other properties besides its purgative action, but each seed can contain only very little nourishment for the sprouting embryo in the form of oil. And no doubt only a small percentage of the seeds do grow into plants, but all this does not fully explain the omnipresence of the Mexican Poppy. This weed has the ability to thrive on very little, a certain native hardihood and a rank lack of sensibility, a quality which is difficult to put in words but which you may observe for yourself if you take the pains to meet any 'self-made man'. That is why it is so numerous and so robust. During the rains, last year, I tried to grow my own vegetables, but nothing came of it. My tomato plants looked ill and had yellow leaves, and my peas were no better. I called in an expert, who announced that I had used the wrong kind of manure, had not supplied enough iron salts and had failed to allow for the calcareous nature of the sub-soil. I followed his instructions carefully and prepared six new plots, with the results that I got two dozen small, orange tomatoes and three pods of pea. And a fortnight after I had given up vegetable gardening, rows upon rows of Mexican Poppies sprung up everywhere, both along the old, abandoned plots and the later ones, every plant bursting with health and greenness and the will to win. I doubt if anyone has ever raised finer beds of these weeds, and still, according to my expert, the soil was full of deficiencies and the sub-soil all wrong. There is much to be said in favour of the less civilized life.

1945

20

Lenin the Lizard

PEEPING FROM UNDER a rafter in the ceiling, I see a pair of eyes—cold, beady eyes that search every nook and corner of the room for something to eat. And I know that Lenin, the fat and rascally lizard who patrols the walls of my room is out on his nightly rounds.

Lenin has been there ever since I can remember. Once, long ago, he was small and lithe, and moved with a swift, easy grace. His tail would twist nervously from side to side, specially when some insect was near, for Lenin was eager and excitable in those days. His body would shine a warm, translucent orange in the glare of the wall-lamp, as your fingers would if you closed them over the bulb of a powerful electric torch. At times he was almost beautiful.

All that is gone. Tonight (for he comes out only at night) he is fat and repulsive. His tail is thick and rigid, with a kink at the end of it, and he is no longer translucent. I never liked Lenin, but in the old days, I used to admire his sinuous speed as he raced about the walls on his career of rapine and murder. Now he has no saving grace: he is just six inches of squat, warty ugliness.

Lenin lives to eat. I have followed his career from the time he was three inches long. He has grown older and bigger, and more expert in the art of catching and eating insects, but he does nothing else. He is silent, and unsociable, resenting acquaintance except with moths. Lizards are not noted for their passionate and affectionate nature, but I feel that Lenin would be considered a sour old recluse even by these cold-blooded reptiles. Once, another lizard came into Lenin's province—a much smaller, much younger lizard: a lizard whose delicately curved tail and elegance of carriage lent a vague feminine touch to the walls.

For a moment I was distressed by a vision of Lenin, his wife, and a young family of Lenins crowding the walls of my room, but this passed like all visions. Lenin's attitude towards the fair visitor was shockingly ungallant and cannibalistic. He chased her round and round, and only her youth and superior speed saved her from a most unhappy end, for lizards are cannibals, and will eat their kith and kin if they are small enough to be eaten. Other lizards might indulge in friendships and family-life, but not Lenin. I'm afraid he is a confirmed misogynist. He never gave up trying to eat her. That brave little lizard, she stuck it out for a week, defying Lenin. In fact she almost conquered the territory for, being quicker than Lenin, she either got the insects or drove them away before he could move. But it was a short-lived triumph. One night Lenin planned a cunning rear attack, and before she knew where she was, he had her firmly by the tail. There was a terrific struggle, and then down she fell, with a whack on to the floor, leaving a squirming tail in Lenin's mouth. I was reminded of Tom O'Shanter's mare and the devil:

> The Divil caught her by the rump.
> And left puir Maggie scarce a stump.

It is a curious provision of Nature that the tail of a lizard, normally pliant, becomes quite brittle when anyone lays hold of it. 'Aha!' cries your inexperienced lizard-catcher as he grabs the tail of his victim, 'I've got you at last!' And the tail, suddenly fragile, comes away in his hand while the rest of the lizard scuttles hastily away to safer regions. And so 'puir Maggie' escaped. I never saw her again. Perhaps she went into hiding— into some dark and secluded corner—till she'd grown another tail, before venturing elegantly out again in the full splendour of a new-grown one. For it is an even more curious provision of Nature that lizards which have lost their tails grow new ones.

Which brings us to the question, 'Do lizards really need tails?' Of course, they do—in fact I think that they'd be utterly lost without tails. The tail is the only organ of emotional expression that the lizard has. It compensates for his voicelessness. There are frogs that pipe shrill tunes and crickets that chirp quite half-a-dozen different notes, but everyone knows that the Lizard on the Wall never says anything beyond laconic 'Tchut, Tchuts'. But then, he has, in the tail, an organ that expresses the entire gamut of a lizard's emotions. Whenever he is excited by any feeling, he twitches his tail. It is true that very few things outside the imminence of food excite him, but that is truly beside the point. Watch a lizard as he stalks a moth and you'll know what I mean. Only the tip of his tail twitches as he advances, carefully, inch by inch, upon his unsuspecting victim. The rest of him is tense and rigid—only the tail betrays his eagerness. Or again, watch him as he passes another lizard and note the gay, friendly wave of his tail as he salutes her. He has another use for his tail— a far more practical use. He clings to the sheer faces of the walls by the suckers in his pads and the tail is his rudder. Without it, his progress against the force of gravity, as he races along the wall, would be most erratic. . . .

I have wandered far from Lenin. Lenin is so unemotional, and unsociable, that perhaps he doesn't need a tail. Life, for him, is one continuous orgy. Beetles, moths and garden-bugs are, to the zoologist, widely different things. But to Lenin they are the same: all things to be gobbled up. Once I saw him actually swallow a small scorpion, with no more fuss than a child would make over sugar candy! It's during the monsoon that he is truly happy, for with the rain the insects come and cluster round the wall-lamp. Just now, as I write, a moth has come in, and settled on a rafter just above the fatal lamp; one of those brown-and-yellow, mottled moths that look, when at rest, exactly like a chunk of wood. Indeed I can scarcely believe that it is not a piece of wood, but Lenin will not be deceived. However still that ill-fated moth may stay, however much it may imitate a chunk of wood, Lenin will get it; for Lenin eats everything that comes his way, chunks of wood included. Why, only the other day, he gobbled up a big, nickel four-anna bit I'd left carelessly behind on the table! You do not believe it? But I have the strongest circumstantial evidence to prove it. Only Lenin and my servant could have got at it; and my servant swears that he has never, in all his life, seen such a coin—it seems the poor, ignorant man simply did not know that the Government of India struck nickel four-anna bits!

1938

21

That Gentleman, the Toad

RECENTLY A MAN I know had what he termed 'a surrealist experience'. Visiting a small town on business, he had returned late in the day to the resthouse and was having a wash when he heard the strangest sounds from just outside the bathroom—deep, disconnected grunts and 'basso profondo' quaverings. Stepping out to see what was making the noise he saw some 50 huge frogs sitting in a circle on the cobbled courtyard behind the bathroom. Seeing him, they stopped their disjointed chorus, but did not budge an inch, and then, to his astonishment, they grew suddenly much bigger right in front of his eyes.

Questioning him, I learnt that they were quite enormous, the size of coconuts, and dark brown in colour, with a close pattern of warts all over. On closer questioning he conceded that perhaps there were only 20 of them, and explained that, when he said coconuts, he had meant the small, hard-shelled coconuts which are stripped of their fibrous covering and given to departing guests at weddings in the South. No, he had not had the curiosity to stay and watch the amphibians, but had left the resthouse soon after.

Undoubtedly what he saw were toads, *Bufo melanostictus*, the commonest and largest toads of India. In places they do attain a quite impressive size, over six inches long and very stout in proportion. They are highly conservative creatures, seldom straying far from home except when the breeding urge takes them to watersides. They are nocturnal and crepuscular, retiring to some cloistered retreat during the heat and glare of the day, and coming out only in the cool of the evening.

They are quite sociable, and numbers may spend the day together and come out in company at sunset, where there are convenient retreats, such as gutters or crevices between cobblestones, but I have not heard of their indulging in a chorus, like frogs. It is well known that when danger threatens them, they inflate their lungs and gain prodigiously in size, an instinctive action to impress and intimidate the enemy.

I know this toad well, having shared my backyard with a huge specimen for years. It is one of the quietest and most unobstrusive creatures one can live with, and is definitely to be encouraged in any household for it preys on mosquitoes, flies, cockroaches and other household pests— I have seen a middle-sized toad seize a large centipede and steadily swallow its squirming prey. Unlike frogs, which leap about and get in one's way, it recognizes the right of way of humanity, and stays immobile in a corner, and when it has to move, it proceeds in a series of small hops with frequent halts, or slowly pulls its mass along in a creeping action, keeping close to the walls. To revert to the old-fashioned imputation of character to animals, the frog is an abounding bounder and the toad is a gentleman, portly, sedentary, unhurried in its movements, and never intrusive.

Its ability to spot prey, when they are in cryptic situations is remarkable—evidently it has what ethologists term 'searching images' of its diverse prey. What that means is easily explained in terms of our own experience; the first time we are shown a picture of some creature in such an obliterative setting that it blends with its surroundings and can hardly be made out, like the picture of a stick insect on thin twigs, we have much difficulty in seeing it, but once perceived, it is instantly seen in subsequent sightings. The toad, apparently, has this ability to distinguish mosquitoes and flies against dark spotted walls, and prey in similar cryptic situations: it just creeps slowly, almost imperceptibly, closer, there is a lightning dart of the tongue, and the mosquito disappears.

It is a long-lived creature, and I believe its life span may extend to well over 30 years, barring accidents. It is not preyed upon by most predators, for the numerous warts on its skin, set into a close pattern, secrete an irritant and repellant principle—predators that seize toads quickly learn to leave them alone.

Is it possible that the toad's habit of inflating itself at the sight of a potential enemy is not merely to gain impressive and intimidatory size, but an instinctive action that serves to express the repellant principle from its warts by the pressure caused by the inflation of its lungs against its containing skin? I do not know but it seems likely—some specialist on the *Anura* might find it worth the while to investigate this line of inquiry.

However that might be, the fact remains that its irritant skin does help the plump toad to survive. *A Passage to India* is now definitely dated, but perhaps some reader may recall the bit in it about the examinee who, asked to annotate the lines from Keats's ode, 'Thou wert not born for death, immortal bird. No hungry generations tread thee down' wrote: 'The nightingale is not an edible bird.'

                                                                              1982

22

The Dinky Desert Fox

THE DINKY LITTLE desert fox (*Vulpes vulpes griffithi*) is only an arid zone variety of the well-known Reynard, the red fox with a wide distribution in many countries. It is about a quarter as large again as the diminutive plains fox of the peninsula (the Indian fox, *Vulpes bengalensis*), and much handsomer in coat and colour—its much longer ears, richly white furred on the inside and with the top half black on the outside, and the whitish tip to its luxuriant brush, are distinctive in telling it apart from the Indian fox, and although it is comparatively larger, it is quite small really, weighing only some 5 kg and being much smaller than a jackal in size.

Depending on locality and seasons, its coat varies somewhat in thickness and colour, but even in March, when I saw it in Rajasthan near Ramdeora and at Makam and Doli, it was richly furred and its brush was very full, and though not red, it was distinctly rufous. In winter its pelt is at its richest, and thickest.

As per the textbooks, it is nocturnal and crepuscular, and a knowledgeable man I met in the desert advised me not to go looking for it except in the evening and very early in the morning. So, being in a cussed mood, I scouted around when the sun was at its hottest—and found it! I even saw one with a fat-tailed lizard which it had just killed in its jaws, and on sighting me it took its prey to a bush and buried it in the earth beneath for consumption later when no man was watching it, smoothing the earth over its buried treasure with its snipy snout.

Thrice I saw two foxes very close to each other, no doubt they were mated pairs. These foxes are said to mate for life. A Bishnoi elder of Doli showed me, from a distance, the earth of a pair of foxes beside an obscuring bush: he told me that on 10 March he had seen the vixen at the mouth of the earth with two half-grown cubs.

Foxes have scent-glands in their feet, and that is why they have been hunted for generations with foxhounds that follow their quarry by the scent-trail left behind, not by sight. These desert foxes are also hunted with sight-hounds. The scent-glands of a beast are of primary utility to it in intraspecific communications, that is, in indicating its presence to other animals of its own kind, but no doubt animals can and do identify other quite different animals by their smell. I think the desert fox has a keen nose and finds much of its food requirements with the help of its nose—desert rodents, lizards, ground birds like the partridge, and also the fruits of some plants.

However, its sight is also keen, even during the glare and heat of the day. When followed at a distance in a jeep (it is useless to try and follow it on foot) it sometimes doubled on its tracks to lie curled up behind a bush, with its brush obscuring its body and only the big head and upright ears betraying it, as if it had gone to sleep—but it slept with one eye open!

Unfortunately for this charming and most interesting animal, it has a soft, silky thick pelt, and nomadic hunters in the desert poach it assiduously, in spite of their quarry being protected by law and by wildlife wardens. I was told that recently a party of poachers had been caught with several hundred fox-pelts. Since it is a solitary animal and not too numerous anywhere, those skins must have meant a substantial depletion of the local population of desert foxes.

The trouble in preventing poaching in open country (and no country is more open than the desert) is that it is hardly possible to patrol such a vast periphery without being spotted from far away, and that, even if one does come upon a party of poachers, they may have cached their ill-gotten goods or disposed of it in some way, to play the part of outraged innocents. They hunt the desert fox with highly-bred, very fast greyhounds of a small, distinctive breed: the dogs run the fox to earth and keep watch till their masters come up to dig out the quarry. Such a method involves no incriminating traps, noses or nets.

It is significant that all the desert foxes I saw were seen not in the uninhabited wilderness but near Bishnoi villages, where the vigilance of their self-appointed guardians prevented any hunter from coming near them. It is a mistake to think that wild animals are not acutely appreciative of sanctuary when they can find it. Many, many years ago, although I am against all forms of shikar and have never hunted, I went to Karwar with a party of shikaris who had licence for some of the shooting blocks there. For the first few days they could find nothing worth shooting at Supa, Virnoli and Dandeli. Then one morning one of them came back to the camp in high excitement with the news that sambar, chital and gaur were just teeming in one of the remoter reaches of a block for which they held licence—it proved to be Birchi, reserved for the Governor of Bombay (who administered Karwar in those days) where no one else was allowed, and with the Governor safely away in Bombay the animals were crowding it, finding peace only within it!

1980

23

Incessant Rain

FOR THE PAST four days it has rained incessantly. The only change we have had from the monotonous downpour has been an occasional bout of more vehement rain, a driving, slanting rain that comes in at unexpected angles through chinks in closed doors and windows. No thunder or lightning, no black billowing rainclouds and dramatic cloudbursts, followed by a dazzling sun, in which one can sense the grandeur of the elements—only dreary unceasing rainfall out of a grey sky.

Railroads have been drowned and passengers marooned, and people in low-lying areas have been forced to abandon their dwellings and seek higher ground. The stormwater drains are great canals, overflowing with swift, red water, and even those who live in high mansions, under waterproof roofs, are not comfortably dry, for the air that comes into their homes is heavily moist, there is a clammy wetness on wall and floor and roof, and in the shuttered, humid, gloomy indoors fungi sprout with epidemic speed over leather and paper and even wood.

I have been spending my time between wiping and drying my possessions and wandering through the rain, looking for lesser life. Where are the squirrels that were so loudly in evidence last week? Where are the crows and sparrows and other familiar birds? They are *rara aves* now, but above the dreary swish of the rain I can hear thousands of frogs from the roadside drains and puddles, even during the day, though it is at night that they are much more vocal.

In a mosque I have passed many times these last four days, the pigeons sit still and huddled within the sharply-arched, sheltering niches in which they nest. From a tea shop across the road I have watched these birds for nearly an hour, through the grey, streaky pall of rain and they have hardly moved, except to shift their static weight from one leg to the other. I was reminded, irresistibly, of a passage from an ancient Tamil classic, 'Nedunalvaadai,' about pigeons in sustained rain:

> The red-legged cock-pigeon, confused between day and night,
> Does not set out with his well-beloved mate to glean the yards,
> But, moveless, mopes within the loft, shifting from leg to leg.

How true to life those lines are! The crows and sparrows, of course, are still there, perching under eaves and ledges and such other shelter as they can find, bedraggled, wet, huddled, but still keenly interested in the prospect of food. Domestic beasts, dogs, cats and cattle react to the weather like the pigeons—they are lethargic, miserable and still. Only the buffaloes revel in the rain. Our buffaloes, incidentally, are direct descendants of that magnificent beast, the Indian Wild Buffalo, which is now almost extinct. The domesticated buffalo belongs typically and anciently to our country, and has well been named the Water Buffalo, to distinguish it from the lesser buffs of other lands.

I saw a buffalo cow sitting in a roadside ditch which had filled and enlarged to a small pond, a private pond that could hold just one buffalo in comfort. Only the top of the head and shoulder of that big beast was above the water, and the eyes were closed against the vertical rain—such a picture of quiet contentment!

Many trees have come crashing down, the soil eroded from between their shallow outspread roots, but certainly the monsoon is conducive to vegetative spread. The way the grasses and weeds have spread is astonishing; even in shallow land under an inch or more of water, these plants have gained ground. Apparently they are none the worse for a drowning over a few days—in fact, this seems to be necessary to swell and revivify their underground stems, baked hard and dry by many months of sun, and to start them on their vegetative growth. Even shrubs and trees suffer no harm from being waterlogged for a week or two—provided the soil is hard and has not been dug up.

I was much impressed by the ability of carpet vegetation and trees to stand long periods of inundation, and come up so quickly immediately the water dried, when I had occasion to study the flora of a tank-bed over two successive years. But that, of course, concerns quite a different set of plants and circumstances.

1957

Nature's Wars

24

Monkey Versus Man

INSIDE THE COMPARTMENT it was crowded and close, and outside too the afternoon was muggy. I bought a 'sweet-lime' at Jalarpet Junction to assuage thirst and lassitude, and balanced it speculatively on my bent knee. Would it be bitter, would it be weak and watery, or would it be sharply satisfying? A hairy grey arm slid over my shoulder, lifted the fruit off my knees, and disappeared, all in one slick, unerring movement.

I jumped out of the compartment, and there, perched on the roof of the carriage, was the new owner of the sweet-lime, a trim, pink-and-grey she-monkey, eating it. My gestured threats had no effect on her, squatting securely out of reach, and she ate on unconcernedly. She jerked the rind free of the top of the fruit with her teeth and detached it in pieces, and having exposed the pulp, bit into it daintily, eating it in small mouthfuls, removing the white, pith-like core with her fingers and spitting out the pips.

I should have felt annoyed, I suppose, but this was the first time I had seen a macaque eat a sweet-lime and I was interested. Years ago an American lady had lectured me on the right and only way to eat an orange; how one should take the bitter rind with the pulp as nature had intended a citrus fruit to be eaten. I had never been able to eat any citrus fruit that way, and I felt gratified to note that this macaque ate the fruit just as I do, rejecting rind, pith and pips with care.

A big, thick-muscled dog-monkey came stalking along the carriage tops, and my she-monkey leaped lightly on to the galvanized iron roof of the platform and from there to the security of the slender upper branches of a neem where the dog-monkey would find it hard to follow, the half-eaten fruit clutched securely in one hand. She did not stuff it into her mouth, to be stowed away in her cheek-pouch till danger had passed, as macaques are apt to do—apparently the acrid rind was as distasteful to this daughter of nature as it is to me!

There are many suburban stations along South Indian railways that hold their colonies of Bonnet monkeys. I could name a dozen such places off-hand and these have sustained their individual macaque colonies from ever since I can remember. This partiality of macaques to railroad stations is not peculiar to the South—in North India, the Rhesus takes the place of the Bonnet monkey along railways. Both are macaques, and look and behave very similarly, the flat, tousled crown of hair and longer tail distinguishing the Bonnet monkey from his northern cousin. The Langurs, no less sacred and therefore equally suffered by men, are rarely colonists at railway stations, though they will settle down in the neighbourhood of suburban shrines.

At these railroad colonies you can see every stage in the evolution of macaque society; the infants at their mothers' stomachs, the big dog-monkeys living as largely by plundering their fellows as by their own pickings, the carmine-faced lepers, the shrinking elders well past their prime. I have noticed that such colonies contain many more individuals than do troops of feral macaques, and I believe these railroad settlements are usually built up of several troops which have discovered that slick hands can come by more things on a congested platform than in the jungles.

There is no recognized leader among them, as there is in a feral troop, and I have often felt amused at the behaviour of two equally powerful, dominant dog-monkeys when their paths happen to cross. Each ignores the other studiously then, and affects some urgent preoccupation, preferring to live and let live rather than fight for mastery. Democracy is an institution that requires one to be unmindful of his individuality at times.

Strangely enough, though naturalists have studied macaques in the jungles, where they are nomadic, there does not appear to be any detailed record of these railroad settlements, semi-parasitic on passing humanity. A study of such a colony would, I feel, amply repay the effort, and perhaps some day an observant stationmaster will give us an authentic account of the social behaviour and habits of these settled macaques.

1950

25

Bashing a Bandicoot

HE LOW MUD wall that divides my neighbour's compound from mine runs east to west, and almost in its geometrical centre there is a crack: a jagged, vertical cleft that extends right down to the foot of the wall. And one morning I noticed a pile of new earth heaped up against the wall, a yard or so away from the crack. The earth was obviously quite fresh—it must have been dug overnight—and had been stamped all over with feet that had left no defined imprints. A miniature mine shaft, wide enough to have taken my arm, opened on one side of the heap, and scattered around it were the pink and yellow particles of some strange substance—particles that might have set a more pedantic man guessing, but which both MacInnes, my sturdy Airedale, and I well knew to be the remains of assortments of dog biscuits. An indescribably musty smell clung to the air around the place and by these tokens I knew that this excavation was the work of a bandicoot.

And more than that for I knew which particular bandicoot it was. All bandicoots are hateful creatures, but this one seemed especially so to me. He had first appeared about a month back, tunnelling his way into the kitchen, taking advantage of a loose tile in the floor. We had discovered the tile, far away from its original setting, a generous quantity of loose plaster and the ruins of what was once a tidy kitchen in the morning. And from time to time, since then, we had had painful reminders of his existence; ruthless exposures of the weak spots in our fortifications, the wrecking of a jar of oil in the bathroom, the wanton destruction of the soap and (this is the thing that still rankles in my mind) the systematic massacre of my beautiful bed of African blue lilies. I had tried every thing—poisoned titbits left seductively lying about, and every kind of trap from rat traps to huge contraptions which might have been intended for elephants. And when these had failed, I had tried MacInnes.

So when I contemplated this heap of newly dug soil my hopes began to rise, for here at last was the chance I had waited for. My trouble all along had been that I could not locate this bandicoot's earth. MacInnes and I, we might not be this infamous animal's equal in cunning, but we were confident that we could get the better of him in a skirmish. My plan was quite simple. Somewhere on the other side of the wall there would be another opening, and in between these two exits the bandicoot, tired with his nocturnal orgies. I would have the farther opening blocked and dig him out, and once he was out of the burrow—well, MacInnes and I would be there to attend to him. Strictly speaking, I would need my neighbour's permission to stop the other opening for it would be in his territory, but I decided to waive the formality and assume an extra-territorial jurisdiction, for this could only mean unnecessary delay. The man had proved to be most unhelpful and casual in the matter of this bandicoot when I had approached him earlier. You see, it was not *his* house that the vandal raided each night.

I sent a couple of men over the wall to locate the end of the tunnel and sure enough they found it, about ten yards away to the west of the cleft, surrounded by fresh earth. They closed the hole with mud and gravel and finally rolled a huge stone over it to seal it against the burrowing claws of the bandicoot. Armed with a long, flexible bamboo, and with MacInnes in attendance, I stood guard over the shaft in my garden while the men set to work with their spades, digging away at it. After a while it ceased to be interesting. MacInnes was obviously bored and so was I. The men dug on and on, right under the wall, and nothing happened. And then we were enlightened, literally. A thin pencil of sunlight appeared slowly in the dark cavity that the men were digging; it was apparent that there was an opening much nearer at hand than the one to the west of the cleft. There it was, right across the other side of the wall under an Ixora bush, barely a couple of feet from the original mine shaft in my garden. The farther opening had no connection at all with this; there was no 'mine shaft'. The thing was simply a subterranean passage connecting my neighbour's compound with mine under the wall. The bandicoot had scored again.

Such is the bandicoot. His nocturnal habits, his profound distrust of traps and baits, his incredible cunning—all these make him an exceptionally difficult creature to deal with. And still he is clubbed to death in the streets and flattened out beneath the tyres of passing cars on the roads. For the bandicoot is anything but agile. He is inordinately fond of the ditch and gutter and will come out after dark, mooching around the garbage heaps and dustbins. And in the open, away from burrows and convenient nooks and corners, he is more or less defenceless. His gait is a slinking hobble and when hard pressed he accelerates into an intoxicated lurch, but at all times his speed is negligible. A rat or mouse will make straight for the nearest cover, galloping along with swift, low bounds; but the bandicoot is handicapped by a certain lopsideness, an inability to run straight. And you can always anticipate his line of retreat for he will never attempt to cross the road or any clear space unless he is forced to; he prefers to have something to run alongside and hugs the nearest wall or gutter, for he seems to be aware of his helplessness in the open (and dislikes to expose himself.) Not that he is a coward. He will fight desperately when cornered. I have seen a bandicoot escape from between the jaws of a Polygar dog, biting and clawing his way to the safety of a nearby drain. His thick body with its cover of loose hide and coarse, straight hair gives little purchase to canine jaws, and it takes a powerful dog to hold and kill him.

However, sticks, and not dogs are his worst enemies. I have not studied the skull of a bandicoot with special attention to the frontals and parietals, but I know (strange metaphor!) that his head is his heel of Achilles. A quick tap with a cane on the head is sufficient to check his disreputable career. And so they kill him with sticks, or else they stone him to death, and then they fling his carcass on to the road to be crushed under the wheels of carts and for crows to peck out the eyes and entrails. I hope I am sufficiently human, and have enough civic sense, to feel disgusted at such things, but I must confess to a feeling of satisfaction when I see the foul remains of a bandicoot flattened out on the road. It is such an artistic end to his life.

1938

26

Death of a Snake

THIS MORNING WE felled a tree in our backyard—an ancient Dak-tree (*Pithecalobium saman*) that had stood timelessly in a corner of the compound, casting a dense, unwanted shade on the roof of the outhouse. But it is not of the Dak-tree, or of trees at all, that I am writing. It is about something else: something slim and dark and sinuous that came down from this tree, before the tree itself came down, filling the backyard with its spread of boughs and leaves.

I was squatting cross-legged like a Buddha on the compound wall, supervising the coolies at their work. It was almost through; a few more strokes of those unwilling axes and the old tree would have been felled. Then something long and slack, like a length of rope, slid down from a bough on to the tiles of the outhouse and slowly down the wall to the ground. At once there was pandemonium—shouts and yells and flying feet on all sides. From my point of vantage I could see quite clearly what it was—a dark-brown snake with yellow mottlings, well over a yard in length. It raised its head a little and looked around in a vague, dreamy sort of way, as if it wondered what all this fuss and noise and sprinting was about. And being quite unable to understand this panic, it slowly lowered its head again, coiled round and went to sleep. I have never seen a more bored and tired snake. Looking at it it seemed to me that this snake, and not the Dove, was the true symbol of Peace.

Some of the men had clambered on to the wall and joined me in my lofty security. We held a council of war and it was decided that the snake should die. I wanted to know if it was poisonous—it seemed so innocent to me. Yes, I was assured that it was exceptionally poisonous. It was a Cobra. It was a Viper. It was a Krait and King Cobra all in one. I said it looked like some sort of a harmless tree-snake; I said it must be a harmless tree-snake since it had come from a tree. It was no good, the men would not listen to my logic. After all, what did the Young Master know about snakes? Perhaps he had read about them in books, but his experience went no farther. And one of them had actually been bitten by a rat-snake in his youth and had survived it! And so they killed it with stones and long bamboo poles, beating it till it became a broken, bloody mess. And even then the tail kept twitching on in a queer, convulsive way. I was still curious. I wanted to open its mouth to see if it had any poison-fangs. It was dead and I was sure that even while it was alive it had wanted to bite no one. But here too the men were against me. It seems snakes never die, not till they are burnt to ashes. It was true that they had beaten this one to a pulp, but it was alive all the same, waiting for just such a foolish Young Master to put his hand in its mouth. Some people would do well to be less foolish and curious. And so on. They became so insufferably patronizing that I went away, leaving them to do what they liked with the snake. The last I saw of it was as they carried it off, dangling at the end of a long pole, still feebly twitching its tail in protest against being murdered violently in sleep.

Thinking of this snake I wonder; what is the true hallmark of a poisonous snake? The cobra has its spectacled hood, but then the cobra is not the only venomous snake in creation. 'The Russell's viper or daboia,' the Zoologist will tell you, 'has a squat, diamond-shaped head and a heavy, thick body.' Not that you need to observe its 'diamond-shaped' head and bloated body and dull pig's eyes to know that it is poisonous. You know it somehow the moment you see it: it 'looks' poisonous. Looking at some men you know at once that they are unpleasant. It is not any particular feature that convinces you of this but a general air of unpleasantness—they seem to exude it. Naturally you do not tell them so, for you are civilized and being civilized, hypocritical and polite. With the Russell's viper, however, you are under no such disadvantage—you may kill it on sight without wasting politeness on it. But that is not the point. There are snakes, besides the Russell's viper and cobra, which are quite deadly and you cannot say, by merely looking at them, whether they are venomous or not. Major Wall has developed an excellent system of identifying snakes by a detailed examination of the scales of their body, but this system is only for the savant—it requires an expert anatomical knowledge of the scales of snakes. Moreover it requires that the snake should be dead, for no live snake will wait for anyone to scrutinize its scales: not even for men like Major Wall. What is the obvious hallmark of a poisonous snake, then? The effect of its bite, of course, but this is not a very satisfactory method of finding it out. The truth is there is no practical way of distinguishing every venomous snake at sight. Perhaps the wisest attitude to adopt towards snakes is that of the cooly: an attitude of grave and impartial distrust.

There may be men learned in the ways of snakes who can tell each breed apart a glance, but I once came across something that would have baffled even those experts. It was a snake's egg, uneven, oblong and with a yellow, leathery shell—in fact it looked more like a ball of old parchment than an egg. Snakes are puzzling enough, but their eggs are positive mysteries. How can you say what sort of a serpent such an egg might hatch? Of course there were some obvious points about this egg. For instance it could not have been the egg of a Russell's viper, for this monstrous snake is viviparous: it brings forth its children matured and alive into the world. And anyway it was a snake's egg: the egg of a bird would have been defined and shelly and a lizard's egg much smaller. Moreover the man who gave me the egg assured me that it was a snake's egg, and why should this man have told me a lie? But that's all I knew about this egg. I kept it in a wooden box in the hope that it would hatch and reveal its secret, but the next morning I found that the ants were having snake's egg for breakfast and so I threw it away. It must have been a very dead egg.

Just think, there are all sorts of deadly serpents everywhere: in villages and in towns, in gardens and in ant-heaps, perhaps even in the dusty, over-fed waste-paper basket that you always mean to clean up next week? Not a pleasant thought, but unfortunately true. Only the other day we had a graphic proof of this when an old gentleman whom I know drew on his shoes. He felt something moving inside his shoe and hastily withdrew his foot, and the something darted out of the shoe and into the garden before any one could observe exactly what it was. The old gentleman swears that he clearly saw the spectacles on the hood of the brute and nothing on earth will induce him to change this view—not even the independent evidence of the three other people who saw the 'brute' and who are almost certain that it was only a mink! And again the cobra–krait–viper we slew this morning. Well, well. 'The land just bristles with these deadly reptiles, girl' as the O.G. said.

Not only the land. If you watch the fishermen haul their nets in of an evening, you will see a flat, ribbon-shaped snake that sometimes gets

caught in their meshes. Very like an eel it looks, and as you watch it flop-
ping weakly on the sands and note the carelessness with which the fishermen chuck it about you begin to lose your respect for the sea-serpent.
And yet the bite of this snake is more fatal than the dreaded cobra's.
Only, it loses all desire and power to bite once it is out of the sea—it gasps
and flounders around the sands and dies, a Samson shorn of his hair.

And they say that in the sandy suburbs of Ramnad, in South India,
there lives a snake thrice as deadly as the King Cobra, that flies around
at dusk looking for poor, ignorant villagers who may be about with their
scalps exposed. For this curious snake will bite only the very top of the
head: in this respect it is more particular than the most fastidious of Red
Indian scalp-hunters. You and I, we may smile and shake our heads over
this, but the villager will remain unaffected by our scepticism. Why else
do the people of these parts go about with their heads swathed in ponderous turbans long after the sun and heat are gone?

1938

27

Bommakka

W HEN FIRST I set eyes on Bommakka she was in a newly-cut field of millet, tethered to a stake. Along with the country schoolmaster who owned her, I had walked two miles to see her: and I could see little in the massive, slate-grey beast to justify my friend's pride in ownership. On the way to that field he had extolled the courage, the great strength and the noble disposition of his pet—and there was this old buffalo cow, disappointingly commonplace in her looks.

Yes, she was bigger than most village buffaloes, bigger and darker, and no doubt she was in splendid condition. But I had expected something more mettlesome than this placid, elderly, cud-chewing creature that allowed me to stroke her Roman nose, and nuzzled closer when I stopped stroking. It was then that I noticed that the poor thing was quite blind in one eye.

However, I summoned a tone of surprise and envy and spoke admiringly of the beast: I know how strong, how strangely uncritical and sensitive, the bond between a man and his buffalo can be. My friend insisted on our crossing and recrossing four spiky fields of stubble to fetch Bommakka an armful of green bean plants, pods and all. And all the way home he regaled me with rambling stories of her prowess.

No doubt I had noticed that she was in an interesting condition—she was getting on in years and this time, at least, he hoped she would bear a cow-calf—unfortunately, on both the previous occasions, in his five years of ownership, she had presented him with bull-calves. Well, to come back to what he was saying, very soon he would have to send her up to the hill-top, nine miles away, where there was lush grass to be had for nothing, and the herdsmen there would welcome Bommakka with joy. For once she was with the herd, the heifers and dry milch-cows were safe from raiding leopards. A full-grown buffalo, of course, is too much for any leopard to tackle, but I should realize that most buffaloes, grazing in the jungles with milch cattle, would be content with making off by themselves when the killer seized a calf. Bommakka was not like that: she understood her responsibilities by the weak. The minute she scented the enemy she would charge him fiercely, and no leopard dared face her onslaught. My friend went on to tell me of the rescues she had effected, and I listened politely, pondering over the amount of imagination that went to make any heroic figure.

Next week I was in the hill-top jungles, along with a shikar party. What took us there was news of tiger—of a tiger that had crossed over into our territory from an adjoining range. We found his pug-marks in the sand of a pool's edge, enormous in their splayed-out spread, but footprints on hard earth told us that he was full-grown, though not perhaps of record proportions—two months later, when that tiger was shot, our estimate was proved right, for though he taped only 9' 9" between pegs, he was in his prime and very heavily built. A deputation from the hill-top cattle pen met the guns with an urgent request to save them from this new menace. The tiger had already accounted for a cow from their herd as also for a big, red Sindhi bullock belonging to the tobacco company at the foot of the hill. As we turned home after assuring the herdsmen of our keenness, I remember thinking idly that Bommakka was probably in that cattle pen, and that even her credulous master could not expect her to deal with a tiger!

A few evenings later, in answer to a frantic message from the school-master, the local medico and I rushed off to a field, where a group of gesti-culating men stood well away from an excited buffalo. The herdsmen who had brought a very lame Bommakka down from the hill gave us a vivid account of the incident. That morning, as the herd was being driven into the jungle, the tiger had leaped out from ambush with loud roars, and the cattle and men had dispersed in terror. But as they ran for dear life to the shelter of a nearby shrine, the men had seen Bommakka turn and charge the great cat. Naturally, they could not see what followed. But for a few minutes they had heard the sounds of battle, the snorts of the gallant buffalo and the roars of the tiger, and then the tiger had gone away, the fainter and fainter tone of his occasional voice telling of his re-treat. When they had gathered courage at last to go back to the spot, they found the old buffalo in a trampled clearing, raging with pain and anger and covered with blood. Beside a bush was the victim, a young heifer that the tiger had killed instantly, with hardly a mark on its white coat.

Some sort of cleaning of the wounds had been attempted, but the men were afraid to go too near the excited buffalo, and blood was still flowing from the deep gashes. The wounds told their own tale. There were four deep, long, parallel gashes down the left hip and thigh, and the right hock was severely bitten and swollen to twice its normal size. Apparently the tiger had tried to hamstring his huge adversary from behind, leaping in from her blind right side and getting a purchase over her left hip with his grappling-hook claws.

Veterinary aid was non-existent where we were, and Bommakka's restive mood complicated matters. She was in obvious pain, but there was no hint of shock or fear: she cropped the fresh, short grass at her feet with fierce relish and glared out of her single eye at us; her nostrils were distended and when we tried to approach her, she tossed her head and snorted low in warning: the four long ropes that had been used to lead her home trailed the earth besides her—I was sure those ropes would have been useless had she not wanted to come home.

Finally, the schoolmaster sent us away, and after a while the great beast suffered him to lead her, limping painfully, to the ramshackle shed behind his cottage. Once she was there, it was possible to syringe out the wounds gently with an antiseptic lotion, and apply the liquid white paste that the medical practitioner provided. No doubt the gashes required stitches, but this was out of the question.

In a couple of days the gashes over her hip and thigh had begun to heal marvellously, but the hock was as bad as ever, and the animal had lost weight alarmingly. The big ribs stood out clearly beneath the hide, and there were deep hollows between and behind them. The trouble was that the great beast could get no sleep or rest for the pain and stiffness of her swollen hock—a buffalo that cannot lie down will waste away, however carefully it may be fed. Some half-a-dozen of us thought furiously of some plan by which the heavy weight of Bommakka's body could be eased off her stiff, injured hock—one of us even went to the extent of devising a sling for the body from gunny bags—but all our thought was futile. The schoolmaster feared that the fact that Bommakka was far gone in calf would complicate things further—however, the immediate problem was to provide her with rest.

This is a true story. I can vouch for every word of it. I state this here because on the third day a miracle happened—the buffalo found the solution that had escaped all of us. She snapped her tether with a casual flick of her head and limped, painfully but with determination, to the watercourse nearby. She waded into the murky, green depth of a pool there, deeper and deeper in till only the nostrils, the eyes and the bump of her forehead showed above water. And at last with buoyancy doing the trick that all our cunning had failed to achieve and her weight off her legs, she closed her one eye and went to sleep. It was a job to get her out of the pool and lead her home as darkness fell, and early next day she was back in the water for sleep.

Being apprehensive humans we continued to fear for her for a while. We thought that the dirty water coming into such prolonged contact with the wounds might result in sepsis, but in a week's time Bommakka's wounds had healed completely and in a fortnight she was her old self, with only the raised scars to bear witness to her adventure. Nor did the experience affect her condition as her master had feared. In due season she presented him with a robust, beautifully pink calf. Need I add that it was a bull-calf?

1952

28

Freebooters of the Air

WATCHING INDIA'S FIRST historic Test victory over England, along with a huge holiday crowd, were a dozen kites. They had followed the game with unrelaxing eyes over the previous three days, and I knew some of them by the close of the opening day.

One had two forward primaries missing from each wing, one had a squarish tail, one was exceptionally light in colour, a bleached golden brown, another was almost black in its swarthy new plumage, and there was a bird that had lost the entire tail quite recently. I was amused by the vigilance of these birds, patrolling the sky above the ground. Whenever drinks were brought out to the players, the air overhead was suddenly thick with kites, swooping and circling low for a minute before sailing away disappointed. During the breaks for lunch and tea there were opportunist scrambles, some birds alighting on the grass to consume scraps thrown aside by the crowd, others flying away with the booty. Quite a few of the spectators, discussing the happenings and prospects excitedly, had the hurried morsel expertly plucked from their hands. Especially was I amused by a sandwich-eater who laughed uproariously at his neighbour's loss, only to have his own bread snatched the next moment—the sheepish smile on his face was worth going a long way to see.

Looting kites are quite a feature of our bazaars and city markets and I know a restaurant in a park, in the heart of a big city, where these birds have grown so audaciously slick that habitues prefer the dull tile-roofed verandah to the charm of repast in the open with colourful shrubs around and grass underfoot. These freebooters of the air come a close second after crows in the list of urban fauna, but there are kites in the country too.

There, with no meat stalls and crowded eating-houses, kites work harder for their living, and are far less offensively familiar. They take to scavenging for their food, a more strenuous and less fashionable profession than picking pockets in cities. And in the remote countryside I have known kites actually hunt their prey.

I know a lake in such a place where I have seen kites fishing. They sail low over the water and clutch at the slippery prey on the surface with their talons, often without success. Here they are awkward apprentices in comparison to the many expert fishermen around, birds equipped with long, stabbing beaks or long, wading legs, other specialized features or at least the boldness to plunge headlong into the water. Elsewhere, I have seen kites chasing maimed quarry or flapping heavily among swarming termites, which they seized ponderously in their grappling-hook feet.

Once I saw a crowd of kites on the ground, in a forest glade. They had feasted with the vultures and were preening themselves after the glut, before roosting. And once I saw a kite hopping along the grass gawkily in the wake of grazing cattle. Hunger had driven that bird into a fresh inroad on the path of degradation, but apparently a kite on *terra firma* can only lose its balance when it tries to clutch with one foot at ebullient grass-hoppers.

That is just as well, for these birds have sunk sufficiently low. They are so common that we do not notice them, and when we do the occasion is often too annoying for us to appreciate their air mastery. Swifts and falcons are faster and more dashing, vultures more effortless in their soaring, but for sheer manoeuvre on spread wings the kite is unbeatable. No other bird has its slick skill in theft—its noiseless descent on the unsuspecting victim and grab with a comprehensive foot. The kite has a strong hooked beak, and a powerful build—it is surprising that it has not developed, beyond petty theft, to thuggery and murder, with its equipment.

But perhaps that, too, is just as well. Those who raise poultry have no love for this bird as it is, and if it took to a more adventurous and violent way of life, the hand of everyone must be against it, in city and in village. And that would be no small waste of national energy considering the kite population of our country!

1952

Cat Fight

O N MAY 11 the dish-faced, grey-and-white tabby with the large grey-green eyes, that my wife had encouraged, presented the world with three undersized kittens.

I had predicted the event, almost a year in advance. When this lean, mild-mannered stray had first sought the patronage of my wife, I had said that if she (my wife) was going to be so foolish as to encourage the animal with food and shelter she would one day regret her softheartedness, because the animal, being female, would inevitably have kittens in her room (this being the best room in the house), and the kittens would make a sad mess of every tidily arranged little thing.

I had gone further. I had predicted, in print, which of the two contesting toms would gain the territorial rights of the roofs of my cottage and neighbourhood and, ultimately, the favour of this pussy. Watching the rival toms, particularly when their contest was acute and for a mate rather than a broad question of territory, I had learned many things. For example I learned that though the courtship proper is both loud and long, the yowling cats that make the night hideous (and, at times, the day as well) are not courting pairs as popularly supposed, but pairs of rival toms. When two toms are of a size, and one cannot just frighten away the other by sheer physical superiority, they go through an incredibly long-drawn process of closely-proximate vocal disputes.

For days on end (sometimes for weeks) they follow each other over wall and rooftop, sitting or lying down close together, and yowling at each other. Apparently neither is willing to chance the first rash move: gradually they work themselves up into a frenzy, the yowling rises in tempo to bloodcurdling shrieks, and then there is a brief, fierce scuffle, fur flies, and they separate—though often they separate before this culmination in physical combat, and the process is repeated all over again. It is so much more a decision by duet than by duel. Naturally any injury to either contestant during this protracted game of attrition leads to its retreat, but the injured tom may recover quickly and resume hostilities. Ultimately one yields the field, after one or more real fight.

Well, everything happened as foretold by me. Only, this wretched tabby chose the lowest shelf of my enlarging table for her accouchement, and not my wife's room. My wife and my cook were both convinced that it would be fatal to shift the tiny, blind balls of fur, squirming about the trays on the shelf—a wholly sentimental and mistaken view, but which man had argued anything successfully against the conjoint opposition of his wife and his cook? Till the kittens opened their eyes, I was denied the use of my enlarger.

Thereafter they were shifted to a small front room, by a tripartite agreement to which the mother-cat (as represented by my cook, who professed to understand the creature) was also a party. This room had a boltable door and small windows high up, through which the cat could gain access to her kittens and to the world outside, as she pleased. The idea was that in the room, behind the bolted door, the kittens were safe from the powerful, semi-wild tom that was their putative father: my wife, and even more strongly the mother-cat (as interpreted by my cook), felt that once their father found them, he would make short work of them. Of course nothing prevented that husky old tom from entering the room through the open windows—in fact, more than once I found him squatting on the floor by his mate, stolidly unmindful of his inquisitive progeny. However, I saw no reason to inform my wife or cook of this.

In a month the kittens had grown infinitesimally—however, they were now able to frisk about and play with surprising speed. Morning and night their mother was at the kitchen, ahead of us, calling in a patient, low, inexorable voice for her milk and rice. She was being allowed generous rations, to provide for the heavy and sustained drain on her resources—and I noticed that several hours each day and most of the night she was away, hunting rats and squirrels, and being an expert hunter she found plenty of food for herself, besides what she was being given. One morning she did not fall to hungrily as usual, when her plate was set before her; instead, she raised her tail vertically, and calling in the same plaintive voice she used for begging food, proceeded to walk in and out of the kitchen, rubbing herself against our feet. Immediately my cook proclaimed that what the cat wanted was to have the plate taken to the front room, so that the kittens, now old enough to eat semi-solid food, could have the meal.

I had just finished reading a book on the scientific investigation of the intelligence of cats and dogs, which said that their IQ was much lower, in fact, than what their fond and fanciful owners thought it was. Reinforced by recent booklore, I explained to my cook, in simple sentences, that to attribute the thought process she did to this cat was unscientific, anthropomorphic and absurd. She persisted in her explanation, and to disprove the woman I took the plate to the room where the kittens were. Immediately the mother-cat stopped her insistent calling; she led her crowding progeny to the plate, took a few quick licks herself, and then retired; by repetitions of this move, the kittens soon learned to lick up the food themselves, though they were very clumsy in their feeding. While her kittens were feeding, the cat sat back, purring like a dynamo—when they had had enough, she ate up what was left. Twice each day thereafter, this process of persuading us to take the plate to the front room was repeated.

Here was a definite and original instance of highly intelligent behaviour—I can vouch for the circumstances, which I verified with the utmost care.

A large, black-and-white, half-Persian tom, with a very fluffy tail, and the high, mournful voice that so often goes with Persian blood, was now paying furtive visits to my room. On 21 June, past midnight when the mother-cat was away hunting, this tom entered the front room through the window and quickly bit all three kittens. There was no doubt about the identity of the killer—his fluffy tail was seen disappearing, through the window when, roused by the noise, we rushed into the room. Two of the kittens lay dead, with two red pin-points just below the angle of the chin and throat to mark the typical, throttling bite of the tomcat: the third was still alive, though also bitten.

This kitten was transferred to my room, which happens to be the only cat-proof room in the house. The dead kittens were removed at once, and the mother-cat, returning some hours later, hunted around for her lost children at intervals for days thereafter, jumping repeatedly into the room and circling around, calling to them in the short, gurgling call that she used for summoning them.

She licked the wounded kitten all over, and cuddled up close by it, tempting it to suckle—but the kitten, probably because of its throat injury, could not suck. For the next two days I fed it at long intervals with a little milk, squirted into the mouth from an ink-filler, and on the third morning it was suddenly much better. It no longer lay listlessly on its bed, indifferent, even to its anxious mother, but started exploring the room. However, its gait now was not the exuberant alternation of crouched creeping and quick leaps that it had been before the injury, but the splay-legged walk of infancy. I put this down to its weak condition, but I was not altogether correct in this. In a week it had recovered completely from its injury and was quite plump again, but its behaviour grew steadily more and more puerile. It refused all food from the plate, preferring to suck its indulgent mother whenever it could; it even went to sleep with its forelegs clasping its mother's belly and a teat between its lips. And like all creatures reverting to an infantile state, it was most cussed in its prefer-ences—for example, it insisted on sleeping inside my slipper when its mother was away, merely because I repeatedly transferred it from the slipper to a more comfortably padded box I had made for it. If ever there was a case of reversion to infancy, after shock and injury, it was that kitten.

1957

30

The Jellicut

I T IS A long time since I saw a Jellicut, but I am not likely to forget it.

The Jellicut is the southern bull ring. There are no horses and lancers here, no flashing matadors with blooded swords. No one waves red cloth at colour-blind bulls; such cloth as there is may be of any colour and is swathed around the bull's horns. The men are unarmed and unprotected, and their aim is not to kill the bulls, nor even to infuriate them.

All the same this rustic sport does not lack spectacle, or excitement, or risk.

Each bull that enters the ring—a circular stockade—has a piece of cloth, often brightly coloured, wound across and around its horns in a loose bandage, and the game consists in the men snatching the cloth clear of the horn as the bulls are driven down a fenced lane. That is, basically, the Jellicut, and explained this way it seems a tame pastime. Let me give a fuller account.

Around Madura, and elsewhere in the south, an active, medium-sized breed of cattle, compact and powerful, is to be found in varying degrees of purity. The Jellicut bulls come from this stock, and are specially reared for the ring. The best type of fighting bull is a beautifully balanced beast, not running to exaggerated dewlap or hump, light and quick-muscled. It is so evenly made, without frills and fancy touches, that its power is not apparent at first sight, except perhaps in a certain arrogance of carriage and gait. A well-trained bull will suffer no stranger to approach close, and is wickedly fast on its feet and with its horns. White, laced with front-grey or a rusty fawn on the head, fore quarters and legs, is a much-fancied colour and is said to indicate fighting blood.

Not all the bulls that enter the Jellicut ring are pure-bred or have the fighting temperament; even steers get in, at times. Some specially dangerous bulls are widely known and respected, and are taken around the countryside for the sport. These are known by the names of their villages, or by the number of years for which they have held their own, unconquered, in Jellicuts. A Jellicut is a major event in rural areas. Men and beasts come to it from all around, sometimes from considerable distances.

The crowd gathers right from the morning for the afternoon's sport. The bandaged heads of the bulls give them a deceptively complacent and domestic look, as their owners lead them in. A number of bulls are driven into the circular stockade—at the farther end is a long, narrow, fenced lane, leading out to open fields.

The spectators crowd around the palings thickly, and the men who enter the arena take up strategic posts in the lane, the frequent gaps in the bamboo fencing allowing them a ready, squeezed, acrobatic exit, should the need arise.

The fun begins with the first batch of bulls—any number up to a dozen—entering the stockade. A terrific din is set up, with the aid of drums and tin cans and loud voices. The bulls career round the ring, the dust rises in a red ground-mist under their hooves and they are off, with waving tails and low heads, down the lane. They are not allowed to enter the lane all together, but one by one, so that the waiting men have a chance.

The men hug the fence, and as a bull goes lumbering past one of them steps in and deftly snatches the cloth from off its horns. A cool head, smooth-moving limbs and perfect timing, rather than bravery or brawn are what make for success in this game, as in all sports of skill. But it is not always that the bull goes tearing blindly past, allowing its crown to be lightly snatched—close holds, and courage too, are often needed.

The Jellicut begins modestly, and the first few batches to enter the stockade hold no really dangerous bulls: some of them are just overgrown, mild-eyed calves still. The bulls with the worst reputations come later; they are reserved for the time when body and spirit have been sufficiently warmed.

At the last Jellicut I saw, staged in a village a dozen miles or so off Madura (I have forgotten its name), there was a notorious bull, a beast that had not been routed in five years, and with the name of a killer. This bull entered the stockade late in the afternoon, when we were tired of watching the sport and were about to turn home. A wave of excitement spread down the close mass of watchers, and five bulls entered the lane in quick succession, giving the men near the lane mouth no opportunity to single out any of them.

I asked my neighbour (never are neighbours nearer) to point out the killer to me, and he waved an obliging hand at the oncoming bulls. There was the bull, right in front, a big fawn-and-white animal with rolling eyes and a large, massive head held threateningly low. As it trotted past, a man leaned out from the fence, side-stepped the sweep of the horns, and plucked the cloth casually off its horns. Joining in the spontaneous applause, I felt my neighbour poking me in the ribs. 'Not that one,' he said. 'Do you see that grey bull behind all the rest? That's the one.' The grey bull was well behind the others, sauntering down the lane and keeping to the middle, the down-held head swaying from side to side to the rhythm of movement. I must say I felt disappointed at the killer's looks and leisurely manner—there were many bigger and more defiant bulls in the Jellicut that day.

A splendid young man, who had distinguished himself earlier, stepped lightly down the lane as the grey bull passed him, and reached out for the cloth. The bull turned in a flash, the young man leaped back from the quick, sideway toss of the horns, and the bull continued its sauntering way down the lane. Only when the man collapsed on the fence, and was helped out of the lane, did we realize that the bull had scored. I had come up to this Jellicut with a doctor from Madura, and we hurried round the stockade to the casualty. The horn had pierced and torn the abdominal wall, and the man was in obvious pain, but I was told that it was not so grave an injury as it looked. We tried, long and ineffectually, to persuade the young man to go with us in the car to Madura, where he could have proper attention: he would have none of our help, and was sure that the aids and medicines available in the village would do.

A week later, meeting a man from a nearby village, we learned that the bull had claimed another victim.

1951

31

The Dying Gladiator

B Y A TWIST of fate the one time I had the chance to acquire a gamecock official prestige barred me. I was a magistrate then, and my fondness for livestock had already drawn comment. My racing homers had been invested with the aura of respectability by the local Boy Scouts using them for their pigeon post (a post suggested and mainly run by me), but the goats were less easily justified.

There had been emergencies when I had to herd my goats myself, and however unostentatiously a magistrate turns goatherd news of the event gets abroad. I had a polite, unofficial note from my chief which said that rumours (which, of course, he discounted) had reached his ear that I had been seen in the scrub jungle piloting a number of goats with bucolic shouts, and that while he appreciated my right to do what I liked outside office, such capricious behaviour on the part of a First Class Magistrate was, nevertheless, ill-advised.

There had been a pompous paragraph on the official proprieties and the dignified and unbending countenance of justice, and, evidently pleased with the etymological aptness of the description, he had repeated the words 'capricious behaviour' several times.

So, when a case of betting on a cock-fight was produced in evidence, I resisted temptation firmly. My clerk, whose adjective law was superior to mine, assured me that the thing to do was to confiscate and auction the fowl besides fining the owner—I still doubt the legality of this procedure, but it had been followed by my predecessors in office, and who was I to try to act wiser? There were people present in the court who would gladly have bought the gamecock at the auction and, after a discreet interval, sold it to me at a formal profit—and somehow they had sensed my interest in this piece of evidence.

But I was firm. I contented myself with sharing my lunch with the haughty bird during the afternoon recess, and with admiring it. The iron spurs, which were also filed as 'material objects' by the police, were interesting, about an inch long, made of mild steel, and really sharp. They were encrusted with blood and had already begun to rust, but I wanted to keep them, as a souvenir of my triumph over temptation. I was denied even this satisfaction. My learned clerk said the rules decreed that such objects, which could be used again to commit an offence, had to be destroyed.

Only once, as a schoolboy, have I seen a cock-fight, and have confused and almost staccato recollections of it—the crowd in the bylane, people squatting and standing in a ring around two gamecocks, the earnestness of the men, the indifference of the birds to each other, then, unexpectedly, the spontaneous flare-up of combat, the incredibly swift and savage attack, flailing legs and flying feathers and blood, the sudden collapse and death of one of the combatants in an unrecognizable, shuddering mess of dishevelled plumes and slashed flesh. I have seen dog-fights, ram-fights, partridge-fights, even a brief tussle between two circus camels, but for sheer shock and impact and savage fury that cock-fight was unapproachable. Blake must have known its violence and gore at first-hand, to have written.

A gamecock clipped and armed for fight
Doth the rising sun affright.

Naturally the law takes a grave view of cock-fighting. It is a rather horrible sport, but even I, who feel revolted by its carnage, realize it is a sport, the kind that stimulates speculation and betting. Once zamindars and other rich, leisured people were much given to patronage of cock-fighting, but those days are past. The gamecock is a rare bird today, and getting rarer.

It is said that domestic poultry orginated in India, and our jungle-fowl go a long way towards proving this claim. However, it is in other countries that fine and specialized breeds of domestic poultry have been built up and stabilized. True we have no native breeds to compare with those tender-fleshed egg-layers, but in our gamecock, purely the product of indigenous breeding skill, we have a bird second to none in looks and power. The gamecock is essentially the same all over India, a tall, hard-muscled, brown-and-black bird with a long, graceful neck, a broad keel, and great, columnar legs—the legs and spurs are the features of the breed, and are most impressive. The hen, as in all gallinaceous birds, is smaller and much more modest in looks.

The reason why this superb and wholly indigenous breed is almost on the point of extinction is that it is of no use except in a fight. Obviously its flesh would be too tough for the table, and the small eggs have no appeal to the poultry farmer. However, a gamecock would make a grand pet, and the race can be saved if only people would keep it for its looks and its temperament. After all, utilitarian worth is as out of place in a pet as in sport, and the gamecock is a bird of real quality. It is capable of deep attachment to its keeper, and intolerant of strangers and intruders. A gamecock parading one's compound lends more than picturesqueness to the place: it lends it security for, believe me, it is a formidable watchdog.

1958

K

KANGAROO

No one has seen a kangaroo
waiting forlornly at a bus stop,
waiting for Number 22
to reach an office, home or shop.

Nor has one seen a kangaroo
waving a frantic paw to stop
some passing motorist it knew
so as to cadge a lift or drop.

Progress by leaps and bounds, no kind of
waiting for transport, is the feature
of locomotion in the mind of
this fiercely independent creature.

Nature Theorized

32

The Vengeful Cobra

ARE COBRAS SPITEFUL creatures that nurse grudges against particular men, bide their time, and take their revenge? Many people in the countryside believe powerfully in not provoking these snakes. Naturally. An attempt at killing a cobra, which is an 'attempt' in the IPC sense of the word, and which therefore results only in injury to the tip of the snake's tail, can have disastrous consequences. Provoked by the injury and cornered, a cobra can attack with determination and speed, and in the countryside (where antivenin is still not readily available) a man well and truly bitten very often succumbs to the bite. But all this, as you would have noticed by now, is no answer to the question originally posed, except to the extent that a bite is reprisal for a blow.

Well, actually there are three answers to that question, as there usually are to most difficult questions—'yes', and 'no', and 'it all depends'. People who believe that the cobra is a specially vengeful snake, and there are plenty, will come out with the most circumstantially detailed stories to prove their point. Here is such a story told me by an educated friend who firmly believes in the vengeance of the cobra. A man who owned a plot of agricultural land went to plough it and found that a cobra had entered into possession during the months it lay fallow; he tried to kill the snake and only succeeded in landing a glancing blow on its 'back' with his stick; months later, when the field had been harvested, this man, along with quite a few others, slept in that field beside his stacks of harvested jowar; he was covered from head to foot in the tough, black 'kumbly' that people use in those parts, but the toe of his left foot alone was exposed; in the middle of the night the cobra bit the man on his left toe, and he died. According to my friend this story proves, conclusively, the cobra's spiteful nature. According to me it proves nothing. I refuse to believe that a cobra, however percipient, can identify a man solely by his left toe—even for fingerprints, you know, they use the left thumb and not the toe. Moreover, the story doesn't go to show that it was the same cobra, or even that the snake which bit that farmer was a cobra.

The school that believes the cobra is not specially vengeful does so because it (the school) argues, fallaciously and energetically, that it is too much to credit a mere snake, low down in the evolutionary scale with the intelligence to recognize and remember a particular man. Actually, neither memory nor the ability to recognize something seen (or otherwise sensed) previously, is always dependent on the self-conscious exercise of intelligence, even in that acme of evolutionary perfection, man. I do not know how you recognize people, but when I see my friend, Chari, coming down the street a hundred yards away, I do not think in these laborious terms: the figure approaching is about five-foot-six in height and almost a yard across; it is clad in a pink slackshirt and vivid green trousers; on its face I can dimly discern an expression that is at once smug, overbearing, supercilious and haughty; therefore it must be my friend, Chari. I know it is Chari straightway, and before he has got any nearer than 99 yards, I already have an excuse ready for my present inability to return that trifling sum of 25 rupees I borrowed from him in November. The idea that all men must seem alike to a cobra and that it cannot distinguish between them is presumptuous; if a man can make out a particular cobra, why can't the snake spot him?

Dogs recognize their masters in the dark (I know this is unpleasant, but the truth will have to be faced in any scientific inquiry) solely by the smell of those same masters. It is a fact that birds and reptiles can get to know particular people, not by their faces perhaps, but by some trick of movement or repose that they have and of which they are probably unconscious. Such recognition is recognition still. It is well known that wounded animals tend to attack those that caused them injury.

Apart from all this, every 'cobra s revenge' story I have investigated has centred around these basic elements: a cobra taking up residence in a locality and a man occupying the same place (whether the snake or the man was first in possession is immaterial, since this is not a legal issue), the man injuring the snake and snake biting the man, usually days after the infliction of the injury upon it. Cobras do have a strong sense of territory and resent all intrusions into the area they have come to regard as their own; especially do they resent attempts to drive them out. The snake's revenge may be due entirely to the fact that having been provoked it becomes aggressive, and bites the man on the spot, who is in the circumstances, likeliest to be the man who injured it. However, I will not rule out the possibility of specific recognition. It is there, but neither proved nor disproved by these stories. I cannot go into the question of animal recognition in detail here, because that would take pages.

Instead of pursuing the third wishy-washy, 'yes-and-no' line of inquiry, let me mention an aspect of colubrine life in our country which is not unrelated to my original question. In many rustic areas, people believe not only that it is wrong to hurt a cobra (for reasons of religious sentiment), but also that if left alone the snake will do them no harm. So, when a cobra takes up residence near them, they do their best to display their friendliness towards it (mainly by leaving it severely alone), and in due course the snake accepts the people around as part of the place, and reciprocates their courtesy by leaving *them* severely alone. Many readers must have come across such a 'vaazhum-paambu' (resident snake) as it is termed in Tamil. You should realize that this amicable truce between a cobra and humanity is not the result of intelligent understanding, or courage, or anything so fallible and flimsy; it is the result of something a hundred times more powerful, of faith.

Incidentally, the practice of 'showing' a lump of burning camphor to a cobra to make it go away is sound—snakes are very intolerant of high temperatures and fire. The offer of milk in a saucer is less sound; snakes do not care for milk any more than they do for water, as any snake-charmer can tell you—if you can get him to speak the truth.

I once knew a resident cobra, attached to the cool, shadowed, peaceful, charming little shrine of Shiva in Sandur. This was a cobra of imposing dimensions, but somehow people did not fear it—it was the temple snake, and would do no harm if one took care not to step on it. I have often watched this snake, seated on a culvert two yards from it, and admired its thick, sinuous grace—once it stayed long enough to let me complete a sketch of it, though usually it would move away with leisurely dignity if subjected to close scrutiny. That was a very old cobra, and strangely enough it loved to bask in the early morning sun (though snakes are intolerant of a strong sun) and warm its beautiful back in the slanting, yellow rays. I used to wonder if it suffered from lumbago.

1960

33

Sleeping Dogs

O N MONDAY MORNING, last week, a dusky pig-hunting Pariah dog was brought to me for a portrait sketch. He was chained to a pillar in my verandah and left with me and it was plain that he distrusted the strange surroundings and longed to be back home. When all my long knowledge of dogs had failed to reassure him, I sat down and looked the other way and waited for the fidgeting and whimpers to cease. That dog was dog-tired if ever anyone was, having been out all night after pig, but he would not relax. I suppose a hunting dog needs to be wary and darkly suspicious by nature, but I must say that this was a specially mistrustful huntsman. After a while he lay down, but with his feet beneath him, ready for instant movement, with every sense alert. Sheer fatigue began to tell upon him, and at last sleep, blessed sleep, overpowered his limbs and closed his reluctant eyes. But even then his native wariness made him hold up his head and prick his ears, and no dog can sleep with head high and ears listening. This compromise with sleep was maintained, relentlessly. His head began to nod and wobble, and his muzzle would sink inwards, but at the point of laying it down on his paws he would pick it up jerkily, cock his tattered ears, and go through it all again. It was the triumph of willing spirit, over weak flesh, so very droll, but also pathetic in a way. I sent that dog back to his hut, back to his well-earned repose.

I cite this drowsy-head in evidence of a theory that in dogs, at any rate, the ears are the last sensory organs to go to sleep and the ones that sleep lightest. The proof of this theory is complicated by the fact that dogs have such odd sleeping habits. Perhaps it is because of centuries of human association, but few other animals go in for so many grades and degrees of sleep. Dogs doze fitfully, indulge in forty winks, siestas, naps and snoring slumber—barring hibernation they know every form of sleep and repose known to every language. It is difficult to say off-hand when a dog is sound asleep, and since deep sleep is necessary for any test of the measure of suspension of normal awareness, one should be slow in surmises. The sleep-postures of dogs tell us little about how soundly they are asleep. The way a dog goes to bed seems to depend upon build and idiosyncrasies, even upon the weather. A long dog, for instance, will curl up compactly for a spell of sleep in cold weather, but in summer he will lie with limbs stretched and spread. Then there is the question of personal preferences. Some dogs like to sleep on their sides, some on their bellies; some with their heads tucked well in, and some again with the chin on the doorstep. I even knew an abandoned Labrador that would sleep flat on her ample back, with all four paws in the air! Furthermore, exceptional fatigue, debility, or a nascent fever, may cause heavy, comatose slumber, or dull some particular sense. In short one should know the sleeper and all his antecedents before predicating anything from his waking behaviour. I have not conducted any sustained experiments on sleeping dogs, preferring to let them lie as a rule. Others can have the joys of investigation and discovery; I am content to raise the point.

What will we find when we do investigate the sleeping perceptions of dogs, scientifically? We will find, I say, that when asleep dogs depend mainly and usually on their ears to warn them. The sense of touch is rarely called into use—a dog is awake and up, generally, before danger can touch him. Sight, of course, is obscured by the thickness of the closed lids, but I believe that sight is a sense that is brought into play only when a dog is wide awake. Switch on a strong light in the drawing room late at night, where the canine sentry is doing duty reclined on the best sofa, and the dog sleeps on, though the glare must filter through the lids to his eyes. If the glare is considerable and direct on the face, he may shift his head, but that is all the notice he takes. But woken suddenly from deep slumber, a dog will often jump up with a surprised 'wuff' and look about him quickly, to locate what roused his sleep-drenched suspicions. Dogs have marvellous noses which they use as much as their colour-blind eyes to explore the world—in fact, many dogs rely more on their powers of smell than on sight. One would expect this sense to function in some way, even during sleep, but I believe that like sight it is wholly dormant then. I have tried placing favourite titbits (some of them quite smelly) right in front of the noses of slumbering dogs, but it failed to evoke any response in them. In one or two instances I thought I noticed increased salivation, but I am not sure of this. Anyway, in no case was the sleeper roused.

A dog's hearing never deserts him wholly, even in deep sleep. I should make it clear that I do not say that his other senses cannot be jolted into awakening a dog, but some violent appeal to them is necessary to rouse him. The ears, however, are sleep sensitive. It is likely that ground vibrations, sensed through the body, may also serve to warn a drowsing dog, but it is on his hearing that he relies in the main. No cognizance is taken of familiar noises during sleep, however loud they may be: it is the same with ourselves. It is not the volume or vehemence of noises that jerk a slumbering dog wide awake, but something unexpected or suspicious about them. Once I spent a night at a railway retiring room, where locomotives had a nocturnal bias. That room was just above the station yard, and a small, mangy dog, belonging to the station generally, insisted on sharing the room with me, with that fine sympathy for lonely strangers that stray dogs have. All night the sudden shrieks and reverberating thunder of the steam engines tore my attempts at sleep to pieces, and that little dog slept serenely through it all! But a strange whisper would have roused him. Any noise will rouse a dog at once, if it is sufficiently sinister; stealthy footsteps, a scraping sound in places where nothing should scrape, anything that squeaks and gibbers like the Roman ghosts. If life compels you at any time to pass a sleeping Bull Terrier on his own ground, walk boldly past, with a casual, assured step, as if he were some harmless, vegetarian creature—never, never try to sneak silently past. The better plan, of course, would be to take a circuitous route, say, some half a mile from the sleeper at all points.

1949

34

The Aquatic Sambar

I N AUGUST LAST year and then in October, I was in two wildlife
preserves over 1500 km apart, one in the Western Ghats and the
other in the Aravallis, wholly different in terrain, flora and even
fauna. However, they had this in common—both held large stretches of
shallow water, and sambar.

I spent much time at these waterspreads watching the animals that
came there to drink and feed—chital in small herds, wild pigs that rooted
in the slushy banks for tubers, a great many water-birds and sambar. I was
particularly interested in the last, for they were there most of the time,
wading and even swimming across to feed on the aquatic vegetation and,
after having their fill, lying up on a flat, open bank to relax and chew the
cud.

Sambar are browsers in the main. They do also graze, especially on tall
grasses, but the bulk of their food consists of green twigs, leaf-buds and
foliage, the bark of some trees, wild fruits and water-plants. In the two
locations I visited, the forests were deciduous and in a resurgent somatic
phase. The trees that were bare and spiky in summer were clothed in fresh
green foliage again with the first showers, and the ground vegetation that
the desiccating heat had withered was now in thick new leaf. Logically,
one would expect sambar to seek aquatic vegetation mainly in midsummer when there is so little green fodder in the forests, and to feed on the
lush green growth that the rain evokes later in the year, and I did notice
the deer browsing at trees and bushes in places, but they were favouring
the waterspreads much more and guzzling the aquatic vegetation with
avid relish.

Like all forest animals, sambar turn fugitive and nocturnal where
there is much human traffic on foot by day in the forests, coming out
only under cover of darkness and lying up dormant in bush cover all day.
Hazaribagh in Bihar, notable for its sambar, is a good example of such

a place. But the deer are mainly diurnal when they are not hunted or harassed by men in their haunts. In both the preserves I visited, sambar were out by day as well.

What made the deer keep to the watersides and aquatic vegetation? I have no firm answer to the question, only speculative theories which, knowing how misleading logical reasons can be in assessing the motives of wild animals, I offer only tentatively. Wild animals are not devoid of intelligence or the capacity to learn by trial and error, but they are more governed by instinctive urges which, in the long run, are of considerable survival value. I should say this first in fairness to my speculations.

In the Western Ghats forest I went to, dhole are the chief predators of sambar. Long ago, in an old shikar book, I read an account of a sambar stag which took refuge from dhole in peck-deep water. Some of the pack then entered the pool, and a few swam to the sambar's front and engaged its attention, while two sneaked up from behind and seized it simultaneously by its ears, securing the quarry by this stratagem. The account, given as that of an eye-witness, may not be factual—I cannot even recall the author's name—but the split-second timing of the dhole seizing their victim simultaneously from either side seems to suggest authenticity. Dhole do often employ pack strategy, some distracting the prey with feints from in front (especially when it is much larger than themselves) while others pull it down by a faultlessly coordinated and covert attack from behind. I have personally observed this in forests far apart.

The point is that in slushy shallow water, when a few sambar bunch together, the dhole hunting them are at a hopeless disadvantage. During my stay at this Western Ghats preserve, thrice a sambar chased by dhole was observed to rush into shallow water fringed with vegetation. It was immediately joined by other sambar that were close by, and then the adults (even the hinds) turned aggressors, walking with outstretched necks threateningly up to such of the hunters as had entered the water after them, and violently stamping to splash the enemy, which immediately abandoned the hunt. So far as I know, this manoeuvre by the deer has not been reported by others, though many have studied the prey-predator relationship between dhole and sambar, even in this very location. Is it far-fetched to suppose that the sambar I observed haunting watersides in this preserve did so because the dhole were there?

Perhaps not, but this could not possibly be the motive in the other preserve I went to, where there were no dhole, though there were tigers. Here, on several successive days I watched a group of sambar stags in the last stages of antler regeneration feeding heavily on water-plants. There were many kinds of plants in that lake; and from over 150 metres away I could spot only a very few—white and pink lotuses and water lily (the leaves of which only were eaten), and a cylindrical alga which was probably *Enteromorpha*. I could not even collect the small flowering plants the deer fed on, because they were in mixed spreads and I could not tell which were eaten.

The hinds were content to graze the lush herbage on the banks, wading in a little way to eat a water-plant occasionally, but the stags fed only on the aquatic vegetation, assiduously. Could it be that these plants contain something that promotes antler growth?

1990

35

Slow-breeding Rhinos

ONE FEBRUARY MORNING, near Bhaisamari bheel in the Kaziranga sanctuary, I saw a big rhinoceros cow closely followed by her almost full-grown daughter. In fact, the latter was so large that from a distance I took this pair for a bull and a cow running together. I saw the pair again next day, and also a few days later. Having no close idea of the age of the young cow, I asked those with me, but they too did not know, and gave widely differing estimates.

How long does a rhino calf take to grow up and until what age does it run with its mother? These are highly relevant factors in assessing the normal breeding cycle among free-living rhinos. I believe there are zoo records of the growth of calves, and these should be useful—such zoo records as exist of breeding would be less reliable, as in captivity the average interval between breedings may be quite different from the same period among wild animals.

Many factors have to be considered to get a sound understanding of the breeding cycle of free-living animals. For example, breeding may be more intensive in some years than in others, and some variation in intervals between successive breedings may be noticed. Again, among gregarious animals, breeding may be less slow-paced than among solitary beasts: I think this is specially so in the largest herbivores. Unlike gregarious animals of near (though smaller) size like gaur and buffalo, rhinos are solitary—that is, they do not live in herds, though a bull and a cow may stay together for a while when mating, and the calf stays with its mother till nearly her size. Among such solitary animals, the cow does not breed till her calf is nearly full-grown and leaves her.

Even if we know it, mere knowledge of the breeding cycle of a wild animal will not help much in effectively conserving it. For this vitally important purpose what we really need to know is the increment to a much-reduced population that may be expected over a period, if it is protected from artificial depletive influences: for this, the number of conceptions and births is less material than the number of young that will survive to adulthood and breed.

From what I have been able to learn by asking knowledgeable persons, and thinking over known facts, I believe a rhino calf is not fully grown till it is some six years old: by that time it is past its adolescence, though it continues to 'furnish' for quite some time thereafter. Among elephants (the largest land mammals—rhinos are the second largest) calves take about 14 years to reach adolescence, but then elephants are gregarious and among them a cow may breed again while her calf is barely half-grown. I do not know how long the association between a rhino cow and her calf lasts, but should think it is about three years. The one thing that can be said definitely about rhinos is that they are slow-breeding.

Is that all we know about the breeding potential of rhinos? Not at all. However, empirical and approximate it may be, we know something much more important about their breeding capacity, that should be of the greatest value in the present attempt, under Project Tiger, to conserve and revive animals wholly unrelated to them.

We know that many years ago it was feared that the Great Indian One-horned Rhinoceros would become extinct in Assam, and that its numbers were then reckoned at a few dozens at best. Rhinos are slow breeders, giving birth to only one calf at a time and breeding only at intervals of years, but we know that what caused the alarming decline of the rhino population of Assam was intensive poaching and nothing else. Dedicated work in protecting the animal from poachers resulted in a gradual increase in its numbers, and now it is definitely saved in Assam and its population in that State is estimated at several hundreds.

Anyone who will take the pains to indulge in a little elementary mathematics will know that irrespective of the slowness of the rate of decline or increment in a population of animals, and in spite of the uniform maintenance of that rate, the actual decrease or increase in numbers is always at continuously accelerated figures. Note that the only depletory factor affecting the rhinos of Assam that was controlled was the entirely artificial one of human interference: losses by natural causes, such as predation (on occasion a tiger may take a young calf), diseases, or the unpredictable exuberance of the mighty Brahmaputra, could not be, and were not, controlled.

In spite of this, and the rhino being a slow-breeding, far-ranging animal, its revival from an almost hopelessly reduced population to safe numbers in Assam is an established fact, and what is more the revival did not take such a long time, after all.

Here is a vital clue to success in wildlife conservation in our country. Provided the environment has not been too badly degraded or damaged, the accord of efficient protection from hunting and human disturbance in an adequate area is certain to result in a notable revival in the numbers of depleted wild animals, particularly of those species that are solitary, though they need not be herbivores as rhinos are—in fact, I think that animals like the tiger, the leopard and the sloth bear, all of which are also largely solitary and also little affected by being preyed upon, will benefit vastly by such protection. Gregarious animals face slightly different problems, but no doubt they, too, would be greatly benefited by such protection.

In theory, it is so simple to protect the wildlife of an area from hunters and overmuch human disturbance, but in practice this may prove extremely difficult in our country. The officials on whom the mantle of protectors of nature falls are, unfortunately, seldom able to resist the temptation to do what they consider, in their ignorance, more positive things, and to try and improve upon nature, so that they themselves turn disturbers so readily.

1973

36

Mixed Issue

A CORRESPONDENT FROM BURDWAN, who shuns the limelight and is keen on anonymity, has a puzzling problem in genetics to solve. He keeps ducks and poultry, and now he has a home-bred cock 'with a peculiar appearance: its body is like that of ducks while it is a cock.' It looks, in fact, 'like a cross between a drake and a hen or a cock and a duck', and my correspondent wants to know if such an off-spring is possible and, if it is, whether the matter is of scientific interest.

The answer is simple. It cannot be a duck-fowl hybrid, but unquestionably it is of scientific interest. I can already imagine frantic letters in the post and Press by geneticists and physicists interested in the way heredity is affected by atom-bomb contamination. Perhaps Burdwan will be under a scientific cloud, and its rainfall anxiously analysed. But all to no purpose. I am old-fashioned in my views on the sanctity of correspondence, and neither torture nor even spot cash can extract from me the name of the owner of the bird of Peculiar Appearance. And without knowing his identity, how can the scientists get at his cuck, or maybe it is his dren?

However, I will answer the very natural question of the reader: how far are these things possible? So far as we know, hybrids are possible only between closely-related animals. But I should immediately add two riders. First, this does not mean that all closely related animals will inter-breed; even animals in vigorous health, of the same species and of opposite sexes, may not breed together, as those who have kept pigeons will know. Second, nearly related animals may look very different, and need not always belong to the same genus. This needs amplification.

All breeds of pigeons, fantastically different in looks as an Owl, a Jacobin and a Runt are, go back to the same ancestor (the wild Blue Rock) and will freely interbreed. The lion, the tiger and the leopard, all belonging to the genus *Panthera*, have been interbred—the progeny of the lion-tiger cross are said to be fertile. The mule and the hinny provide familiar examples of infertile hybrids between the horse and the ass, both belonging to the genus *Equus*. The issues are more interesting when we consider the dog tribe. No one knows precisely how the domestic dog was bred, but it is thought that both the wolf and the jackal contributed to man's best friend. Utterly dissimilar-looking breeds like the Great Dane and the Old English Sheep-dog can be interbred—in fact, the only limitation to interbreeding different breeds is the physical one of size, and such dogs as the Bull Mastiff and the Dobermann Pinscher are examples of recently manufactured breeds. Moreover, the domestic dog will breed not only with the wolf but with the jackal also. Note that all three belong to the same genus, *Canis*.

With cattle we come to more interesting hybrids. As everyone knows gaur can be interbred with domestic cattle, and the Mithun of Assam is the result of such sustained outcrosses. Recently I believe someone succeeded in breeding a zebu-buffalo hybrid—the word 'zebu', which is rarely used in our country is, unfortunately, the only specific name for our humped cattle. Here the parents belong to different, though closely allied genera. The limits of mixed blood in animals, in actuality, seem to be indicated by these examples.

In mythology there are no such limits. Apart from exotic hybrids like the unicorn, the hippogriff and the griffin, our own legendary fauna can boast of the lion-elephant Yali, the two-headed Gandaberunda (though this is no hybrid), and a highly decorative creature, part-fish and part-reptile, found in old temples and incorrectly identified with the crocodile by art critics. Were my correspondent's cock carved in stone instead of being a thing of flesh and blood, it could be easily explained. That suggests to me that if the bird was referred to a gourmet with a truly discriminating palate, he could probably pronounce judgement on its ancestry.

Only twice, in my experience, has it been claimed that animals belonging to unrelated families could be interbred. In the Madras Zoo there is a small but most interesting bunch of albino blackbuck—I believe albino buck have been recorded even in wild herds, but these confined buck are pure white and breed true to colour. I was surprised to find the statement, in the guide-book of this zoo, that these animals were produced from imported (albino?) Fallow Deer, by a process of hybridization. Tactful inquiries elicited the information, from the Superintendent, that the buck as well as the information regarding their ancestry were presented to the zoo by a certain Governor. I rarely presume to rise superior to my station in life, but I was overpowered by curiosity, and so addressed His Excellency explaining how, being a naturalist, I was consumed with a desire to know the authentic ancestry of his gifted albino buck. That was close on three years ago. I still await a reply. Not that I suggest, for a moment, that H.E. is capable of purposely frustrating scientific curiosity—perhaps a discreet Private Secretary, after considering all the circumstances, decided it was wisest to consign my letter to the w.p.b.

And the second instance? Well, that was not a genuine one, either. It is only that, when I was young, my brother and I decided that a certain gentleman, who exercised authority over our lives in those days, so much partook of the physical and traditional attributes of two totally unrelated creatures that he must be the outcome of a misalliance between the two. And so we coined the word, 'pigasse', the terminal 'e' being added out of a delicate sense of style. For years, afterwards, I used a hand-drawn crest on my letter-paper, displaying a pigasse rampant, and gave it up only when this whim cost me a lucrative job, when I used my letterhead in replying to a businessman who had made me a handsome offer.

1956

37

The Aggression of the Vegetarian

I T IS HARD TO say who first expounded it, but the thesis that among Indian wild animals the larger herbivores are, as a rule, more aggressive towards men than the carnivores has been the conviction of more than one naturalist-shikari who knew our fauna intimately.

We are, of course, speaking of normal attitudes and bents—not of exceptional reactions or abnormal, cultivated tastes. The man-eating tiger and panther must be left out of this consideration, and also the rogue elephant (which is often an animal maddened by the abiding pain of a man-inflicted injury). And we should also leave out the fright reaction of animals closely confined and provoked; a captive tapir, probably the most timid of all beasts, has been known to savage a man who caused it pain.

Even with all these limitations the thesis might seem absurd at first sight. We think of carnivores as specially savage animals—in spite of the fact that Man's Best Friend is a carnivore. That they kill to live is something that makes people think of them, at all times, as likely killers.

But normally no carnivore attacks man. When excited, as when courting, or when apprehensive, as when guarding cubs, a tiger or panther may attack a human intruder, but being equipped with exquisite senses, and being swift in their nervous controls, they almost invariably give a timely warning, often several warnings, before they attack.

I can easily find support for this view that it is the chance-met herbivores that are more dangerous by citing the evidence of zoo experts. Any experienced zoo man will tell you that the greater cats give him little cause for worry, and that it is some of the old dog-monkeys and, in particular, old bucks and stags (and we always think of antelopes and deer as such harmless, lovable creatures!) that are really dangerous. But I will not cite this testimony. In my opinion, animals, especially mammals, live under such artificial restraint in even the best-run and planned of zoos that observation of these captives helps little in understanding their true nature.

It is especially the adult male that is aggressive, among the herbivores. The bull elephant and the lone bull gaur can both be really dangerous on occasion. The bull gaur is normally a most peaceable beast, very shy of man, and rarely attacking except under extreme provocation—it is the bull wild buffalo that is truculent by nature. But there are authentic instances of an old lone bull gaur attacking men without provocation, and I myself knew for a ticklish week a young lone bull that was so restive that to approach him was to ask for trouble.

When a bull gaur does go for a man, he is persistent and savage in attack, continuing to trample, gore and toss the victim long after death. This is generally true of herbivorous aggressors, which lack the mercifully swift and clean efficiency of the carnivores in killing.

Ask any true jungly, living on the outskirts of a typical forest area holding elephant, gaur, deer, tiger, panther, bear and pig, and he will tell you that it is the elephant that he fears most. Being mainly nocturnal and crepuscular, being so early with their perception of the approach of man and so quick to get away from him, or at least to give him due warning not to approach closer, the greater cats rarely cause humanity in the jungle any anxiety. Sloth bears (which are vegetarian in the main) can be dangerous: being shortsighted and given to deep preoccupations, at times they take no notice of one till one is almost upon them—and then their behaviour is unpredictable. Pig in the jungles usually give men a wide berth, but on occasion an old boar may stand his ground and turn aggressive—when there can be no two opinions on what the human intruder should do! However, it is the mighty elephant that people whose business takes them through elephant jungles really dread. In places where they have not been disturbed or molested, as in some sanctuaries, elephants may be very tolerant of humanity. But elsewhere, in the Nilgiris, for example, they can be aggressive and dangerous.

It is usually a lone bull that one has to beware of, but I have heard of an entire herd attacking transport lorries. Personally, I think this truculence is a comparatively recent development, caused or stimulated by the constant disturbance of human invasions of their territory, probably also by occasional injury inflicted by men—elephants are both long-lived and intelligent. The fact remains, however, that though one can find reasons for a tusker turning aggressive, he is a singularly dangerous beast. The uncanny silence with which he can move, the deceptive seeming casualness of his movements, his persistence in attack and the fact that unless one can jump down a steep bank it is hardly possible to outrun an elephant, and quite impossible in bushy or grassy cover, all make an encounter with a misanthropic tusker specially risky and terrifying. Luckily, he is shortsighted, and if one gets quickly behind a tree or bush, hugs the earth and freezes, chances of escape are excellent.

1961

38

The North-South Rule

IT IS A generally accepted principle that when an animal has an all-India range, it attains its best development in its northern reaches and declines in size in the southern. This has been endorsed by eminent ornithologists with reference to many species of resident birds—obviously the rule cannot apply to migratory birds that come to our country, both to its northern regions and its southern, from outside. Naturalists have also applied this rule to some of our mammals, such as the common langur and the blackbuck. Now any rule, to be valid and viable, must be true of the overwhelming majority of a class of animals, though there may be an exception or two—these are termed, somewhat slickly, 'exceptions that prove the rule'.

I do not think the rule holds for our mammals: it does not exhibit a demonstrable general trend when applied to them. Naturally, animals limited either to the North (like wild sheep, goat-antelopes, the clouded leopard and the caracal) or the South (like Nilgiri tahr, the lion-tailed macaque and the slender loris) cannot be compared, because they do not live in both parts of the country. It is only those animals that are found in both the North and the South, in the same species or in regional sub-species or races, that can be compared.

At this stage it must be realized that individuals of exceptional size may occur anywhere in the all-India distribution of an animal: only the relative sizes of the average adults of different regions can be taken into account for establishing, or disproving, the rule. If it is found that it is neither the northern nor the southern population of an animal that displays this maximum average adult size, but a population living in between or markedly to the west or east, then also the rule breaks down.

Now, quite a few mammals with an all-India range display such a wide variation in adult size in all their regional populations that there can be no comparison of the relative size attained in any of them. Examples of such animals are the leopard (very big and very small adults are to be found in most regions), the tiger (in which individual variation, where it is perceptible, appears to be no question of latitude but of environment), palm civets, the porcupine, and other rodents.

It has been suggested that the rule applies to our deer. Sambar, chital, muntjac and mouse deer are the only deer species which occur both in the North and in the South. I have seen impressively big sambar in the deep southern hill ranges, and noticed that in parts of Uttar Pradesh (such as the Corbett Tiger Reserve) the sambar are not only quite average in size but also notable for their very poor antler development: the most robust populations of sambar in India (where this deer with a wide distribution in south-east Asia attains its best development) are probably to be found along the Bihar-Orissa border. It is claimed that it is in sub-Himalayan tracts that the chital attains its best size. It is true chital in this region do come very big, but I am very sure that elsewhere, too, in the south, they are no less impressive, though only in specific locations. For instance, in the Moyar-Masinagudi area of the Mudumalai Sanctuary of Tamil Nadu, the chital (both hinds and stags) are as big as they come anywhere. The other two deer show no latitudinal differences in size.

All this does go to show that there is no demonstrable superiority in bodily development in the northern populations of many of our animals, but what is much more damaging to the rule is the provable existence of animals which attain their best size in the South. The most notable example of such an animal is the gaur. The gaur, like the sambar, has a wide distribution in south-east Asia and is also there in some northern States, but nowhere does it attain the truly magnificent size it does in the southern reaches of the Western Ghats, in Karnataka, Tamil Nadu and Kerala.

The Indian hare is differentiated into a northern and a southern subspecies: the latter is the larger. The giant squirrel, too, seems to be larger in its southern hill forest range. Finally, the most magnificent of our land animals, the elephant. There does not seem to be any demonstrable superiority of size between the regional populations of this somewhat discontinuously distributed giant. In fact, adults of distinctly different bodily conformation are to be found in the same herd, and the elephant is probably the farthest-ranging of our mammals by nature—given the space, it traverses well over 200 km of forests in its seasonal treks.

A man I know, who has a rabid antipathy to the north-south rule, cities the elephant as conclusive evidence disproving the rule. Taking the elephant in southern Kerala to start with, he traces its ascent northward up the Western Ghats right up to Goa, without disclosing any increase or decline in average adult size, and then goes farther north to Gujarat, where its sudden and swift diminution in size is so drastic that it disappears altogether from view!

1981

39

The 'Pinch Period'

IT IS NOW, in midsummer, that forest-living animals go through a taxing period of adversity, termed the 'pinch period' in contemporary Indian wildlife literature. It is the mammalian herbivores, like deer, gaur and even antelopes, that are most affected by this month of want and stress, though the other animals also experience hardship.

It is mainly in the deciduous forests, where at this time there is hardly any green fodder in the ground vegetation and the trees have shed their leaves and still not fully renewed them, and where the water has dried up and sources of the life-giving fluid are few and far between, that the animals are sorely handicapped. Undoubtedly, they suffer much during this month, and some may even grow so weak that they fail to survive it. But is this a natural recurrent disaster against which conservationists provide artificial relief (like artificial water-holes, in a few places even the provision of green fodder), or is it something that also has an ultimate beneficial influence? After all, it is no hardship newly imposed on the animals of such forests, but something they have survived for centuries.

This question has intrigued me for decades. Naturally even a partial understanding of the problem cannot be gained by arm-chair theorizing, and as opportunity offered itself (quite adequately), I have been investigating it in the field in suitable habitats all over India, in the north-west, central and southern regions. I think the 'pinch period', while never beneficial to an individual animal during its currency, does benefit its species as a whole. I shall try to set out my view broadly, in non-technical language, resisting the temptation to cite instances from my field observation, and omitting all mention of quite a few fascinating aspects of animal behaviour arising out of the study.

What happens in a typical setting is that early in summer (which is spring in our forests) the grasses and other ground plants wither and turn dry and brown. There is a prodigal flowering of the trees, usually preceded or accompanied by leaf-shedding, and by April the trees are still not in thick green leaf (though the leaf-buds are opening). But the natural consequence of the flowering is the fruiting, and most trees are in fruit. Many of these fruits are eaten by the animals, some even by men. Forest pools and ponds dry up, and the nullahs also are dry, except for a few small puddles along their course. A notable feature of the wild mammals of such habitats is that they do not shift *en masse* to a greener and less parched tract—as birds do, when the finding of sustenance in a habitat becomes harder and harder. This is because beasts lack the swift coverage of distances of flight, traversing hundreds of miles in a day. Some large herbivores, like gaur, are given to ranging far in their feeding, and even monkeys shift feeding grounds seasonally. Animals like gaur and elephants may cover considerable distances in the course of such treks, but over a period. They go on from one feeding ground to another and then to a third, and take months to go far out and return.

Moreover, the gain in fodder by such shifts is only slight because they traverse much the same kind of forests, similarly affected by seasonal rigours—though there is very considerable gain in the maintenance of the balance of nature by such shifts, important faunally and floristically, but outside the scope of this inquiry. Furthermore quite a few animals do not move out at all but stay put in their settings.

Most wild beasts prefer still water, or slow water, to drink from, and will go long distances to a puddle or a muddy water-hole rather than to a river that is nearer. But during this period it is not that the herbivores (including the ruminants which crop fodder quickly and in bulk to lie up in safety and chew the cud) are wholly without food or water. In places the dry leaves forming a carpet on the forest floor provide a natural silage that is edible and freely eaten, and some green leaves not browsed when on the plant are eaten after they have been shed and have turned yellow. Moreover, there are fruits and bulbs and tubers, and along the dry nullahs (which still retain some subsoil moisture) brakes of succulents serve to augment the failing water resources.

Two things in the way the animals are affected by this month of rigours are significant, and neither seems to have been considered by faunists. First, there is a forced change of diet and a limitation to the food intake, with green fodder no longer there in plenty. Secondly, and no less important, it is at this time, when their physical reserves are at an ebb, that many animals undergo a change of coat, shedding their old coat in ragged patches, and regrowing the new—a great strain on their bodily resources.

The benefits from this period of attrition and want are twofold in the main. The lame and the halt, the too old and the infirm, often succumb to the 'pinch period' and thereby the community as a whole is rendered more healthy by the non-survival of the unfittest—to adapt a phrase from Darwin—this is specially a benefit to gregarious animals. Neither predation nor epidemics are selective and serve to weed out the unfit, whereas this seasonably imposed set of hardship and change does serve this purpose—I mean, all the factors combined, a forced change of fare, severely limited food and water resources and the change of coat.

The second benefit, although I have no proof of it, is that a spell of austerity serves to tone up the system. Note that with increasing loss of body weight during this period, the basal metabolic requirement is also reduced, enabling most animals to survive. It is an age-old belief in many human communities that the periodic spells of fasting and austerity imposed on its members by tradition benefit them not only spiritually but also physically. I believe that this period of want and change of fare does serve to improve the powers of endurance of the wild animals and also conditions them to increased bodily vigour when the days of plenty return.

1987

Nature Domesticated

40

My Distinguished
Neighbour

FOR SOME TIME last year I lived next door to an elephant—I mean literally next door. Only a low brick wall separated us, and there was nothing to prevent his reaching out and grabbing the precious vegetation of my garden or even me, but of course he never did such a thing. For he was an orderly, law-abiding sort of elephant, who knew the laws of property and trespass and respected them. He would stay all day in his trellised stall or else come out into the sun and air and stand towering above my garden wall, but as I said his exploring trunk never crossed it. He could not come farther than that, for his foot-chains held him, though perhaps it was unnecessary to shackle such a well-behaved creature. Each day I would rise to the sound of bells as he was led out for his wash in the pond, and afterwards, sitting idly in the verandah, I would watch Jadhav returning from the bath, black and fresh and newly scrubbed, the little gun-metal bells at his throat tinkling with each movement. All that is gone with the past year. I live once again amidst commonplace men, but I often think of those far-off days and of my distinguished neighbour.

Jadhav was a fine animal well over eight feet high. And I suppose he would have grown taller still, for he was only a dozen years old and an elephant is still young at 40. His ears were rounded and whole, with none of those tears and leprotic patches that make their appearance on the ear-folds of most elderly elephants. His youthful tusks were barely a foot long, and his hide was sleek and smooth, with a scattering of thick bristles over the back and face. He walked on inaudible feet, in spite of his magnificent bulk. Elephants are remarkable for the utter silence of their movements. Cattle and horses go past with a clatter of hooves and you can hear the thud of the galloping feet of a dog yards away, but elephants and cats—you never hear them move. They both walk on cushioned feet.

The huge, circular sole of the elephant's foot is a pad of loose fat, except for the horny rim of toes. When the foot is pressed against the earth this pad is drawn in and up, but its weight lowers it when the foot is lifted, so that it is the first thing that comes in contact with the ground when the elephant puts down its feet. And that is why these massive animals move noiselessly even over ground strewn with dry, crackling twigs, and leaves: their cushioned soles muffle all sounds.

But what used to surprise me even more than the silence of Jadhav's gait was its apparent slowness. His walk was a languid dawdle, but I found it was all I could do to keep up with him on the rare occasions when I accompanied him on his early morning strolls. The elephant, by the way, bends his hips legs outwards and behind at each step, like a man.

Whenever I saw my neighbour I used to be reminded of an ancient school text from which I had learnt all about the domestic uses of the elephant—about the timber-dragging elephants of Burma, stacking and carrying teak, lordly State elephants marching in royal processions, shikar elephants, performing elephants, and the war elephants of ancient and more recent times. Elephants were used to carry heavy guns in the Indian Army till very recently, as anyone who has read 'The Servants of the Queen' will remember—

> We lent to Alexander
> The strength of Hercules,
> The wisdom of our foreheads
> The cunning of our knees.
>
> Make way there, way for the ten foot team.
> Of the Forty Pounder Train!

Of course my encyclopaedian school text had not forgotten those gun elephants, but it had omitted all mention of Jadhav and his kin. Jadhav belonged to a temple. He was painted, decorated and taken along the streets during festivals, but otherwise he did nothing beyond belonging to the Gods. At times he got quite bored with his tethered inactivity, and then he would swing himself from side to side for hours on end, a recreation that seemed to amuse him in some strange way. Occasionally he would succeed in working himself up into a frenzy, and the swinging would change to a violent, jerky dance, but a word from his mahout was always sufficient to restore order and calm. It was only very rarely that Jadhav indulged in such antics—ordinarily he was suave and dignified, serene and nonchalant as only an elephant can be. I have not seen a gentler, more tractable creature than this elephant. His strength was incalculable—I have seen him toss a boulder aside with a casual flick of his trunk—and still he never rebelled. His mahout was devoted to him, but at times, when Jadhav was particularly stupid or inattentive, the man would lose his temper and then a truly comic scene would ensue. The mahout would stand in front of his charge and lecture to him on the gravity of his misconduct and then he would deal out the punishment, deliberately, almost unwillingly, like a man discharging an unpleasant duty. And Jadhav would stand penitent and still throughout, and at the end of it he would throw up his trunk in a huge *salam* and trumpet shrilly to announce that the episode was concluded. . . .

1939

41

Amrit Mahal

TODAY THERE IS a welling enthusiasm for mechanization in our country, especially in regard to transport and agriculture. I hope I am not atavistic in my values, but I cannot help feeling at times that we are rather carried away by this new-found enthusiasm. Quite recently I overheard a friend explaining to another the virtues of a particular make of tractor, suitable for small holdings, about which he had heard.

No salesman, boosting his stock, could have been more full of rosy words, but listening to my friend the conviction grew upon me that two or three pairs of Amrit Mahal bullocks could do all that was claimed for the tractor, at less cost and without needing replacements and spare parts. And they could supply manure, solve the problem of inter-village transport, and be useful about the farm in a dozen other ways, in addition.

Writing in 1818, the Commissioner of Mysore said, of these magnificent bullocks: 'They are active, fiery, and walk faster than the troops. In a word they constitute a distinct species, and possess the same superiority over other bullocks in every valuable quality that Arabs do over other horses.' Long before this, and long afterwards, the speed, stamina and mettle of the breed were highly valued by the armed forces—Hyder Ali and Tippu Sultan used them as pack animals in their rapid campaigns, these bullocks distinguished themselves with the English Army in Afghanistan, and the Iron Duke (who knew his Mysore well) missed them in Spain during the Peninsular War.

Amrit Mahal bullocks were used in Mesopotamia during World War I, and the GOC Force 'D', Baghdad, reported: 'They can walk as fast as a mule on the march, and are steadier when crossing pontoon bridges and over bad roads, and in spite of the difficulty of giving them the rations to which they have become accustomed, have stood the climate well.'

The transport corps of armies are less dependent on pack animals now, but the Amrit Mahal breed is by no means outmoded or just an interesting relic of a military past. Thousands of miles of winding, intersecting cart tracks mark the Indian countryside, often merely a pair of parallel ruts worn through scrub and hill jungle. The man who thinks that mechanized transport will soon displace bullock carts here must be singularly motor-minded, unrealistic and unobservant. Bullocks for the plough and cart are a vital and integral part of life in India, and in this country of small, detached holdings, draught bullocks are good for centuries to come.

It is hardly surprising that in a country where bullocks have always been valued even higher than milch cows, a number of draught breeds should have been evolved. Apart from dual-purpose breeds like the Ongole, Nellore, and Sindhi, we have specialized draught breeds in the Kangeyam, Hallikar, and a number of less stabilized strains, including the miniature 'rekla' breeds. None of these can compare with the Amrit Mahal, except perhaps its close cousin, the Hallikar. Amrit Mahal bullocks are unbeatable, unapproachable, as draught animals. The Commissioner of Mysore was just and temperate in claiming a superiority for them as patently superlative as the qualities of the Arab among horses.

The Amrit Mahal is a long-horned breed. Even the stud bulls and the cows have long, tapering, sabre-curved horns. The breed is marked by a long, lean face, a muscular build combining size and strength with active speed, and real endurance. The bullocks continue to flourish after they are five years old, and reach their prime about the age of eight years; they are good for hard service for many years thereafter. A full-grown bullock stands nearly five feet high (the official average is 52 inches) and has a girth of about 70 inches. Such an animal should weigh about 800 lbs. Long, tapering tails, ending in a bushy tuft of black hair, well below the hocks, are characteristic of the breed.

The bullocks are typically iron-grey in colour, darker on the head and forequarters and almost white on the flanks; the cows are grey, or white at times, and the dark grey deepens to black on bulls. The bullocks stand over a lot of ground on firm limbs—they are big, powerful beasts, endowed with a mile-eating stride and tireless, quick muscles.

My head-piece,* sketched from life, shows a pair of bullocks in repose, and has a placid, decorative bias. It gives no indication of the fiery, high-mettled temperament of these animals. The Amrit Mahal and Hallikar

*Not reproduced here.

breeds seem to have had a common ancestry, but whereas the Hallikar handles easy and has a more amiable temperament, Amrit Mahal bullocks are high-strung, resentful of strangers, and wild, a quality which is at once their chief asset and handicap. The hardihood and quick temper of the breed is largely due to the fact that they are raised under natural conditions, the young herds being grazed in the jungles and exposed to wind and weather. It is said that a herd in the jungles can take care of itself against all comers, including the tiger, and knowing the dislike of tigers for a massed attack of determined, spike-pointed horns, I can well believe this.

It should be possible, by careful, selective breeding, to eliminate the stubborn wildness of the breed without loss of spirit or stamina. This is not so difficult as it may seem at first. Those who have followed the progress of the Coloured Bull Terrier in the last 20 years will know what I mean.

It is unfortunate, and all wrong, that this superb breed of cattle, whose hardihood and abilities have been tested and proved here and on foreign soil, should be so little known outside its native Mysore. But Amrit Mahal cattle have so long enjoyed the patronage of the rulers of Mysore, that it is reasonable to hope that governmental recognition will now be available to them in enhanced measure. Perhaps, in the near future, these superlatively useful bullocks, which provide so many answers to the problems of our rural economy, will be appreciated and made available on an all-India basis.

1951

42

Versatile Neem

SOME TIME AGO, there was a report about the neem being introduced into a distant country from India, as a quick-growing shade tree with potent medicinal and germicidal properties. And, reading it, I recalled the adage about the prophet not being honoured in his own country.

That is not quite true. Even today people in the countryside are alive to the neem's versatile virtues. It is seldom cut down and is still planted in and around human settlements. Tradition decrees that, when the Indian new year comes round about midsummer (in April) and the neem bursts into prodigal, fragrant white bloom, its tiny flowers mixed with jaggery should be cooked into a special side-dish, both as a tonic relish to mark the commencement of a fresh year, and to remind people that life is an admixture of sweet and bitter experiences. The latter sentiment seems largely imaginative, for neem flowers are not bitter, though the leaves and fruits are. They have a characteristic resinous aroma and are mildly astringent. In the South, the flowers, which fall soon after opening, are gathered, dried, stored and used as a garnish to impart a distinctive gusto to mashed greens, and especially to 'rasam', the thin, clear dal-soup that is taken with rice and which is the most demanding test of culinary skill in Tamil cookery.

The neem comes up readily from seed, but is not really quick-growing. It is a close cousin, the 'wild neem' (*Melia composita*), that is noted for its rapid growth. The neem is a long-lived hardwood, thriving for a century or longer, and remarkable for doing well in very different soils—in dry, sandy tracts, black cotton soil, and even humid areas where the drainage is good. Since it is an evergreen, and its finely-cut foliage does not form too dense a crown, it lets the air freely through while providing a sun-proof shade. Few trees can rival it for the roadside. The pleasantest avenue I have ever known is a 3 km section of the road leading from

Badami to Pattadakal in Karnataka. This stretch is flanked on both sides by great old neem trees, planted a hundred years ago perhaps, that almost meet overhead, providing an airy, cool, vaulted shade for which we were truly grateful on a sweltering summer afternoon.

Many trees prized for their fine, beautifully figured furniture woods belong to the neem's family—mahogany in the West, red and white cedar in our own country, and some others, including the fragrant, lustrous, soft-red chickrassy (*Chukrasia tabularis*) and satinwood (*Chloroxyion swietenia*), the handsomest of all blond hardwoods, though cross-grained. All contain aromatic oils, and are very durable and termite resistant. The neem's heartwood, heavy, very dark red, oily and with a disagreeable smell when fresh-cut, is also used for furniture and construction, but there is no need for this with many more attractive timbers of its family available. All the therapeutic and preservative products for which the neem is renowned come from its foliage, bark and seeds, and for these the tree need not be cut down.

From time immemorial the neem has been valued in our country for its religious associations, and the medicinal and germicidal efficiency of its twigs and bark, the heavy-smelling oil extracted from its seeds (a powerful antiseptic) and the preservative and disinfective potency of its leaves. Sophisticated techniques have been employed to derive cosmetic products from the neem, like soap and toothpaste. The green twig, chewed into a fibrous brush at one end, is an excellent toothbrush that contains its own cleansing paste, and is widely utilized in the countryside.

The use of shade-dried neem leaves to preserve books and clothes from destructive insects has long been practised, but their enduring efficiency in preserving foodgrain stored in huge earthen bins (as grain is commonly stored in rustic tracts) merits wider publicity. I can personally vouch for this property of the dried leaves.

Long ago, I lived in a valley in the Deccan where jowar was the staple grain. One year, when unseasonal rains ruined the jowar harvest, and the grain was in short supply a farmer remembered that his grandfather (who had died 30 years ago) had buried the surplus from a bumper crop stored in bins in a 12-foot deep pit in the dry earth of his backyard, and thought of digging up the buried treasure. Everyone said it would be a wasted effort, for the grain was bound to have gone bad in all those years and, moreover, the imprisoned air within the crypt would be poisonous and dangerous. However, the crypt was cautiously opened up, and the bins with their sealed, baked-clay lids were also opened.

There was a thick layer of dry neem leaves on top, beneath the lid, and another at the bottom of the bins, and the grain between these neem-leaf layers was plump, dry, pale yellow and seemed quite sound. Still some of the doubting Thomases argued that, until the grain was ground into flour and baked into rotis and eaten, one could not be sure. I was one of those who volunteered for this test, and I must say I have seldom eaten better jowar-roti, something I like and have subsisted on for over a year. Finally, the excavated grain was sold at a handsome profit.

The long-held belief that it is good to have a neem tree or two growing close to one's house to purify the air around was pooh-poohed by two scientists I know, but has not been disproved. It is only in recent years that we have come to be aware of the hazards of air pollution that we cannot readily detect. Neem leaves on a tree do have a distinctive, faint smell from close by. It is by no means far-fetched to think that some volatile principle in them may permeate the ambient air, or that it may have a purifying potential. This is something that a painstaking scientist, duly qualified and adequately equipped, has yet to investigate to prove or disprove the belief.

1992

43

Jungli Phal

ABOUT THIS TIME of the year, for many years, my elderly cook used to warn me of the dangers of eating all sorts of 'jungli phal' by which term she meant the custard-apple, the jamoon (*Eugenia Jambolana*) and the wild, sharp Carissa, fruits now in season in many places. Particularly was the good woman against the first two.

The custard-apple, I was told, promoted phlegm and the rheumatics; it was a fruit one should guard against at all times, but especially in seepy September. The jamoon was worse. It caused, besides sore throats and bronchitis, sudden, debilitating fevers; a distant cousin of hers, who was fond of the fruit, had died young. Moreover it was infra dig for a man of my years and status, an officer of the Government to indulge such immature, boorish tastes. Latterly these sermons became so insistent that I had to use much furtiveness in my fruit eating.

I am no longer under Sita Bai's motherly surveillance, for I have left that place and she this world—and I am an officer no more. I eat my fill of custard-apples and jamoon, with abandoned openness. But somehow they have not quite the old relish.

There was much truth, though, in the elderly advice. A surfeit of custard-apple is not calculated to improve one's health. However, it is not often that one takes it in any quantity, for it is a fruit of which one tires quickly. If you like its somewhat musty flavour and have not eaten it that way before, you should try it in an ice-cream. Much of the prejudice against the fruit is due, I think, to the fact that people often eat it overripe and are not choosy over their custard-apple. The polygonal 'cells' on the rind (denoting each carpel) should be few and large and the fruit of good size.

It should be taken off the plant while still firm and stored in dry grain till just ripe—much of the charm of this artless fruit lies in its being properly ripe. The way to get good custard-apples is to collect them in person from carefully selected shrubs or, if one is an officer, to employ a confidential agent for the purpose. People rarely sell the best custard-apples they can find. They eat them.

Of the jamoon I can speak with greater enthusiasm. This, too, varies considerably from tree to tree, even more than the custard-apple, and is often eaten over-ripe. What is sold is fallen fruit with bruised skin, collected from under the tree. The jamoon must ripen on the tree and is at its best when just about to fall, pendent and a glistening purple-black. An ideal arrangement would be to wait beneath a tree of known quality and catch the fruit in one's mouth as it falls, but ideals are hard to achieve in this cussed world. Therefore, pick your tree and get someone to climb it and bring down the ripe fruit.

The jamoon differs as much in size as in quality. On the hill slopes it is possible to get a long, thick variety twice as big as the fruit of the plains, dark-fleshed and exquisitely flavoured. To my plebeian palate no lichi or mangosteen has the sweetness of this fruit. On the plains the trees yield smaller and more astringent fruit and some of these are hardly worth the eating. However, one need not despise the jamoon of the plains provided it is of fair size and good flavour. Sprinkle salt and powdered red chilli over the fruit and wait for an hour and its astringency will be cured—this treatment is not to be thought of for choice hill-grown fruit.

The world consists of those who like the jamoon and those who do not. Among the addicts are the aborigines, the shaggy Sloth Bear and other denizens of the jungle. The people who cannot abide the fruit are often highly refined and intellectual—they find no joy in life.

Another delicious and wholesome fruit, now in season, is the guava. Being marketable, it is frequently cultivated in orchards and there are 'improved' varieties, mild, white-fleshed, yellow-skinned and big—excellent for conversion into jam or jelly, I think. Give me the small, green-skinned, red-hearted country guava. I believe I am correct in saying that the country guava is far richer in vitamins than the cultivated varieties. Anyway it is better eating. There is a pear-shaped kind, very small and red and often grown in the backyards of villagers. The tree is little better than a shrub and its yield very scanty, but make friends with the man who owns it.

There are many other trees and shrubs in the jungles that are in fruit just now, but I shall mention only the spiky *Carissa carandas*. It is very sour when green, less sour when ripe, and too acid for consumption as it is— there are other Carissas that bear sweeter fruit. However, the green fruit of this bush can be converted into a piquant and stimulating pickle with powdered chilli and other spices and just a little oil. According to South Indian traditions this fruit (even in a pickle) is superlatively good for the liver. I think there is sound sense in many of our traditions regarding things to eat and I am sure that even my old cook would have agreed that it is very important to keep the liver in good order!

1953

44

Walchand

A SUDDEN CLAMOUR FROM the nether regions, the brassy clang of tumbled vessels, shrill and shocking language from my elderly cook and the thud of stick upon hide proclaim that Walchand has broken bounds and entered the kitchen again. I rush to the cuisine where Walchand, unmindful of the feminine stick, is steadily consuming my dinner, and diving beneath the upraised arm of the cook I grab him by the beard. And I lead him back to the goat-pen, grumbling and protesting, and tether him up securely.

Walchand is a Surti buck and hornless by virtue of his pedigree. This does not prevent him from butting wickedly, but of course he can effect no serious damage. Whoever evolved the Surti goat did wisely in breeding out horns, and even better in breeding for the thick ridge of hair from nose to tail. By this ridge I know what sort of a mood Walchand is in. It lies flat to one side of the back, when he is on good terms with the world, but when he contemplates a change it bristles 'like quills upon the fretful *porpentine*'. Walchand grows suddenly bigger and 'bristlier', and I know what to expect. It is the beard, however, that is the true index of the breeder's cunning and genius. Walchand's beard is at once his pride and his undoing. It is no goatee, no mere straggling tuft of hair, but a full and fluent beard long enough, thick enough and (except on the days he is washed) dirty and orange enough to delight the heart of the most fanatic fakir. At the same time it affords a most convenient hold—in fact I would be as helpless without it as he himself. Walchand is difficult at times, when he thinks he has not had his due share of 'bajra' or when there has been dissension in the harem. It is useless to seize his ear at such times, for an ear is yielding and pliant and he can twist round and butt. But once I have him fairly by the beard all arguments end abruptly. He still protests in a quavering treble—his voice is surprisingly thin and high considering his lusty looks—but all fight leaves him.

I remember Walchand as a year-old kid, when first he came to me. The four-foot wall that separates the pen from the kitchen-block was no obstacle in those days. He would jump lightly on to it and go skipping along its edge, rearing and bucking for the sheer joy of being alive. He is too heavy now, and crusty and dignified, to do such things. It is only by a feat of will that he can hoist his bulk on to the wall these days, and he is too sensible to put himself out for no purpose. When he smells dinner, my dinner, however, he is impelled to the effort.

His zenana is his chief preoccupation—a dozen does, of all sorts and colours. There are two evil-looking country-breds in the lot who can, if they choose to, rout Walchand in battle, but they never do. It is his beard, I think, that subdues them, and they suffer him to butt them and bully them and put them in their places. In return for this acknowledgment of mastery, Walchand leads them all, at home and abroad. At times he grows ambitious and sets out to acquire fresh conquests for the harem. Walchand does not come home, though his indifferent wives return, and we search far and near for him: and find him at last disputing possession with the lord and master of some other herd, dirty, bedraggled and bested by the horned buck, but still willing. We bring him home and bathe him and it is then that I find that old Wallie has not changed one bit in his heart of hearts. He detests a bath as cordially as he ever did.

I use warm water, the best of soaps and persuasion, but he fidgets and struggles. Force becomes necessary. I get my goat-boy to souse him with the water, and holding his beard in one hand proceed to soap him with the other. The rich, white, frothy lather spreads like the crest of a wave along his side and something in the sensation seems to quieten him and he stands till. It is an old trick, but I fall for it. I relax my hold on the beard to get round to the other flank. Walchand springs forward with irrepressible suddenness, floors the boy with a savage butt and we dance around in a shower of lather and warm water, a strand of the beard still clutched in my hand. I secure my hold, and the bath is resumed, leaving the soaping of the vital beard to the very end, for we dare not let it get slippery. At last the ordeal is over and a white and gleaming Walchand, washed and towelled is tethered to the verandah to get quite dry. But we are a sorry sight. The goat-boy is wet to the skin and has a bump at the back of his head. I have soap in one eye and both ears. . . .

1945

45

The Pariah

THE INDIAN PARIAH dog, according to the professors, is nearest the greyhound-type in the way it is made. It is all a question of the relative girths and lengths of the bones, the nice adjustment between skull and jaw. Incidentally the pundits write with far greater certainty when writing of the Pariah dogs of countries other than India, Turkey or Java for instance. They are less sure of their grounds, their bones, I mean, when on the subject of the Indian Pariah, which is perfectly natural and understandable when one thinks over the matter. It is extremely hard to write with precision or authority on anything Indian. There are always varieties, too many varieties. It is so with our foods and languages, our costumes and castes. It is so with our Pariah dogs. And so the dogologists have been content with saying that these dogs, generally speaking, more or less approximate to the greyhound-type, generally speaking, that is.

I have always felt a certain native reluctance to enter into disputes with Colonels and Professors, and men who can quote massive Latin names in support of their views, but I just cannot accept the theory that the Indian Pariah, taken by and large, is greyhoundy in any way. Mind, I do not deny the existence of races and colonies—these dogs live in colonies—that are greyhoundy. The 'Pariahs' of cities and cantonments are often so, long-limbed, deep-chested, with hungry tucked-in bellies and lean faces. You find them furtively reconnoitring the purlieus of garbage heaps and bins, or haunting railway stations, I have a powerful suspicion that this is the dog that the dogologists have taken for their type—this is the only way I can reconcile expert opinion, for which I have great respect, with facts, for which also I have respect. And the fact is that these muddled mongrels are no more Pariahs than they are blue-blooded Salikis. A great variety of breeds, modern and ancient, have gone to make them. Perhaps they are greyhoundy because among dogs, as in pigeons, when breeding is promiscuous and uncontrolled there is an atavistic tendency towards the old type, and the greyhound-type is undoubtedly a very old one. I do not put this forward as a complete explanation—only as a suggestion. What I do say is that the City-and-station Pariahs are no Pariahs at all. For one thing they run much to whites, piebalds and black-and-tans and these colours are foreign to the true breed. I admit that I would not know the jaw bones of a jackal from those of a champion Fox Terrier, and that my ignorance of the canine cranium is profound, quite profound. But I have played with the Pariah dogs of our country when I was a child and still have esteemed friends among them. I have seen and known them in all sorts of places, on sweltering plains and cold hills. And my point is that they are, in no way, like a greyhound.

I take the Pariah of the Bellary district, the herd-dog of these parts, as the type. I would like to reiterate the fact that type varies, even locally, but on the whole this dog is representative, having had few chances of getting mixed up with other breeds. It starts life as a remarkably solid puppy, very like a drop-eared Chow in miniature, except that it is less hairy and heavily boned. The Chow, by the way, can be fairly described as the Chinese Pariah, standardized and improved in England. The puppy quickly outgrows the resemblance, developing a snipy muzzle and thin straight limbs. The adult dog has a short-coupled, thick body, wide across the chest rather than deep, a massive neck and a head notable for its wide, domed skull and thin muzzle. The ears are pricked and the tail usually carried gaily. Tail-carriage, however, depends much on the mood of the moment and the Pariah is a dog of many moods. The coat is moderately smooth, longer on the neck, and the tail has, at times, just the suspicion of feathering. The colour ranges from yellow to deep brown and some dogs are brindled, but it is very likely that the brindled coat (which usually goes with heavier jaws and a taller stature than usual) is the result of an outcross. White as a dominant colour is the hallmark of mongrel blood, in my opinion, and I view black-and-tan or even black with suspicion. White streaks or a white splash over the chest do occur specially in brindle dogs, and fawn and red dogs may have black masks. The dog stands about as tall as a Bull Terrier but is lighter built, and would stand no chance with the latter in a fight. Bitches are not much shorter, but are noticeably slighter, with a longer body and much finer head.

It should be obvious from the above description that the Indian Pariah has few claims to looks. There are authentic accounts of the use of packs of Pariahs to worry and hold a leopard by aboriginal hunters and

I myself have known these dogs being used for hunting wild pig. But I would not call the Pariah a courageous dog. It may do great things in packs but a single dog will never face odds if it can help it. However it has other and rarer virtues which should outweigh its lack of looks and 'conspicuous gallantry in action'. It is tractable, clever, even sagacious, self-reliant and absolutely incorruptible. It has an extremely hardy constitution and costs next to nothing to feed. There is no better house-dog. It is so clever and willing, you can teach it practically anything, it never makes friends with strangers whatever the bait, and will wake and give voice at the slightest suspicion of anything wrong. It does not keep howling all night, nullifying all attempts at sleep, but barks only when there is good reason. It is this quality, rather than the desire and ability to maul, that is wanted in a watch-dog and the Pariah has it.

As a shepherd's dog the Pariah does its job neatly and well. The flocks are small, a couple of hundred at the most, and the dog is not required to do anything spectacular, as the Collie and Kelpie are. However it can and will do all that it is called upon to do. I suppose the Pariah can be stabilized as a breed and improved in appearance—it cannot be improved in brain—but frankly, I see no future for this dog. In a country where the Poliga and Mahratta hounds have been allowed to die down, practically, is it likely that the Pariah will succeed in attracting notice or support?

1944

46

Chocki

C HOCKI CAME TO me from 500 miles away, over road and rail.
I had wanted a Poligar puppy that I could raise for the show
bench—the intercession of a friend and the generosity of a
southern landlord, known for his strain of Poligar hounds, had brought
me Chocki. I still remember my disappointment on seeing her first, a
runty, dirty puppy with no promise of size or power, yapping at me from
a bamboo basket. Only in the dark, bold eyes, and the exquisite feel of
the skin, were there any signs of blood. I said to myself that no eastern
hound puppy looked its best at six weeks of age, and that if I had any
breeding in me I would see at once to the comfort of the poor little thing
that had come all that way in that basket. I lifted her out and set her down
beside a bowl of egg-flip. She bit my hand.

Nine months of care and nourishing, and bone-building food saw a
very different dog. Chocki was almost full-grown now—she stood 22
inches at the shoulder and weighed 42 lbs. There was power and quick
grace in her build, and refinement in her narrow, chiselled features; she
looked an obvious thoroughbred. But I had given up all idea of showing
her, for she was undersized in spite of her symmetry; I wrote a guarded
letter to the landlord who had bred her, telling him that the puppy he
had so kindly sent me was now a grown dog, and lacked size; and that
while he was perhaps the one man who possessed and understood the
true, old-type Poligar hound, I sometimes wondered if my dog's sire, or
dam, was somewhat on the small side. His reply, received months later,
was brief and just to the point. It said that some men were just five-foot
tall, but were men all the same.

Early in our acquaintance, I gave up Chocki's education as well.
When she was old enough to learn I began to teach her the many and
useful accomplishments that a house-dog should own. It was soon apparent that she had a stubborn, fierce will, but I, too, do not lack the quality,

and the obedience-lessons progressed at a crawl. When my slow patience had prevailed on her to sit and lie down at the command, follow to heel, and come up when called, I began to feel a violent revulsion towards her further education. Chocki had the simple dignity and poise of truly ancient races, and expressive brown eyes. There was a look of infinite resignation in her eyes when she sat down at my word, and if I kept her at heel too long, out walking, she would sigh audibly. I stopped her lessons, and somehow we felt closer to each other thereafter.

Except when kept to heel with frequent admonitions, Chocki would run ahead or loiter behind, though she would never let me go out of sight. Returning home belated, one night, I noticed that she kept close to me of her own accord. Later I noticed that whenever I took her for a walk at night she kept by my side—she would come closer still, with a low warning growl if anybody passed us on the road. I put this down to a young dog's misgivings of the dark, and desire for support. One pitch-black night, with my flashlight dead and the dog practically guiding me over the road, the truth dawned slowly on me—she was escorting me, alive somehow to the decreased self-confidence of a man in the dark. Her nearness to me at nights had all along been protective!

At a year-and-a-half Chocki was no longer rowdy, and had acquired a certain indefinable fineness without loss of strength, as if her lineaments had changed to tempered steel. Her ivory-coloured coat wrinkled in a delicate network over her sides when she bent them, and her limbs seemed slimmer and harder. She retained her stormy vivacity, and could be self-willed, or idle, or full of animal spirits, as the mood took her. A bath was still a thing she would suffer only at my hands, and she would allow no one else to groom her. She had learned, unfortunately, that a menacing display of teeth, or a snarl, was sufficient to restrain the zeal of most people. However, she had developed a surprising tolerance towards the very young. There was no love lost between Chocki and my goats, and she would snap at them if they disputed the way with her, but she was uncommonly gentle to the optimistic kids that sought milk from her, being content to take herself away if they bothered her too much. My six-year-old son and Chocki spent quite a lot of time together, and it was most amusing to watch her enticing him to resume a game of hide-and-seek that he had grown tired of. However, he used to try her patience sorely in spite of our warnings, and at times she would growl at him— my wife and I felt that sooner or later the dog would bite him, in self-defence, and she could bite wickedly. One evening, returning home from work, I was confronted with a strange sight. Chocki, vividly marked all over in blues and greens and reds with primitive representations of motor cars, stood on my front verandah, looking like no dog on earth; and my son sat on the floor beside her, his tongue between his lips, absorbed in decorating her stern with my pastels. Seeing me, the dog advanced to greet me, and vexed by this sudden departure of his surface, the artist jumped up and kicked her in the stomach. The long-suffering animal spun round with a yelp of pain and rage. Taking my son by the shoulders I shook him and spoke angrily to him—may be I was rougher than I need have been in my anxiety for him. Chocki turned on me in a flash, and tore the sleeve of my coat with a slashing bite. I know enough about roused dogs to know that only the instant removal of my hands from the person of her playmate saved further developments. She transferred her loyalties to my son that day, and till he left the place, years later, I remained only second-best in her affections.

Even when a sober matron, Chocki retained her fierce individuality and whims. At times she was a source of acute embarrassment to us. It was only with great difficulty that I cured her of the habit of greeting my wife's friends by circling all around them, and snapping playfully at the hems of their sarees. When I was there, she would behave herself, but she was not the dog to resist fun in earnest. Once she jumped straight for the magnificent turban of a gentleman who had called on me, lifted it deftly off his head, and ran round and round the house in sheer devilment, with eight yards of orange, unwound mull trailing in her wake. After retrieving the turban and handling it back to my guest, with my most voluble apologies, I took Chocki aside and lectured her on the enormity of her conduct. On such occasion I would speak severely to her, taking good care not to relax the reproach in my voice—the words themselves, usually the Latin names of plants, mattered nothing. Chocki dreaded the ordeal even more than a beating. She would lift her head and howl in a thin, melancholy voice, and when this failed to stem the unrelenting flow of nomenclature, she would grovel on the floor; if this too did not move me to forgiveness, she would sit up and get quite lost in frantic search for an imaginary flea. Diplomatic relations, severed after these lectures, would be resumed after an hour or two, and I always took her out for a romp to mark the close of the episode. I must say that Chocki never repeated an offence after being spoken to sternly—but then, why should a versatile dog repeat herself?

As years went by a deeper understanding grew between us, till I felt

that I could read her every mood—no easy thing with such a tempera-
mental creature—and I dare say she felt the same way about me! When
Chocki was six years old, in her prime, she took to ranging the scrub and
hill-sides on her own, getting back in time to give me a tempestuous welcome on my return from work. Sometimes, in the excitement of pursuit,
she would forget herself, but she was home by nightfall invariably. Twice
she brought in hares she had hunted down by herself, tributes to her
speed and woodcraft.

When finally, I had to leave the jungle-clad hills amidst which my dog
and I had spent eight happy years, Chocki was a major problem. I could
not take her with me to the cities for which I was bound—it was unthink-
able that a dog who had never seen a chain, except round a goat's neck,
should live tied up, or cooped in a kennel, the best part of the day; and
given her freedom she could never have survived metropolitan traffic.
What I wanted for her was a home in the countryside, where a dog with
an independent nature, and a will of her own, would be really welcome.
This was not easy to find. In the end a friend came to the rescue, as friends
will. He was frank about it. He did not like Chocki's manners, and
doubted her intelligence, but he did not like to see me worrying either,
and offered to ship her to his estate in the country, to which he was retiring shortly, and give her a home. The parting was brief, and hurried.
Chocki's reactions to her new home were typical: she broke away and
lived in the surrounding scrub-jungle for a week before she would return
to it, but is now firmly established there. I hear that she is very happy in
her unrestricted life, and new loyalties, but has grown fat and less active.
And I believe my friend no longer thinks that parlour-tricks and the
domestic manner are the best indications of canine intelligence or charm.

1950

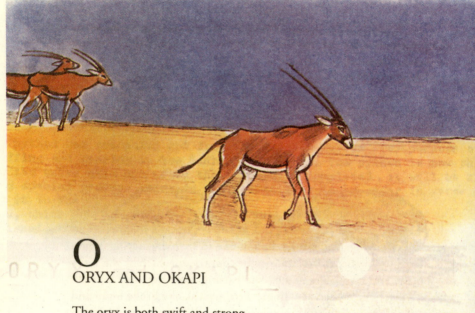

O
ORYX AND OKAPI

The oryx is both swift and strong,
with sabre horns a metre long,
and it is wild and wary.
It is a desert antelope
that loves in little herds to lope
across the Kalahari.

Okapis, on the other hand,
are forest beasts that cannot stand
the open sands and sunlight.
They live within the humid, dark
Ituri, and their limbs are stark-
ly banded black-and white.

Nature Desecrated

47

Captive-bred Mugger

I WAS A MEMBER of the Indian Board for Wildlife for three decades. Soon after its inception, M.D. Chaturvedi and I were asked to draft the pledge that members should take, a pledge of commitment to our wildlife. Chaturvedi was high up in the north and I low down in the south, so that we had to draft the pledge by correspondence. I felt it should be short, simple and sincere—it is so easy to be solemnly pompous over a pledge of commitment—and as I was writing to communicate this view to my masterful colleague I received a letter from him containing the pledge fully drafted and already sent in to the IBWL, thanking me politely for my cooperation! It was a fulsome pledge, and I cannot remember its precise wording, but recall its first part. 'Born in the Land of the Buddha and Mahavira, I solemnly pledge myself to. . .' In due course it was replaced by a shorter pledge (on a Western model) free from pious sentiment, but three years ago I was reminded, irresistibly, of the old pledge.

The IBWL is an advisory body with no executive powers. Its recommendations are implemented, or not, by diverse Governments. It is a large and colourful body, with a preponderance of the top brass of Governments, but also with a sprinkling of representatives of institutions and members of the public. Its sessions are lengthy and decorous, and usually culminate in a substantial lunch. Perhaps because of all this, the minutes of its widely spaced meetings are brief and usually omit the opinions expressed by members.

Early in the 1970s, when Dr Karan Singh was in the chair, the precarious position of our crocodilians came up at a meeting. We have three kinds of crocodiles. Much the commonest is the mugger, for some reason also called the marsh crocodile though it inhabits, not marshes, but rivers and deep waterspreads. The second is the estuarine crocodile that favours saline waters along the coast and is much the most powerful and aggressive of the three, alarmingly dwindled in India by the 1970s, but still there in Malaysia and Australia. The third is the uniquely Indian gharial, the fish-eating crocodile, which had almost reached the brink of extinction by the 1970s.

At this meeting I said that while the gharial could probably be saved only by captive breeding, and possibly also the estuarine crocodile in our country, all that the mugger needed was stricter protection, and that where human sentiment guarded it, it was still there in the south, safe from the crocodile skin trade and its predatory poachers. Naturally, neither what I said nor what others did figured in the minutes, but immediately on coming home I wrote to the secretary of the IBWL to say that if captive breeding of muggers was permitted, it would be disastrous, for the public would oppose the release of the teeming hatchlings into rivers. Perhaps that letter is still there in some file of the IBWL—my own copy was lost long ago when my house was flooded.

By 1984 what I apprehended had come to pass. The thing about the captive breeding of muggers is this. In nature, the female lays 30 to 60 eggs on a river bank in a clutch, covers them up with earth, and stays close by most of the time guarding them. However, something like 90 per cent of the eggs and young hatchlings (which enter the water at once) are destroyed by natural predators, monitors, mongooses, jackals, even other crocodiles, and only about five per cent survive to reach the size when they can fend for themselves. Under captive breeding 90 per cent of the eggs may hatch and the hatchlings reach the size when they can be released into wild waters.

By 1984 huge stocks of mugger hatchlings had already accumulated at various captive-breeding centres and, because of opposition by the vote-holding public to their release, they were still held in captivity. At this meeting of the IBWL it was proposed that a pilot project for trade in crocodile skin should be tried out with this 'surplus' stock. I pointed out how dead against the Indian ethos, and the avowed principles of the IBWL itself, this proposal was, and suggested that Governments might kill this huge stock of hatchlings quickly and mercifully and sell their skins and flesh too, but that the ban on trade in crocodile skin should be strictly enforced to save the wild muggers still left. I added that, as in the ivory trade, poachers would definitely find ways to circumvent all attempts to confine the trade to Government supply.

Many sided with me, but one, a good naturalist and specialist in our reptiles, rose to say that since I had argued that in nature only 5 to 10 per cent of the eggs survived, there could be no harm in utilizing the 90 per cent going waste for pecuniary gain. This was the argument of an elementary mathematician and not of a naturalist. In nature the great mortality of the eggs and hatchlings is not just a waste, as suggested, but goes to sustain other Indian animals. However, I could not argue the point, and a few others as well that are quite relevant in rebuttal, as by that time people were getting visibly restive. The aroma of lunch, being laid out in the next room, pervaded the air, and as an experienced ethologist I knew how futile, even dangerous at times, it was to stand between gustatory arousal and its consummation. I therefore asked for the matter to be left undecided, and asked the secretary for an opportunity to present my arguments fully well before lunch at the next meeting of the IBWL, and he ceded this.

Then, when the IBWL was reconstituted in June 1985, the embarassment I was causing was neatly circumvented by leaving me out of it. I cannot have any objection to this manoeuvre, since Governments have the prerogative in such matters, but may I suggest through this column that the IBWL pledge should once again be revised as follows? 'Born in the Land of the Buddha and Mahavira, and Mahatma Gandhi as well, I solemnly pledge myself to flay the captive-bred mugger and sell its skin for profit.'

1988

48

Hounding the Sloth

W HAT HAS HAPPENED to the bear with a ring through its nose, that the wandering bear-trainer used to bring to town and village? I believe both the beast and the man are still to be found in places, particularly in the North. Recently, a probationer who had travelled along sub-Himalayan railways, told me how he got down at a station at midnight; a number of men, bundled up against the cold in rough, black *kumblis*, were sleeping on the platform; he took a close look at the sleepers, then a closer look, then finally appealed to his companions. 'Do you see what I see?' he asked them, for three of those slumbering men were bears in fact, stretched out besides their masters and hardly distinguishable from the *kumbli*-swathed humans.

I also read a thrilling newspaper account about a North Indian landlord suddenly visited with bandits; he fled for protection to the nearby camp of a party of gypsies, who had arrived at his village that day with some performing bears; the bears were unleashed, and attacked the enemy with such zest that some of the bandits were killed on the spot, and the rest bolted into the landlord's house, and bolted themselves in against the retributory bears, so that the police had no difficulty in arresting them later.

Such happenings prove that the bear-trainer and his impressive pet are still very much there, in places, but it is true that they are no longer the familiar sight they used to be all over the country. Just as well, I think. I can never see a performing bear, however amusing its antics, without feeling sorry for the shaggy, grotesquely semi-human beast. Some captive wild beasts do suffer domestication without losing heart or character, especially those (like the elephant and the civet) which can be given a large measure of freedom. But the Sloth Bear (which is the bear-trainer's bear) is never happy tied up all the time and fed rations. What a fate to overtake a great natural wanderer and gourmand!

Even apart from its trainer and nose-ring, what has happened to our

Sloth Bear, in its native jungles? This is the bear of peninsular India, and peculiarly our own. Most other bears have a wide, almost a worldwide, distribution, and have bigger or smaller brothers in other countries. Not so our Sloth Bear. There is a race of it in Ceylon, but it is found nowhere else. It is unique in its anatomy and habits, and so has been assigned a class, all to itself, by zoologists.

And it is a creature associated with our oldest folklore and mythology. There is no countryside adjoining boulder-strewn hill-jungles, where bears once lived or still live, where they do not tell the story of the male bear abducting the village belle. From available evidence it seems clear that the bear, though devoted to its mate, indulges in a rough courtship—however, in the story, the bear always treats the girl it has abducted with the utmost consideration, and lavishes gifts upon her that are valuable to a bear, such as honey and queen-termites and jungle berries! Our Puranas, too, have their bears, and our classical poetry knows them well.

How is it that the rapid disappearance from the country of an animal so anciently associated with our culture, and so peculiarly distinctive of our fauna, has been viewed with such complacency? I know many places named after the Sloth Bear, whose favourite haunts they were till recently—Bear Sholas and Karadi Kollas. Where, now, are the bears that gave these places their names?

Perhaps I am unduly apprehensive, and there is no likelihood of the Sloth Bear becoming extinct in India, no imminent likelihood, anyway. However, I must point out that the disappearance of this bear from many places where it was known a generation ago is not a question of opinion, but of fact. Moreover, it has happened time and again in the past that people have realized the need to protect some wild animal a trifle belatedly, when the species has been reduced to beyond the biological minimum necessary for its survival.

The Sloth Bear should be strictly protected where it occurs, and introduced into sanctuaries from the neighbourhood of which it has disappeared in the recent past. Many of our animals have become locally rare or extinct due mainly to the increase of the human population, rather than to being shot out. The bear, however, has been shot out. It is neither the conversion of its homes into agricultural land (it lives in stony hill-jungles) nor the professional trapper that has been the main cause of its disappearance in places. For generations the 'gentleman sportsman' has thought the bear fair game, in any circumstance, and even found its ululations in mortal agony killingly amusing.

It is true that, when stumbled upon in its jungles, an early bear may attack a man in its panic, and that occasionally it has inflicted grievous wounds on some careless woodcutter poaching in the jungles. However, it is no more harmful to man, left alone, than many other wild animals, and definitely less harmful than transport buses, trains, and the like. The Sloth Bear is mainly nocturnal and crepuscular, and causes no great damage to agriculture—it is not a crop-raider in the sense in which pigs are crop-raiders. Those who have studied its habits agree that it is one of the most interesting denizens of our forests, and it is wholly ours. If a strict ban on the shooting of this bear, except when the authorities may consider it necessary, is enforced, it would be easy to save our bear.

1958

49

The Vanishing Bustard

RECENTLY I READ a book on the common game birds of West Africa, and was surprised to find quite half-a-dozen bustards mentioned. I could not help comparing our one bustard with these exotic cousins, and pondering over its fate. I noted with pride that the Great Indian Bustard is far larger than any of its West African relatives: but, unlike them, it is doomed. I have met men who will not admit that the Hunting Leopard is virtually extinct in India, because they cannot bring themselves to believe that an animal they knew in their youth is already gone. But even they realize that our bustard is going, going, though not quite gone.

The Great Indian Bustard is a bird of the open country and very large, so that its presence anywhere is not hard to locate. It is a big fowl, nearly 40 lbs when full grown (a prodigious weight for a flying bird) and four feet tall on its thick, yellow legs. It takes off with some difficulty and after the manner of an aeroplane, with a long run assisted by flapping wings. Once launched in the air, it gains height with lubberly beats of its sail-like wings, then soars on their stretched spread with surprising ease. However, it comes down to earth after a while, for it is essentially a ground bird. It carries its boat-shaped body like a boat, horizontally, and runs with its head and neck flung forward; it runs far more readily than it flies, and at a fair pace.

In spite of its dull brown back and dull, earth-bound habits (no one will call it a vivacious bird), the white in its plumage against the dark ground and its size give it away from afar. It has not many enemies in the flat, bare country that it loves, but unfortunately it is excellent eating, and man has never forgotten this.

Man (especially the man with the gun) is entirely responsible for the fact that this wholly Indian and magnificent bird is on the verge of extinction, and only man can save it now. Let me explain that statement.

Animals do not become extinct because they are shot down to the last pair. In nature, every species faces certain hazards, and survives in spite of them because if some of its members succumb others live to reproduce the species. There must be a minimum population for any species to survive, and the hazards of nature seldom reduce its numbers to below this minimum. This is what is implied in the much-used phrase 'the balance of nature', and this is not only a phrase but a proved fact as well, the principle underlying the running of any large sanctuary.

By shooting them, by infringing on their territory and driving them to fresh, unsuitable grounds or overcrowding them, and in many other ways that may not be intentional, man reduces the numbers of some species to below its biological minimum. Then it becomes extinct. When such a fate is about to overtake any creature, only by preserving it jealously, by helping it in all possible ways to breed back to its biological minimum strength, can we save it.

I have reason to believe that in a dying race the reproductive instinct is exceptionally strong, but unless sufficient living space, food and protection are provided (artificially, by man) this last-minute resurgence cannot save the species.

Our bustard is a useful bird, besides being ours, on the brink of extinction, and one of the largest of its tribe. It feeds mainly on locusts, grasshoppers, a variety of insects, and the like—the damage it does to cultivation is more than offset by its beneficial influence.

Can we save it? I think it is possible, if governments will enforce protective measures without too long deliberation. The bird is already on the protected list—on paper. The penalties to be imposed on people shooting the bird should be made stricter—and they should be enforced. A fine will not deter a gourmet, especially when he does not realize that the bird he is shooting is not merely illegal game, but a representative of a dying race that is a hundred times more valuable than it would be otherwise because it is struggling to breed up to the biological minimum necessary for the survival of its tribe. Something must be done, harshly, effectively, to make the flesh of the bustard have a bitter taste to the man with the gun. Only governments can do such things—but is not the Great Indian Bustard a fit challenge to the resources and responsibilities of our national administration?

It may be thought that already the bird is too far gone for any attempt to save it, however resolute. I do not think so. Someone told me, last week, that there were not half-a-dozen bustards now in Mysore State.

Perhaps that was a highly exaggerated statement, but even if it was true, no matter. The Great Indian Bustard is not such a *rara avis* as it may seem at first sight. Last year I counted seven of these birds in the flat country surrounding the village of Hagedal, near Gajendragad in the Dharwar District. These bustards, I was informed, had defined beats. Two of them were noticeably subadult, with dark streaks on their necks: very likely these birds breed in that area. I do not know how many of those seven are extant today, but surely there must be other places like Hagedal?

Experienced sportsmen need no appeal not to point their guns at our bustard but how many gun-license holders know that the bird is rare and dying out? It is quite necessary to inform public knowledge on our vanishing fauna, and the need to preserve it. This, again, is something that only governments can do well. Private enterprise can make little headway in this direction; nor have I seen many appeals to the public on behalf of this bird. The only notice of it that I have seen, outside the writings of a few naturalists, was in an old drawing-book for schoolchildren, and here, too, the bird had been ill-served, for it had been defamed, in thick black type!

1952

50

A Lament for Lost Wood

DURING THE PAST year I travelled many miles along the great arterial roads radiating from the urban heart of Madras, and along their rural branches. And once again I noticed the ruthless destruction of trees all over the countryside.

I do not refer to our forests. Rarely did I get much farther than 50 miles away from Madras City, and within that radius forests, in the botanical sense of the term, do not exist. Such forests as we do have in our State are sadly depleted, the 'clear felling' of areas without any compensatory, enforced plantation having been permitted in them for generations. Light jungles, of the kind that one may hope to find on minor hills, are rare in the neighbourhood of Madras: there were such jungles, but most of them have disappeared in the recent past. Why, Mylapore, so anciently a part of the City, and now so unrelieved an expanse of crowded architecture, was wooded in the Nineteen Twenties!

In the old days people planted fruit-trees and shade-trees, and nurtured them in groves and on roadsides, so that succeeding generations might enjoy the comfort and charm of their maturity, and rest in their shade. From remote times it has been typical of the culture of India to care for trees, and to take good care of them.

Many passages from ancient classical Sanskrit and Tamil prove this, but let us not look into them—particularly as I have no Sanskrit! Instead, let us look nearer our times. As recently as the last century, and even during the early years of this century, people still took a pride in trees. It was during this period that many exotics were introduced into the country—some merely because they had the appeal of novelty, others from a deeper motive. Our two chief hill-stations, Kodaikanal and Ootacamund, will serve as examples. Many foreign trees and herbs were introduced into Kodaikanal, irrespective of the country of their origin, but in Ooty, where the Englishman felt most at home in South India, English flowering plants and even English weeds were planted, to satisfy a deeply-felt sentiment.

I sometimes think that the disembodied ego of the Abbe Jean Paul Bignon, Librarian to Louis XIV, would feel deeply gratified if it could visit South India today. Excepting *Millingtonia hortenis* (the one tree of acceptably native indigene common alongside roads here), the trees of the family *Bignoniacede* that have found favour with our avenue-planters and gardeners are all exotic; *Spathodea campanulata* and *Jacaranda mimosifolia* probably flourish as exuberantly in Bangalore as they do in their native tropical America and Argentina; another African tree of this family, common on roadsides in and around Madras, is *Kigelia pinnata*.

Other exotic avenue trees are no less common here. We do not know who planted them or when, but judging by their girth and growth they must be 50 or a 100 years old, some older. Who planted the magnificent avenue of *Ficus benjamina* that adds so much to the looks of Vellore Town? On a common adjoining the main road at Meenambakkam is a small group of African baobabs, whose swollen boles and stature suggest mature years—this tree is also to be found in old gardens in Madras. Late in the nineteenth century or earlier it must have been harder to get a plant from afar than it is now. There must have been real interest in sylviculture then, for such trees to have been established here.

But of course this interest in sylviculture, by the road and beside human settlements, was not confined to exotic species. I cited these foreign examples only to establish the comparatively recent data of their importation. A number of indigenous trees have been valued as specially suitable for plantation in groves and avenues, from time immemorial. In Book 1 of 'The Sacred Books of the Hindus' by Professor Benoy Kumar Sarkar, I find the following among the species listed in the *Sukraniti:* the custard-apple, the champak, the pear, the Punnai (*Calophyllum inophyllum*), the Ber (*Zizyphus jujuba*), the mango, the red silk-cotton (*Salmalia malabarica*), the sandal, the Asoka (*Saraca indica*), *Pongamia glabra*, the tamarind, the lime, the wood-apple, the bael, the neem, the Vakula (*Mimusops elengi*), the Kadamba (*Anthocephalus indicus*), the country fig (*Ficus glomerata*), the peepul, the banyan, the mulberry, and the date, the betel and the coconut palm.

This citation is by no means exhaustive. I have merely listed the species mentioned in that ancient text (as per Sarkar) which are common in South India—many more are mentioned. From old Tamil works, and from personal recollection of the southern countryside I may add the following, as typical roadside and villageside trees: the guava, the jamoon (*Syzygium jambolanum*), the Illuppai or Southern Mohwa (*Bassia longifolia*), the white silk-cotton (*Eriodendron pentandrum*), the coral tree (*Erythrina indica*), the Sarakkondrai (*Cassia fistula*) now largely replaced near dwellings by the imported *Peltophorum pterocarpum*, *Odina wodier*, the Nettuligam (*Polyalthia longifolia*), *Ficus retusa* (occasionally) and, of course, the ubiquitous palmyra.

Noble trees of these species are still to be found in the countryside, and even in towns, but, exotic and native, they are disappearing rapidly. Unless popular feeling and governmental authority step in, right now, to save them, there will be little left in a few years.

Unluckily, the feeling for trees that there was a generation ago is no longer there. I compute that within the past 30 years, more live wood has been cut down, root, bole and all, than was nurtured to maturity in the previous 200 years. At first that may seem a wild exaggeration, without any factual basis. How I wish that were true! The sad, the depressing thing is that my estimate is soundly based, and very near the truth.

Growing populations and the need for more and more firewood has been the main cause; the expansion of suburban and rural settlements and industries a lesser cause. Well-grown trees, 30 or 40 feet high and proportionately thick, were not grazed down by goats; nor were they cut down with many regrets and sighs because of a rot in the wood that had killed them. You can see the sap dripping from the cut logs even while they are being carted to the yards, and from such stumps as have been spared, thin new shoots spring up in due course, though they can never again attain the stature of trees.

You have no idea of how quickly wood is cut and removed by our fuel-hungry citizens. No trace of a big tree felled in the morning remains by nightfall, not even a few leaves; swarms of men, women and children descend on the fallen tree, armed with saws, axes, bill-hooks, and even kitchen knives, and in no time at all it is gone. It is as efficient a disposal as the disposal of a carcass by vultures, except that no tell-tale bones are left behind.

Some seven or eight years ago, thousands of trees (among them many fruit-trees) stood in the great grove known as 'Nav-lakh Garden', a mile or so from Ranipet—perhaps there were nine lakhs of trees here once, as the name suggests. Only a barren, parched expanse of flat land without cover of bush or herbage now remains; even the roots of the slaughtered trees have been extracted.

Limbless and beheaded boles are depressingly common along all our roadways. To whom do these trees belong, and why were they not protected? Such questions are futile. I presume that ultimately or immediately Government exercises some control over our roadways and commons ('poramboke' lands). But, if I am correct in this, the blame for failing to save trees from the predatory axe is not assignable to any particular department, but to Government as a whole. Where the administration has not yet realized the urgent need to protect roadside and villageside trees, such things will happen.

When the British Raj was there, we blamed the callous, foreign Government for such damage to live wood. Let me quote a passage by Dewan Bahadur R. Raghunatha Rao, written about the year 1906—I concede its language is quaint, but its sentiment is strongly-felt: 'I am afraid this is not generally known to the European public what the feelings and opinions of the Hindus are regarding forests and trees. Their religion tells them that trees have souls like men; that cutting down a living tree is as bad as killing a living man; that their twigs even branches and leaves, when absolutely required, should be removed without harm to the trees; that only dried trees should be cut down for fuel. Any indiscriminate destruction of trees is very abhorrent to a true Hindu.' Well, where is this allegedly Hindu regard for trees now? More trees have been cut down within the past 10 years here than in the previous two decades.

Unfortunately, our Vanamahotsavas, which can be constructive and compensatory remedies, do little good because those in charge of this ritual insist on planting the wrong kinds of trees. Is it unreasonable that I, a citizen of India, should wish to see the trees of my native soil around me, when they can serve just as well as, or better than, queer, foreign importations? The prosopis that was imported to reclaim the desert in Rajasthan, and bind the shifting sands of Hagari, did its job all right—but why plant this ugly and useless bush all over Madras? Is it not because it needs no care once sown, and grows rampantly and spreads apace that it has found governmental patronage? Very soon it will develop into as smothering and troublesome a weed as the lantana, allowing nothing else to grow where it holds territory.

Why plant *Giricidia sepium* so very extensively at Vanamahotsavas? What claim has this exotic flowering tree to recognition as a species that stands pollarding well and supplies green manure, that a dozen indigenous trees do not have? I like the show of Mexican white Plumerias along the Marina at Madras, but what happened to the no less ornamental, wholly native *Calophyllum inophyllum* that was there in my boyhood? It belonged so truly and traditionally to the coast.

I realize that the fuel problem is a formidable one. For a while, it looked as if the solar cooker might yet save our trees. But now it seems clear that only sustained governmental (or private) effort, and the plantation of hundreds of thousands of acres to supply quick fuel, can save the trees still left on our roadsides and commons. Meanwhile, such trees as there are must be protected efficiently, and soundly-planned plantation work done, to provide tree growth to replace lost avenues and clumps. And in all such sylviculture, the indigenous species (which have suffered by exotic competition, apart from being cut down for fuel) should be preferred. It is true that some exotic trees grow quicker and need less care than many native species, but the latter should be preferred, if only to lend a more Indian look to the countryside.

1957

51

Gilding the Lily

T HE SPORTSMAN INTENT on the kill, the poacher seeking his meat from the furtively-laid trap and gun, the wasteful and unnecessary spread of agriculture and transport routes into the outlying scrub and jungle, and the relentless pressure on our wild vegetation for fuel and building materials to meet the needs of our ever-growing population—all these have been potent influences in the depletion of our once-wonderful flora and fauna. But, it has been said, these were not all: the apathy and cynical neglect of protective duty of a foreign Government have also been responsible for this sad state of affairs.

Today we have been awakened to the pressing need to save what is left of our great national wealth of nature and for the past few years there has been a noticeable governmental and popular enthusiasm for wild life. And with this enthusiasm, arising out of it, is another influence, seemingly constructive which could be as harmful as the gun and trap and callousness and greed of the past, because its power to deplete is so largely unsuspected.

No hint of cynicism or presumption of superior knowledge lurks behind this criticism, but only certain homely, well-founded misgivings about human nature. What should we do, what can we do, to preserve the flora and fauna of any area where there is still sufficient left to save? Why, nothing at all, beyond making quite sure that that area is freed from human interference and possibly, the consequences of past interferences. Leave well alone is the proven maxim of all wild-life conservation. It has been shown, time and again, that well-meant attempts to add to the natural richness of any place by the introduction of plant and animal species not native to it have ended in disaster. But it is not in human nature to leave well alone.

We want to do something about it, once we have taken on any responsibility, we want to gild the lily. While this is true of humanity everywhere especially is it true of us today, when so many in India are thinking in terms of national reconstruction. Of course this constructive zeal is heartening, and natural to a re-born nation. But we are a very ancient nation, too, and there are vital matters in which we need to be conservative rather than constructive.

Particularly we are given to the introduction of exotic plants in our desire to beautify the countryside and make up by plantation for the annihilation of jungle and woodland that we have been responsible for during the past fifty years. This is not the place for a survey of the foreign plants introduced by man and by accident into India, but it may be said that for several miles around our towns and cities it is difficult to find any sizable patch of scrub or jungle which does not feature exotics.

Our wastelands and open spaces teem with Tropical American herbs and weeds—the Mexican Poppy, *Alternanthera echinata*, and *Croton sparsiflorus* are only a few of these. Lantana, the ugly, assertive and ubiquitous *Prosopis juliflora*, and other shrubs from abroad dominate the scrub in large patches and even penetrate into the forests; and in parks and compounds and roadsides in Madras State, we find the tree-growth featuring many exotics—*Gliricidia sepium* (neé *maculata*), *Delonix regia* (the Gul Mohur—and that in a country to which three of the loveliest of all red-flowered trees belong: *Butea monosperma* or the Flame of the Forest, the Asoka, and the Red Silk-cotton), *Peltophorum roxburghii* (in replacement of the entirely native and much more graceful *Cassia fistula*) and *Kigelia pinnata* among them. The Madras Marina is, perhaps, one of the most telling examples in the country of this systematic favouring of exotics: it is dominated by the Australian casuarina and Mexican and West Indian white-flowered frangipanis!

No country in the world has a flora so rich in exotics as India.

Many of these have been intentionally introduced by well-meaning people, and have completely altered the complexion of the countryside over wide tracts. And still we keep on propagating them. That these introduced plants are hardier than the native species and need less care (often no care at all) is not a consideration in any sort of national planning, however constructive.

All of us will readily appreciate the point that we cannot shift the fauna of a specific forest to an equally wide tract of open country and expect it to do well there. We realize that animals are highly dependent on their environment, on particular environments to which they have become accustomed and suited through the centuries, and that any radical change in those surroundings will prejudice their lives seriously. But still people suggest the planting up of a denuded area with plants not native to that soil, to provide cover for the fauna of the place, without realizing that this will lead to no less radical a change in the environment. Apparently the change must be sudden, complete and obvious, and not insidious, for people to take note of it.

When a thing can be stated in general terms, there is no need to cite examples, though such citation will lend the verisimilitude of fairness. . . . It is so profoundly true that the best way to preserve the indigenous flora and fauna of any tract is to leave it severely alone, confining our care to the exclusion of all alien and artificial influences, that the temptation to provide examples can be easily resisted here. But that is not to say that no suggestions have been made, in fact, that as part of our wildlife effort species of plants and animals not native to a tract should be introduced into it—some quite fantastic suggestions have been made. The majority of suggestions for the 'improvement' of our wildlife, however, do not concern the wildlife at all: they are suggestions for the provision of amenities to visitors at some of our sanctuaries and parks. No doubt we do need these amenities, no doubt they will serve to attract the foreign tourists to India, but first and foremost we must secure the effective preservation of the attractive force, i.e., what wildlife there is still.

Permit me one example—because it did happen, really, and because it is so very illustrative of the lengths to which some people can go in trying to improve upon imperfect Nature. My photographic assistant, who has often accompanied me on my field trips and who has seen most of our wild animals in their natural setting, was talking to me about a recent trip to Mysore. Krishnaraja Sagar was spectacular, and in its way, Bandipur was no less magnificent, especially in its herds of chital; how grand it would be if only the two could be combined. Given a limited woodland, in which chital and blackbuck and peafowl would have to stay (because they had nowhere else to go), and given the lighting up of the entire area twice a week with powerful, multicoloured beams that would play impartially upon the ebullient fountains and the prancing buck and deer—why that would be Paradise, no less.

I felt too deeply shocked for words then, but will say this now. Personally, I do not believe in any sort of existence after death, but if there is a paradise let us wait till we are decently dead before we aspire to it.

1958

52

A Warning to Aesthetes

SOME 30 YEARS ago, an aesthetically minded gentleman in the Andamans had an inspiration. The islands offered few social pleasures then; remember, it was settled with desperate convicts and inhabited by aborigines described, by an encyclopaedia of those days, as 'savages of a low Negrito type'. However, there was vegetative beauty enough, and gazing at opulent plantations and woods, it occurred to this gentleman that what was needed to transform the vista to a scene from fairyland was a herd of chital in the foreground.

Only those who have seen this most decorative of all deer in a forest glade can know the charm they can impart to a woodland setting: I have always felt mildly surprised that Hopkins wrote 'Glory be to God for dappled things...' without having seen chital. Anyway, this gentleman lost no time in gilding the lily—he imported a few chital into the islands from their native home.

Frequently it happens that impulsive importations have unexpected consequences, and these chital were no exception. Any competent naturalist could have predicted the result—chital are very hardy, very prolific, and large enough to resist the smaller predators (the Andamans contain no greater cats). I quote from a recent news item featuring the tour-report of the Inspector-General of Forests to the Government of India, after a visit to the islands:

'The introduction of chital (spotted deer) from the mainland 30 years ago is regretted. In the absence of their natural enemies they have become as great a menace as rabbits in Australia. The report announces the arrival of two female panthers in the islands to check any further increase in the number of chital.'

Well, that sort of thing will happen. However, it is obvious to the critical reader that if all that is now sought to be done is to check further increase in the chital population, the comparison with rabbits in Australia is exaggerated. I have never been to Australia—for that matter, I have never been to the Andamans, but I understand the rabbit position there is really menacing.

It has happened, almost invariably, that wherever man tries to improve nature by importing exotic plants or animals, they have perished from inability to acclimatize themselves, or else they overrun the land. Take the Lantana, for instance. Its conquest of India is surely the most rapid and complete in the history of our much-conquered country—and it was never actually introduced into India; it was brought to Ceylon, and just leapt across the ocean in the gizzards of migrating birds.

Why must men upset the balance of nature? The shooting down of animals ruthlessly, without thought of the survival of species or the way it upsets the well-tried equilibrium of God, is something that is even more reprehensible than thoughtless importations. It is going on all over India, but it is only the animals that perish, and so no óne cares. When they flourish overmuch, as these chital in the Andamans do, it is then that we are moved to quick action.

I would like to point out the soundness of the action taken in this ease. Panthers are the natural enemies of chital, all right. They have an appetite for chital flesh that is not easily satiated. Chital are not shy of human neighbourhood and enter plantations freely; in fact, that is why they are a nuisance in the islands. They can be shot down easily; the introduction of natural foes that will give them a chance of survival, in preference to massacre, is a laudable action.

But why 'two female panthers'? Of course what follows is largely guesswork, but I think they are going cautiously. Apparently the instance of the importation of mongooses to check the rat menace in the sugarcane plantations of Jamaica is being remembered, besides rabbits and Australia. Those mongooses did their job well and suppressed the rats: then they turned their attentions to the poultry runs. Too many leopards in the Andamans can lead to highly unpleasant consequences, for panthers turn quite often to domestic stock when other hunting fails them, as I who have lost many milch-goats to them, know well. I grant that the application of the analogy is hardly apt or direct, but perhaps the story of King Log and King Stork has also been remembered!

1952

53

On Shikar English

THE FOREST RESTHOUSE was right on top of a hill, a little cottage with two wings. One wing was occupied by a high-ranking English officer retired from the Indian Army, and I occupied the other wing. At the foot of the hill, in the lantana and teak, lived a party of 11 chital, a very feminine bevy; some of these beauties came uphill to visit us each morning and evening, with that charming confidence that animals in a sanctuary often develop towards humanity.

The Brigadier had done a lot of shooting in his time, and was now keenly interested in wildlife preservation—a gentleman of the old school, active in mind and body in spite of his years, and unrelaxed in his standards. He had come there with permission to shoot any wild dog he could find in the sanctuary, and though he found traces of his quarry he never caught up with it. I was there to photograph Gaur, and was having a run of singularly poor luck.

We were sitting in the back verandah after dinner, and in reply to a query I said I had seen nothing all day, except for the 'tame' chital hinds. Promptly he corrected me. Does, not hinds, he informed me; sambar hinds, but chital does.

I assumed my most pompous manner. 'I beg your distinguished pardon, Sir,' I said to him, 'but I stick to my "hinds"; after all, you always say "chital stag", not "chital buck".' I wanted to add that the young of chital were invariably termed 'fawns' and not 'kids', but refrained from doing so, in view of his absolute certainty.

He did not say that after all this was a matter of English idiom, and that English was his language, not mine; he did not refer to his longer years and experience and his reputation (of which I knew nothing, being a non-shooting, vegetarian sort of man) as a shikari. Does, always does, he pronounced with brusque finality, and that was the end of the matter.

In a number of shikar books, written by European officers in India, you can find this confusion. The chital, after all is a medium-sized animal, and as in all Asiatic deer the females are smaller than the males and wholly hornless. To call them 'does' might seem natural, but it is definitely incorrect. I must add at once that the more informed and authoritative of these authors have never made this mistake—men like the brothers Burton, Dunbar Brander and Champion have always called female chital 'hinds'.

I have so often, and with such sincerity, paid my tribute to the magnificent work done by British officers in India in building up the natural history of the country, that I can afford to be critical of the minor faults of some of these 'sportsmen'. Before doing so, however, I would like to take the opportunity to point out, once again, what an uphill task the building up of the scientific literature on India's fauna and flora was. For one thing, there was no reliable background of indigenous natural history to help: for another, the vast territory involved, its varied climates and soils, and the exuberance of plant and animal life, required the close co-operation, over generations, of professional and amateur naturalists, many of them British Civilian or Army officers who took to shikar as a relaxation and then became interested in the fauna. The collation of the knowledge gained was always done by expert biologists, but the collection and observation work was often done by amateurs—still, the scientific integrity of the effort was never relaxed.

I am convinced that the greatest achievement of British rule in India, the one undeniable and wholly admirable achievement, has been the evolution of our natural history and the systematic study of our fauna and flora. Towards this, particularly towards our understanding of animal ways, a number of 'gentlemen sportsmen', without the professional biological equipment of IFS men, have contributed quite a lot. But they have also contributed many misnomers, some deplorably imaginative literature, and the kind of English that would have supplied Fowler with material for yet another book.

Who was responsible for calling our Gaur, wholly unrelated to the bison family, the Bison? Who named the Tahr of the South the Nilgiri Ibex? Who coined the utterly misleading name, Lion-tailed Monkey, for one of our most distinctive macaques and who referred to our langurs and macaques, indiscriminately, by the term 'baboon' when no baboon is found in India? The British 'gentleman sportsman' was responsible for all these misnomers, and, besides, for some quite wretched natural history.

To return to those chital, when does one use the term 'hind' and when 'doe'? Is it a question of the kind of animal described, i.e., would one always say 'doe' of the female of all antelopes and 'hind' of the female of all deer?

The rule is quite simple, and, like many rules, subject to sudden exceptions. To some extent the kind of beast described seems to determine the term, but size also plays an important part. It is generally true to say, of Indian antelopes, that the male is the 'buck', the female 'doe' and the young 'kids' (though 'fawns' would also pass muster), but when we speak of our one large antelope, the nilgai, the size and somewhat bovine looks of the animal bar these terms—we use 'bull', 'cow' and 'calves' instead. 'Stag', 'hind' and 'fawn' are safe for all our deer except the very smallest. Speaking of the Mouse Deer, and sometimes of the Barking Deer, we use the terms 'buck' and 'doe'—note that in such small deer the males are either hornless or have small horns which cannot possibly be termed 'antlers', even by the imaginative.

For all really large animals, whether bovine or not, 'bull', 'cow' and 'calf' would apply—to whales, elephants and rhinos, for example. Luckily the distinction between the sexes and between young and adult specimens is clear and easy when writing or speaking of the greater cats and the dog family. However, one cannot lay down hard and fast rules with regard to such things, in view of the exuberance of some English and American gentlemen sportsmen—one of these, in a recent book, refers to a 'bull hyena'!

1958

54

A Red Test for the Young

RECENTLY I HAD occasion to ask a number of young university graduates, at an interview, a question which I thought a fair test of their knowledge of India and general awareness. I asked them to name two red-flowered trees, or at least one.

Mind you, it was not a tricky question. We have no less than seven common red-flowered trees, the Flame of the Forest or palas (*Butea monosperma*); the Indian coral tree (*Erythrina indica*) and its cousins, including the dadap of tea plantations; the Asoka (*Saraca indica*); the magnificent red silk-cotton (*Salmalia malabarica*); the Gul Mohr (*Delonix regia*); the tulip tree (*Spathodea campanulata*); and the frangipani (*Plumeria rubra*, and varieties)—the first four are native to India and the rest exotics now common here. We have besides, quite a few other red-flowered trees, such as species of *Sterculia*, that are less common.

Well, I asked this question as they came up, one after another, and after a while I grew introspective. Am I, I asked myself, too biased by my preoccupation with the flora and fauna of our country, and asking too technical or difficult a question of these bright young people? On reflection it seemed to me that any country bumpkin, asked the same question, would have named the Indian silk-cotton unhesitatingly, and I asked my question again with renewed hope. However, I added a rider to it which I felt would help.

The rider was a bit of factual information—that the rose was not a tree. The first few candidates had triumphantly named the rose, and I felt it would save time all round to eliminate it straightaway.

Occasionally, when my question flummoxed them, I asked if they could name one yellow-flowered tree instead—the lovely Indian laburnum and other casias; the babul (*Acacia arabica*); the portia or umbrella tree (*Thespesia acutiloba*); and the opulent-flowered yellow silk-cotton (*Cochlospermum gossypium*) among native trees; and the rusty shield bearer or copper pod (*Peltophorum roxburghii*) among exotics, all have conspicuous yellow flowers, and are familiar trees. I had no better luck.

One of my victims (he was one among the four who had graduated in botany) named the Indian coral tree: three named the gul mohr which, however, they called the flame of the forest; one named the rain-tree (*Enterolobium saman*) which has pink and not red flowers, but it was near enough to please me.

One said he could not give me the English name of a yellow-flowered tree but knew its name in Telugu (vernacular tree names were allowed, of course) and then went on to describe what I felt sure was the mohwa, which is white-flowered.

I could not keep an accurate count as my question was purely an incidental one, but out of some 30 graduates, only four really gave any answer which could be called correct, and most of them did not answer it at all. Not one named two red-flowered trees.

I asked many candidates at this interview an easier question, the name of an exclusively Indian animal—I asked this mostly of those to whom I did not address my floral question. In assessing the peculiarly Indian claims of any animal, a slight overlapping of distribution into a neighbouring country in a distinct race is to be ignored. Leaving out reptiles and birds, and mammals like the lion-tailed macaque which only naturalists are likely to know, we have well over a dozen mammals, none of them rare, though some are rather local in their range, which are peculiarly Indian: the bonnet money; the common langur and the Nilgiri langur; the Asiatic lion today; the charming little Indian fox (*Vulpes bengalensis*) which is by no means uncommon; the sloth bear (it extends to Ceylon in a race); the striped palm squirrels; Indian blacknaped hares (very common); the wild buffalo; the Nilgiri tahr; the chinkara; the blackbuck; the chowsingha or four-horned antelope; the nilgai; the swamp deer or barasingha and the chital—I would also include all races of village buffaloes, and all breeds of Indian humped cattle in this list, though both have now been exported to many other countries.

In due course I felt the need to add a rider to this question as well—that the Royal Bengal Tiger was not a distinct species of *Panthera tigris* or even a recognized race, and that it was to be found in many other countries besides India. Even with this rider, no one gave me the answer to my question, among those that tried to.

One tough customer neatly turned the tables on me by claiming that 'the Indian black ant' was exclusively Indian—I do not know whether or not the large black ant of the countryside is peculiar to India, and it is certainly an animal within the meaning of the act (in this case, the Indian Penal Code!).

The question now is this: is there something radically wrong with the education and culture of our young men and women that they should not know the answers to these reasonable questions, or is it that I have become a monomaniac and am therefore unable to perceive how unfair my questions are?

1967

55

Nature Study

I STILL HAVE VIVID recollections of the terrible nature-science classes we had when I was at school. All the nature we saw was confined to a grey book, full of grim words and execrable, black-and-white illustrations, and a blackboard. Our teacher, a gifted impressionist, would draw bones and stomachs and the innards of men and animals on that blackboard in coloured chalk—and that was nature-science. He told us that the blood got flamelessly burnt in our lungs, like rusting iron, and that a cow's stomach is divided into compartments. The only time that nature had a chance to enter those gruesome classes was when some of us were asked to go out, and catch a butterfly for a demonstration. At the end of the 40-minute period the butterfly-hunters returned, flushed and breathing hard from a game they had played on the road, and reported that no butterfly was to be seen in or around school. We were, very naturally, believed.

I know that nowadays they try to make nature more objective, and a trifle less stale and weary, in schools, especially in primary schools, but the approach is still the same. The plan of study, which graduates from Nature Study in primary schools through Elementary Science in high schools to Natural Science in colleges, follows what is known as the Concentric System. The idea behind it is to teach more and more of the same thing as the faculties of the young student develop, an excellent plan, no doubt. The first year the child learns that the cow has four legs (quardruped), gives us milk, and eats grass (herbivore). The next year, may be, there is a lesson on milk and another on how the cow is a Mammal. And in Form IV the young naturalist learns how and why the cow chews cud (ruminant), and that its stomach is cut up into compartments. If you follow the cow carefully through the syllabus, as I have done, you will find that that is all you learn about a cow in school. There is nothing about glue or leather or cheese, you do not hear of the relations of the cow, even its nearest ones, what prejudices and fancies a cow has or on what it thrives best. In fact, except that the cow is such a common animal that you can't escape seeing it, you would have had all your cow from a book and on the Concentric System. Nature comes to the class room, in selected bits and on the instalment plan. Oh yes, there are Experiments, Demonstrations and Specimens. Properly used they can be invaluable aids to teaching, but they are only that, and often not even that because they are not properly used. Let us be honest, rather than polite. There is never any experimental work in school—only set demonstrations, based on the Concentric System. Early in his life the scholar makes his acquaintance with the Bean Seed and its germination, and very naturally concludes that all seeds have fleshy cotyledons, are exalbuminous, and epigeal in their germination. The 'experiment' is never prolonged to show the need for light, or soil salts, once the leaves are out. They do not take you out to a field of seedlings to study germination, or tell you why the farmer ploughs his lands. They teach about metamorphosis, but I wonder how many schoolboys have watched a caterpillar pass through the chrysalis stage, or tadpoles grow into frogs. All they teach is a prescribed text by mastering which you can pass examinations.

If you want to know how inhibiting these methods can be, you have only to meet a number of educated young men and women. The average educated adult knows little or nothing of the teeming plant and animal life of the country, and cares less. Livestock does not interest him, and the world is to him a place which holds only human beings. He can never make friends with a hill or a dog, and if he has no one to talk to, no book to read, and no gadget to turn and unturn, he is quite lost. School education is solidly to blame for all this—children are not taught to know and appreciate nature at first hand, only terms and explanations from books. They think of nature as something necessary for passing examinations, as something unfortunately necessary. And when they are grown they are unaware that they have missed half the joy of life.

The school approach to nature study is fundamentally unsound. It is based on the theory that one must proceed from elementary, understandable things. There is simplification and selection, and logical, reasoned steps guide the approach. But the fact is that nature is not simple, logical and reasoned—thank God it is not. There is no need to fully understand anything, in all its structure and complexity, to be alive to its charm. Systematic knowledge, morphology, anatomy, physiology all are essential to the study of natural science, especially of advanced classes, but the stress should not lie solely on structure and function, right from the beginning and all along. What makes living things fascinating is their behaviour, not their anatomy. Children in primary schools should get to know the common wild plants and birds of the locality; birds because they are so easily watched. They should learn, a little later perhaps, the stories of the domestic animals. They should be taken out to see nature for themselves, and be given pleasant books, with gay, coloured illustrations, telling them about these things. The coloured illustrations are costly, but they are vitally important. Children love them, and will readily interest themselves in any text if it is free from morals and illustrated in colour. That may seem a faddist's view, Show me the child who can resist the Pete Castor series of animal books and I accept defeat.

It is in high schools, however, that nature study can be made really interesting and worthwhile. Occupation and instruction, without dullness, can be provided by giving the students a plot of ground for growing things in—not a bed for the bean seed only, but a miniature market garden. I am convinced that if the school could go to the trouble, and trifling expense, of maintaining a poultry-run, a goat-pen (not too near the miniature garden) and a pigeon-loft (pigeon post could be made a regular part of the training of the older scouts), and a middle-sized School Dog, the scholars would acquire virtues and knowledge that a whole board of teachers cannot help them to get. There must be variety and choice in such matters, of course, and they would have to be extra-curricular. More than all these, regular nature-study outings, supplemented with lessons in field identification and methods of observation, will help to develop a keen, live interest in nature. Obviously, these outings and classes would also be extra-curricular—one never knows beforehand what one might see when setting out, and much of the value of such study lies in its being as per no set plan. Whoever is in charge of these classes must have a genuine enthusiasm for nature study and be utterly honest. Again and again he will come across things that puzzle him, and there will be questions to which he does not know the answers: if he is an observant man, he will learn quite as much as the students. And he must realize that there must not be that insistence and forcing in these outings that one associates with curricular classes. Too much discipline, in nature study, tempts the students to dishonest methods, and an approach that is not absolutely truthful (to the extent of one's perceptions), is as worthless and hypocritical as the sentimental, sloppy approach. The importance of this was brought home to me in an unforgettable way, some years ago, when I was allowed to try out my methods in a school. We were collecting material for the school exhibition, and some of my trusted lieutenants had been deputed to procure birds' nests for a section of the show. All sorts of nests came in, including the nests of a sybarite tree-rat, and it was heartening to see the enthusiasm of the boys. But one of them seemed unwilling, and he could produce nothing but a succession of sparrows' nests. Now, there is a limit to the number of nests of the Common House Sparrow that one can use in an exhibition, and I lectured that boy severely on laziness, how everyone should pull his weight in a joint effort, duty and similar topics. By evening he returned, staggering beneath the weight of a ponderous nest wedged in the fork of an enormous green branch. I was completely flummoxed, to put things mildly for I could not imagine what sort of fowl, barring the Roc of Sinbad the Sailor, could have built that nest, and the Roc as everyone knows, builds no nest but rears its brood on the edge of a precipice. There was a neat symmetry, geometrical pattern, and tidiness about that nest that I could associate with no large bird. I asked questions. There were evasive answers. Finally I took the nest to pieces, and beneath an underlay of jowar stalk I came across indisputable evidence of the identity of the nest-builder—there were stout twigs at the foundation, firmly lashed into place with string, and reef-knots. Yes, overmuch discipline should be avoided in nature-study classes: it tends to defeat itself.

1947

Wombat: Burrowing herbivorous marsupial of genus *Phascolomys*,
native to S. Australia and Tasmania, with thick, heavy body, short legs,
rudimentary tail, and general resemblance to small bear.
—The Reader's Digest Great Encyclopaedic Dictionary

WOMBAT

The fat Australian wombat
does not indulge in combat,
or work, or argument, or any quest.

It feeds on what it feeds on,
it finds a mate and breeds on,
and then recuperates in sleep and rest.

Nature Protected

56

The Bishnoi and Blackbuck

THE BLACKBUCK IS exclusively Indian. It is the type-specimen of the antelopes and the handsomest of them all. It is also the swiftest long-distance runner among animals and can keep going for 10 km, at 60 km per hour. And it is well known to our classical art and poetry, and there are separate names in our regional languages to distinguish the graceful, hornless, sand-brown doe from the arrestingly black-and-white buck, with spiralling horns as long as the animal is tall.

There are other superlative claims too that can be made for the blackbuck. During the eighteenth, nineteenth and the first half of the twentieth century, it was the most numerously shot of our much-shot wild beasts, and also baited and snared, or otherwise killed, by meat hunters all over India. Further, it was the animal to hunt which cheetahs were used in a royal sport, practised only in our country for centuries till the cheetah became extinct here. Later, when the plains country (the natural home of blackbuck) was intensively and extensively occupied by our exploding humanity, it was one of the animals most seriously affected by deprivation of territory. The open, level scrub it had roamed from ancient times was colonized, cut up and cultivated by men everywhere, and everywhere the blackbuck was hunted down as a crop-raider. Whether or not it really did much damage to cultivation, its flesh was much relished. Today, blackbuck are locally extinct in many locations where they were known in great herds for centuries, or else reduced to a few straggling parties. Even in sanctuaries like Kanha, Point Calimere and the tiny Guindy National Park around Raj Bhavan in Madras, the buck lead fugitive lives and are poor in size and horn.

How delightful it is against this factual background to find that there are still agrarian communities and settlements in our country where the blackbuck is not only not hunted in spite of the trifling damage it does to the crops, but also actively protected! And here one finds it in fairly large herds, and it attains as splendid a bodily size and horn development as it ever did.

Tal Chhapar in Rajasthan, about midway between Ratangarh and Sujangarh, is perhaps the most notable for its blackbuck of all such Bishnoi villages. The Bishnois are a predominantly agricultural Hindu community who follow their own ancient 20-point programme. Two of the important tenets of their faith are that they feel bound to prevent killing of all wild animals (including birds) and to prevent greenwood from being cut. They practise kindness towards all living things as their creed, and provide water to wild creatures around their settlements in arid tracts.

It is only around Bishnoi settlements that one suddenly finds blackbuck, chinkara, peafowl, partridges and other shy, fugitive wild animals being quite confiding and unafraid of men—proof positive of the potency of a strict policy of non-interference towards the local wildlife (except of course when occasion arises to protect it from human predators). And at Tal Chhapar, a fairly populous settlement, it is the blackbuck that dominates the area.

There were mixed herds too, containing adult does by the dozen and many young from the previous breeding season, but in March when I was there it was the all-adult male buck parties that were specially notable. At other Bishnoi villages too, I saw such buck parties (for instance, at Makam, Ramdeora and Doli, and beyond Jodhpur) but the largest of such parties was at Tal Chhapar, consisting of some 60 to 70 bucks, all running together.

Soon after Independence we have had the Indian Board for Wildlife, and the Wildlife (Protection) Act of 1972 and regional Wildlife Advisory Boards and Wildlife Wardens formed and appointed under the Act. They certainly represent a constructive and real step towards implementing the growing Governmental awareness of responsibility towards the nation's wildlife. We have knowledgeable societies and associations willing and able to offer advice and information on various aspects of wildlife conservation. And we have a vast and varied multitude of wildlife experts, Indian and exotic, so keen on helping in the good cause that it is difficult to escape them, and their cliques and coteries and theories. But if you want to know how conservation can be really effected successfully in the field without all this fuss and bother, by illiterate rustics through dedicated and sincere effort, and faith in the policy of leaving well alone, go to Tal Chhapar.

1980

57

Vedanthangal

VEDANTHANGAL IS IN the Chinglepet District, a little village not shown on the smaller survey maps, some 55 miles from Madras and six by road from the nearest place to which bus or train can take you. And perhaps the oldest bird sanctuary in India lies here.

There is a small seasonal lake here (or a large tank—call it what you like), 74 acres in extent excluding outlying low land. In summer, and till the rains arrive in August or September, the lake-bed is dry—a shallow mud basin with little grass or other small growth on it, but with about 500 Barringtonias growing in massed clumps near its middle and singly along the inner edge of its palmyra-topped bund. The trees (all *Barringtonia acutangula*, except for a handful of thin acacias) are mature and stout-boled, with spreading, evergreen crowns, but they are not tall—not much over 20 feet in height, some not even that high. When the rain-fed lake is full, it is about 10 feet deep in the middle and the trunks and lower boughs are submerged, with only the leafy, much-branched crowns showing above the thick green water, in darker green mounds. And thousands of birds come here, to nest in these crowns.

From time immemorial they have nested here, and been effectively protected by the villagers. The motive of these good people in protecting the birds is not wholly altruistic, but I do not believe it is wholly selfish either. The droppings of the mixed assemblage of parent birds, and the rising generations, enrich the lake water, endowing it with manurial potency. It is this water that is used for the neighbouring paddy-fields.

Both the Indian and Madras Wildlife Boards have accorded recognition to Vedanthangal, but it was a sanctuary for centuries before the boards were there, and officially recognized long ago. The records of such official cognizance are interesting.

Late in the eighteenth century Mr L. Place, Collector of Chinglepet

(1796-98) appears to have given an original 'cowle' to the local inhabitants, who asked for official recognition of their age-old 'prescriptive right' to protect the birds against all-comers. This document stated that no birds might be shot or snared in the Vedanthangal tank area.

On 7 January 1858, George G. Tod, Chief Assistant Magistrate of the district, renewed the sanction at the request of the villagers, who had lost the original given them by Mr Place. Mr Tod's 'cowle' is in rather quaint Tamil and runs as follows:

'Whereas it has been represented that in the Kadappai trees of the lake of your village of Vedanthangal a variety of birds nest and live freely and that the Hon. Placesaheb had long ago given you a cowle prohibiting the shooting or capture of these birds, which document has been lost, and whereas you have now asked us to give you another in replacement, this has been issued to you.

Should any persons, Europeans or hunters or such people, come to the lake and attempt to shoot or capture the birds in contravention of the above-mentioned order, show this to them and prevent them from doing so.'

More than three-quarters of a century later this order of 'Todsaheb', carefully preserved by the villagers, was produced before another 'Todsaheb' for renewal—only, this second saheb chose to spell his name with a double 'd'. On 10 February 1936, Mr A.H.A. Todd, Collector of Chinglepet, issued an order which says:

'Vedanthangal tank is a birds' sanctuary and has been kept as such by the villagers for over a century. Notice in English and in Tamil in bold characters should be painted on wooden boards and set up at each end of the tank bund. The form of notice to be put up is enclosed. The expenses should be met from office contingencies.'

I saw no wooden boards carrying prominent notice when I first visited Vedanthangal in June 1954, nor during four subsequent visits made late last year and early this year. But I saw the lake area dry and birdless, and later water-filled and teeming with nesting birds, and was able to collect sufficient observation material for this note.

Asked to guess now many trees grow in the middle of the lake, people would be hopelessly out in their estimates. Most would put the figure around 50, the more reckless might even go up to 100. No one who did not know the actual number would think some 300 trees stood there, so closely are they massed and so confluently do their tops run into one another, when seen from the bund. A clump that from the bund looks as if it were made up of two or three trees actually represents 20. I have taken no census of the trees, but on a rough reckoning I made out there were 300 in the middle.

The trees, as I have said, are old. During summer the seedlings that sprout in the shade of their parents are grazed or trampled down by cattle, but I think they would need transplanting to the periphery, some distance away, to develop into vigorous new clumps, even if they are otherwise protected. So much for the history and topography of the sanctuary. Before going on to the really interesting feature of Vedanthangal, its nesting birds, we may briefly consider the probable origin of its name.

'Vedan' in Tamil means 'hunter' or 'fowler' and 'thangal' is an old Tamil word that has two relevant meanings in this context, viz. 'tank' and 'the act of protecting or guarding'. Those who construe the place-name to mean 'fowler's tank' must surely realize that they have hit on a singularly inapposite rendering. Vedanthangal having been a bird sanctuary for so long, it seems reasonable to presume it was named so because its birds were protected against fowlers.

Now for the bird life. I list the species I noticed nesting here during the latest breeding season, still 'on' as I write. But first I must point out that I may have missed a few species that go about the business of securing posterity unostentatiously, that my observation was limited to the few clumps I could watch through binoculars and the fewer clumps I could get near to, and that sustained observation over a long period (not half-a-dozen random visits) is necessary for any appraisal of the species, numbers, and priorities in a large, mixed heronry, and the nesting habits of the birds.

I found no migratory birds here, excepting a few teal I saw on the afternoon of 12 February flying over the lake. That afternoon I also saw a pair of pelicans here, but these are not migratory birds, and are common near Madras where there are broad sheets of water, for example at Pulicat lake, to the north of Madras (Vedanthangal is more or less to the south). However, I heard persistent reports from local inhabitants of the occasional visits of large, swan-like birds that rode easily on the water—not pelicans, surely. What I heard strongly suggested Barheaded Geese to me, and if they have visited Vedanthangal during certain seasons, that would mark the southern-most point of their migration.

Hundreds of Openbilled Storks were nesting in the Barringtonias, but no other storks—I was rather surprised at the absence of the Painted Stork. All the egrets were here, the Large Egret, the Smaller Egret (which

G.M. Henry so rightly terms Median Egret), the Little Egret, and a few Cattle Egrets on the periphery—I don't know if the last nest in the lake, but perhaps they do. An interesting point I noticed was that though the first three were breeding actively, and there were nestlings and even eggs in their nests, some of the Large and Smaller Egrets were not in breeding condition. . . .

Night Herons, Pond Herons ('paddy-birds') and a few great, gaunt Grey Herons were prominently in residence, as also White Ibises. Spoonbills sporting full nuchal crests, the tokens of their breeding condition, were nesting in large numbers. Apparently they breed here right from November to March—my mid-February photographs show week-old young in the nest and also three-quarter grown spoonbills, one of them obligingly displaying the cause of its name.

Little Cormorants and Darters ('snake-birds') complete my list of breeding birds, somewhat incompletely! I thought I saw a few shag, but could not get near enough and am not sure I saw dabchick near the shore, and was told that some sort of moorhen or waterhen also resides here.

Common grey-necked crows and Brahminy kites were very much in evidence over the lake; common kites, neophrons, and an occasional bird of prey were also to be seen. In any large nesting colony, a few eggs and nestlings fall into the water while their parents dispute territory, nests may be left unguarded momentarily, and opportunities for scavenging, thieving and fishing are not lacking.

I can give no estimate of numbers. The Little Cormorants, Smaller Egrets, spoonbills, openbills and night herons were the most plentiful. Thousands of birds nest here, and their young survive the bustle and crowding of the breeding enterprise to continue the species, thanks to the protection they enjoy.

Soon after the first rains, some time in October, the birds start arriving in small flocks, and rainfall being normal, they keep coming till January! The nesting species do not descend on the lake full strength, in sky-obscuring flights, but arrive in small successive flocks. Many of these start breeding at once, colonizing some tree of their choice before the next flight reaches Vedanthangal, so that once breeding has commenced, young at various stages of development may be found at any inspection. The position, however, is not quite so simple for while some species (and possibly flocks) arrive ready to breed, others are not in breeding condition on arrival, and may take their time nesting.

Breeding goes on for almost five months, from November to March,

and many of the birds raise more than one clutch. They nest here, as they
do elsewhere, in mixed companies. However, there is a tendency for
birds of a feather to keep together in locating their nests, one part of a
tree-top being largely utilized by one species, another part by some other
species. White Ibises sometimes run their nests together, as observers
have already pointed out, and at Vedanthangal I saw large, machan-like
platforms consisting of the communal nests of this ibis—there were no
eggs but the young on them served to identify the machan-builders
surely.

Openbills, the smallest and almost the most awkward-looking of our
storks (the palm for such looks must surely go to the largest, the adju-
tant!), and spoonbills tend to occupy special trees of their own; the
openbills build their nests pretty close, on a sort of flat system. Incidentally, they are capable of the most dexterous turn of wing; not only do they
soar, stork-fashion, but they also dip and shoot off in the air at acute
angles, at dizzy speed. Young openbills have no gap between their man-
dibles (it is this gap in the adult beak that gives the bird its name); they
have comparatively short, gapless, wedge-shaped beaks.

Paddy fields around and sheets of water not too far away provide the
parent birds with feeding grounds, a most important factor in the communal breeding of water-birds, for the quick-growing young have insa-
tiable appetites. This, the shade provided by the Barringtonia foliage
(even the young of most diurnal birds cannot stand the sun) and, more
than all, the protection they enjoy are what make the birds arrive here in
such numbers, soon after the rains. The great Madurantakam Lake is
only a few furlongs away, there are minor sheets of water close by, and
I observed egrets and ibises feeding in paddy fields eight miles from
Vedanthangal, a negligible distance to a bird.

However, the potentialities of Vedanthangal Lake itself as a feeding
ground appear to have been overlooked by observers. On the village side
the water is shallow and merges into cultivation—flocks of egrets and
spoonbills, and paddy-birds, may be seen feeding here all day. Cormorants and darters fish in the lake, though from time to time the former
sally out to feeding grounds and return to their nests in large, thick,
quick-winged flocks. I saw openbills prodding the shallows at Vedanthangal, not far from their nests, and from the manner in which they threw
up their necks and gulped, every now and then, the occupation seemed
rewarding. Undoubtedly the regular feeding grounds of the nesting species lie outside the lake, but the water below their nests, rich in algae and
aquatic insects and other small fry, is not a larder despised.

Vedanthangal is one of the most picturesque and interesting breeding grounds of water-birds in our country. A naturalist can spend a lifetime here, profitably observing the local avian life, but even to the layman the lake during the nesting season is fascinating, the compact field of observation, the teeming colonies in the water, the constant passage of birds to and fro, and the rural setting combining to capture and hold his eye. It is perhaps just as well that the sanctuary is off the beaten track, but it deserves to be much wider known than it is now. Used to a village within a furlong, the birds can take no fright, or other harm, from being observed. Unfortunately, though they are safe on their nesting ground, they are ruthlessly shot all around, when they set out to find food for themselves and their young. The Madras Government, interested in the sanctuary, will no doubt devise means to prevent such cruel slaughter. Vedanthangal can do much to stimulate a now apathetic public interest in our bird life, and I hope that more and more people will get to know of its charms and that it will soon develop into a centre of national and international interest.

1956

58

The Charm of Chilka

IN THE FIRST week of January last year, I sepnt a whole day in a fishing-boat on a saltwater lake some 60 km from Madras. Boats here depend on directional winds—one has to set out early in the morning to get the wind right to sail out into the lake, and in the evening the wind turns right round and brings one back. Nowhere is the brownish green mire-bottomed lake deep and in places flat sandspits rise just above the thick, dark water. One is transported at once into a different world, a world of total flatness where an egret wading in the shallows stands taller than the distant, hazy palmyras on the horizon, a world with no verticals. And throughout the day I was thinking of Chilka lake, ten times as large but otherwise so strikingly similar—I was hundreds of miles away from where I was.

I do not know why it is so, but when governmental minds think of nature preserves and sanctuaries, they seem to think only of forests or else of the nesting sites of water-birds and freshwater tanks to which migratory waterfowl arrive in numbers such as Sultanpur jheel, Nalsarovar and even Bharatpur. The importance of lagoons and saline lakes as highly distinctive and valuable wildlife habitats does not seem to be realized by them. Chilka is the largest and most interesting saltwater lake in India, and even its shores have their faunal and floristic distinctiveness. Recently, the human need for wildlife recreation, and the value of habitats with their own, individualistic character, have been realized all over the world. Surely we cannot afford to overlook the most expansive world of flatness in the country in planning our national preserves.

In 1968, utilizing an unforced opportunity that came my way, I suggested to the Orissa Forest Department that it was imperative to set apart a good portion of Chilka lake as a nature preserve, and to protect this preserve efficiently. From my father's diaries I knew that very early in this century a variety of professional meathunters were systematically trapping, netting and shooting the water-birds at Chilka lake, and I noticed no lessening of this activity in 1968 and further learnt that Calcutta was the main market for these poachers. I could spend only two days on Chilka lake, but made out as good a case as I could for my recommendation from my observations—and nothing came of it. In 1970, finding myself briefly on the Government of India's Environmental Commission, I again pressed for recognition of Chilka's claims, and offered to do a field survey and provide a detailed plan—and nothing came of that either. Subsequently, the Indian Navy has acquired certain interests in the lake, and I believe other claims have also been made on its natural richness.

Apart from the fishes, crabs and lesser life of this vast spread of shallow saltwater and its vegetation, it is of major importance as the wintering home of many migratory water-birds, from plovers and sandpipers to many kinds of duck and both kinds of flamingo—the lesser and the greater. So far as I know, this is the only place anywhere where the Ruddy Shelduck (the Brahminy—the *chakwa-chakwi* celebrated in our legends) can be found not in pairs and small parties but in teeming flocks. Chilka's mouth has its own distinctive faunal complexion, featuring the dolphin. And more than everything else, Chilka is Chilka, unique in its charm as a world of vast flatness, where wildlife recreation and organized tourism, for once, need not have any deleterious effects on the wildlife.

I believe some measure of conservation by the State Government does now obtain in a part of Chilka, but the sustained and relentless slaughter of the water-birds goes on still and surely such an extraordinary natural asset merits the assurance of its future being recognized, over an adequate and representative area, as a national park, and protected strictly against poachers.

1979

59

Planning a Park

O N 5 DECEMBER 1945, a small group of people stood on a terrace right on top of Ramgad in the Sandur Hills, and gazed
north-westward at the plains beyond. One could see for miles
across the flat country, and the cerulean smudge of Narayanadevarakere,
beyond the middle distance, dominated the panorama; the nearest haunt
of blackbuck lay around it. The Tungabhadra Scheme was then mainly
on paper, as you may remember, and the site of the dam was not visible
from that terrace; still, the people who were there saw the gleam and rip-
ple of prospective water in that landscape. The present Regional Secretary for the South of the Indian Board for Wildlife and I were in that
group, and everyone was thinking of the great lake that would drown all
that expanse of brown earth, and bank against the ancient hill we stood
on.

We know that each winter brought many kinds of duck, barheaded
geese and other aquatic birds to the small rain-fed lakes in the plains.
When all of it was one vast sheet of water, right on their migration route,
would more birds settle here? That was a speculative question then. It is
still one. But it was as we stood there, staring and speculating, that the
idea of utilizing this unique feature for a wildlife sanctuary was born.

There was no Indian Board for Wildlife then, and the territory involved lay in three separate States. Much water has flowed through the
Tungabhadra sluices since, and there is no longer any political barrier or
uncertainty over the water spread area of the reservoir. Moreover, thanks
to the initiative of its Southern Regional Secretary, I understand the idea
of locating a national park here has already been approved by the Wildlife Board, and that a scheme will soon be drawn up.

This is not that scheme for I have no knowledge of the Board's inten-
tions beyond what I have said. In February this year, I was presented with

an opportunity for a reconnaissance of the Tungabhadra area and purlieus to collect further material for this article. I am no stranger to this
country and know parts of it intimately, but February is the driest month
within the Sandur Hills, and outside them, too, there is little rain, though
the water in pools and minor lakes has not yet dried up. It is a good time
to study conditions in the field. Moreover, no plan is the poorer for a little spade-work, and so I utilized the opportunity to have a good look at
the terrain around the Tungabhadra Dam.

What I thought were the basic arguments in favour of a national park
here nine years ago still hold. I shall give them to you briefly before giving
you more briefly a plan for a possible national park around the Tungabhadra Dam.

Wildlife preservation in every country has certain common ideals, but
the practical lay-out and working of sanctuaries and parks must vary
from country to country. This fact, I am afraid, is not always appreciated
even by the small minority of people interested in our wildlife. It is all
very well to talk of vast tracts being reserved for the herbivores in America,
the sowing of buckwheat for the animals and the carefully regulated
shooting permitted to prevent overpopulation—yes, they do things very
well over there, in America and Africa and other countries, but those
methods may not suit our country. No man truly interested in a country's
fauna will deny that the ideal is where there are no parks or preserves, but
where the beasts and birds are ceded territory and unmolested by virtue
of a highly informed national consciousness. I myself am convinced that
our traditional modes of agriculture and transport are quite as much to
blame as firearms for the alarming decline in our wonderful fauna, and
the rapid increase in our human population is unquestionably the most
potent cause for this decline.

The fact remains that now and in our dominantly agricultural country, the scattered small holdings and network of cartways sustain human
life, that the public (both literate and unlettered) has no interest in the
great national heritage of wildlife, of which it knows little and for which
it cares less, and that our cultivators will bitterly oppose all attempts to
consolidate their dispersed holdings. But in one cause the Government
has no hesitation in dispossessing the cultivator, even in dispossessing
entire villages. This is when a river valley project is taken up. Here is a
great opportunity, then, for adding a small margin to the area already re-
signed to the water spread of the dam's reservoir, and so to benefit the
creatures of the open country.

Leaving out the Bombay State area, with which we are not concerned, the Tungabhadra Reservoir claims 75½ square miles in the Mysore area and 57½ square miles in the Hyderabad area with the elevation of 1,630 feet at the dam. Now, all these 133 square miles of flat land were not agricultural fields before they were marked for submersion. The fields were here and there, and only dry crops were grown on most of them. How about the fields outlying the present water spread line? They, too, are scattered and only dry crops are grown on most of them. If we add a half-mile margin all round to the present water spread boundary, no great damage would have been done to agriculture in the area. And a truly reviving belt would have been created for the fauna of the plains.

The second main argument for the founding of a national park here is the topography of the place. Just look at the land, or even at a map of it! At the Dam there are buildings on either side and all things necessary for accommodating and attracting tour-traffic; good roads, superb views and easily seen country. The Dam must be the centre of any proposed national park.

Now for the barest possible outline of the proposed park. I reiterate that these are only my suggestions; no doubt whatever is ultimately done will be much better done. The broad principle here followed is that the proposed boundary line should go along the almost continuous belts of reserved forests and hill forests, so as to encroach as little as possible on cultivation. Starting from the Dam, this boundary line could be carried south-east, almost in a line with the axis of the Dam, along the inner foot of the Ramgad hill in the Sandur area till it meets the Narihalla (the stream that cuts through the Sandur Hills south-westwardly); the boundary could then turn west, at right angles, and follow the stream to the southern edge of the Bandri Reserve Forest and proceed along that edge to the Sivapuram Reserve Forest and proceed along the edge of that forest around it and then northward, to the north-western corner of the Nandibanda Reserve Forest: from this point it could be carried along the reservoir's south-western contour to Basarakodu, crossing the Tungabhadra here to Mattur in the Hyderabad region. This would be the main body of the park in the Mysore region.

In the Hyderabad region, the boundary could be carried more or less around Mattur, Nirligi, Katarki, Hyati and Mundergi (i.e. along the north-eastern contour of the reservoir), then north to Hire Bhogamhalu and east to Lingapur, then right around the northern edge of Agoli State Forest and then south along the eastern edge of Benakal State Forest,

then further south to the Tungabhadra. Re-crossing the Tungabhadra
into the Mysore area, the river could then be followed back to the Dam,
so as to include Hampi within the park's ambit. All this is roughly shown
in my map.*

The above proposal would include not only a margin of flat country
around the reservoir (both in the Mysore and Hyderabad regions) but
also many forests. These are hill forests or else reserved, so that cultivation will not be seriously affected by their inclusion. Moreover, these forests should be guarded against decline, and, therefore, should be included. Every February, man-made fires rage across the Sandur Hills,
devouring the undershrub and saplings. These fires spread far out along
the Bandri and Nandibanda forests. On 24 February this year I saw them
roaring across the jungles around Chilakanahatti, when I passed that
way. These fires are started by men for the sake of the young grass and
beedi-leaves (the leaves of a species of ebony) that sprout in their wake,
and can certainly do no good to the large forest tracts they scorch. Further, the cutting of greenwood by contractors on licence is not conduct-
ive to silvicultural welfare in places where there is little active plantation
and where the wood depends for its existence on natural regeneration.
Apart from faunal considerations, these forests should be included in any
national park scheme if their ancient charm is to be saved.

Beyond the Nandibanda forest begins the flat country, skirting the
reservoir. Here is the sanctuary of the future for blackbuck, foxes, a few
wolves, floricans, sandgrouse and the Great Indian Bustard. I have mentioned animals known to have lived here not long ago, and the Great
Indian Bustard (threatened with extinction) is still to be found not very
far from this area. The country is ideal for blackbuck, especially on the
Hyderabad side. On the Mysore side it should be possible to establish
belts of mangrove in the tracts periodically inundated by the water spread,
to make up for the cleared wood (practically every tree has been cut here)
and to provide roosts for the waterside birds. Strangely enough, we found
far fewer water birds around Narayanadevarakere this February than in
past Februaries, though the water was so very much broader. However,
the birds will come back when conditions are more settled. I think the
Barringtonia (the tree that sustains bird life at Vedanthangal, near Madras) would do very well here, and attract ibises, storks, spoonbills,
herons, egrets and birds of like feather. But beware of the Prosopis!

*Not reproduced here.

Introduced into Hagari to bind the sandy, shifting soil, the Prosopis did all that was asked of it and more, then proceeded to the conquest of the neighbourhood. Goats do not eat its finely dissected foliage, but they munch its fleshy legumes and scatter the seeds abroad. I saw these spiky, bushy trees flourishing in the Tungabhadra Dam area recently, where they had not been on a previous visit some two years ago. As a food plant for blackbuck Prosopis has not many claims, and given half a chance it will inherit the earth.

One last word. Whatever else is done or not, let not the chital (spotted deer) be introduced into the future park. Chital are undoubtedly beautiful (many think them the loveliest of all deer), and now that the water supply is assured, they should certainly do well in this area and get quickly established. But for all that, and the additional fact that there are predators here that will limit their numbers, I think it would be wiser to take a conservative stand, and not bring any animal into the country not known to have been an authentic native till recently. Chital, like the Prosopis, rather tend to inherit the earth.

In fact, there is only one interesting importation that could be made, and that too was definitely known to have lived in these parts not so long ago. I refer to the cheetah or hunting leopard, now virtually extinct in India. If a national park is founded around the Tungabhadra Dam, and after it has been developed for some years and the blackbuck are well settled and prospering, the hunting leopard could be imported from Africa and released here in a tract long known to it and for many years its stronghold.

1955

60

Animals of
the Dwindling Forest

OVER THE PAST 35 years, India's wildlife has dwindled to a mere fraction of its former strength. The decline began much earlier, but was so insidious between 1900 and 1935 that it was hardly noticed even by most of those concerned with the country's wildlife, the officers of various regional forest departments, taxonomists doing stupendous work on the flora and fauna of India, and the more experienced hunters interested in the forests and their animals.

In animal populations, the tempo of decline accelerates after a gradual fall to a low level; once the local population of a species is much reduced its ability to recoup deteriorates progressively, and with the fall in numbers often the factors of depletion gain lethal potency. Broadly speaking, the main factors causing depletion of wildlife in India are: greatly increased demands on the forests by people and governments as a consequence of the great increase in human population, the destructive exploitation of natural forests to serve political ends and the recognition of village rights in the forests, sustained and poorly controlled wood and flesh poaching and (to a lesser extent) licensed shooting, and industrialization and its consequences. These factors have become stronger during the past 35 years, and it is in this period that the decline in the country's wildlife has become flagrantly noticeable. Many common species have become locally extinct and a few (the cheetah or hunting leopard is the best known example) extinct altogether in India.

It was during this same period that in the more depleted West a widespread feeling for wildlife was developed, gaining impetus from a war that left people profoundly disillusioned with the sophisticated norms of civilization, and that a number of national and international organizations for the conservation of nature were established. Whether or not it was inspired by the growing concern for nature abroad, it was only after independence that a national body for wildlife was set up in India (the Indian Board for Wildlife), as also state wildlife boards. However, there were already some fine sanctuaries established in what was then British India, and in a few of the princely states.

All that has been said so far is wellknown and undisputed, and is a brief introduction to the assessment here attempted of India's current wildlife crisis and its probable future course. Before proceeding further, two things must be stated. First, it will be necessary to go back to the past again to trace some of the trends of depletion that have led to the present crisis; second, the lack of reliable statistics will have to be explained, and made good to the extent possible.

Although the flora are as integral and important a part of the wildlife of any region as its fauna, in this note (if only for considerations of space) a heavy faunal bias has been adopted intentionally. However, to explain the lack of the statistics that could provide a more objective basis for assessment, and also to explain the main cause for the dwindling of the fauna, it is necessary to consider the flora first.

During the past four decades thousands in India must have noticed the deterioration of large tracts of forests into barren scrub and wasteland, and their conversion into plantations, roads, agricultural holdings, human settlements, depots and the like—I speak of forests directly in the charge of the state forest departments (as almost all forest land in the country is), most of them reserved. Many examples of such denudation, and the conversion of natural forests to other uses, can be cited from all over India. And yet, allowing for territorial adjustments following the formation of new states and changed inter-state boundaries, and also the taking over of zamindari and princely state forests by governments, the astonishing conclusion emerges from official records that there has been hardly any change in forest area in any state over the past four decades, and even earlier. That is to say, there are no official records to show the denudation of forests by departmental exploitation, or wastage by the public or other agencies.

Here is a fair sample of the most reliable official statistics available, provided by a knowledgeable senior officer of the Indian Forest Service, Mr P.D. Stracey, in the course of a newspaper article published less than a year ago: 'The total forest area in this country, on the basis of 22 per cent of the land area, is about 78 million hectares, of which about 75.4

million hectares are broadleaved and 2.6 million conifers. The total commercial forest area is about 45 million hectares. About 17 per cent of India's total land area is wasteland and remains unutilized.'

An analysis of these figures is interesting. Obviously, the 17 per cent of the total land area that is unutilized waste is not included in the 22 per cent of the total land that is forested (and in the charge of forest departments). One might think that the broadleaved forests, comprising 96.6 per cent of the total forest area, consist mainly of tree forests, as the 3.4 per cent of Himalayan coniferous forests do. This is not so. Mixed tree forests, deciduous or evergreen in the main but always mixed, with their undershrub much varied, meadows, belts of tall grasses and bamboos, swamps, nullahs and ravines, hill tops and slopes clad mainly in herbaceous vegetation, streams, rivers and lakes all go to make up the total area.

It is this diversity of biotopes that makes the forests of peninsular India such valuable and versatile homes for the wild animals, for they provide habitat suited to all seasonal and other changes and needs. And these natural forests have, for over a century now, been felled selectively for a few species of timber trees, clear-felled in coupes for fuel, cleared for roads and settlements, cut down by wood-poachers and encroachers, hacked and hewed by forest-side villagers who have established, or arrogated to themselves, the right to collect small timber and fuel and graze their cattle in them, worked for minor forest produce such as bamboos and thatching grass, and converted into plantations of exotics and a few indigenous softwoods and timber trees, *without any successful attempt to re-establish the natural vegetation lost by all these operations*; and exotic weeds have colonized large tracts of them in the past 35 years.

Taking 1935 as an arbitrary point of time for comparison, we had roughly 75 million hectares of broadleaved forests then, too, and for obvious reasons they were then much less denuded and even quite primordial in large tracts. How much of the natural tree forest and scrub jungle, swamps and grasslands, valleys and nullahs that we had 35 years ago do we have left now? We do not know, and the official statistics available cannot give us a fair idea of the extent of loss of habitat to the wild animals over these years.

Plantations, it will be seen, constitute quite a large part of the total forest area; actually much peripheral wastage and clearings for roads have not been taken into account in reckoning the total area of plantations. A few of these are plantations of indigenous softwoods, such as *Ailanthus excelsa* or *Ceiba pentandra* or of timber (almost entirely teak); these are usually sited in the heart of natural forests, which are clear-felled to provide space for the plantations. For instance, in the Anamalais, where some of the finest mixed deciduous montane forests in the country have already been ravaged by the setting up of the Parambikulam hydro-electric project in their midst, both on the Kerala and the Tamilnad sides of the forests vast tracts have been clear-felled for the sake of stump-planted teak.

The great majority of departmental plantations, however, are of exotics, eucalyptus and wattle species and casuarina from Australia, cashew and rubber from tropical America, and others. The forest department of one state went so far as to try out planting pineapple, and in Tamilnad the forest department has taken up tea. None of these exotics (in particular the most widely planted of them, eucalyptus) has any value as fodder or cover for the wild animals, and they only serve to deprive them of territory. How such plantations are reckoned as part of the forest land is a mystery that no one so far has solved.

Perhaps this is the place to mention the most overlooked major depletive factor applying to the wildlife of the country, the constant disturbance that the animals are subjected to in their homes by men: even in sanctuary areas, this factor is very much there. In forests where men are busy working on forestry operations, or collecting produce, or grazing cattle, or doing some of the many other things that they do, the animals leave the area (often for less suitable surroundings) unable to bear the disturbance, or else the diurnal animals turn into apprehensive, fugitive creatures of the night.

I must add that it is not as if no one foresaw until recently the effect of sustained exploitation of the natural forests or of converting them into plantations. Writing as far back as 1910, S. Eardley Wilmot, who had just retired as the Inspector General of Forests, devoted an entire chapter in a book of shikar memoirs to the disastrous consequences of exploiting the forests of India to meet public demands. F.W.F. Fletcher says, in his *Sport on the Nilgiris and in Wynaad* (1911): 'The grand indigenous *sholas* have been cleared to make way for interminable forests of ugly eucalyptus and wattle . . . over the portals of modern Ootacamund . . . let there be written *Sic transit gloria* (Ootaca) *mundi*.'

Trustworthy faunal statistics are much harder to find than figures for flora. They involve population counts of free-ranging animals, sometimes of shifting populations, and counting gregarious animals in the forests of India is often an impossible undertaking. Further, the rapid diminution of the more exposed communities has to be taken into account. In the early 1940s I would see many herds of blackbuck, some over a hundred strong, around the Tungabhadra Dam (where Mysore and Andhra Pradesh meet in a hydro-electric project); by the 1950s every last little buck in the area had been snared or shot to death by professional meat-hunters and amateur 'sportsmen'.

Currently, some faunal counts are being made in some sanctuaries: these will yield fairly reliable figures over a course of years. In the past, the only significant counts attempted were limited to important species threatened with extinction, in areas where the animals were localized, such as the lions in the Gir Forest, the great Indian rhinoceros in Assam and north Bengal, and the hard-ground barasingha in Madhya Pradesh. Doubts have been expressed over some of these figures, but it should be remembered that what a faunal census seeks to achieve is a near approximation to the truth and not mathematical accuracy.

In assessing the decline of India's fauna, it is customary to list the species which are on the brink of extinction or quite extinct in the country, such as the cheetah, the pygmy hog, the hispid hare, the two lesser species of Asiatic rhinoceros, the pinkheaded duck, Jerdon's courser, and the great Indian bustard. A better and more indicative way would be to point out that in most places where they were familiar creatures till recently, even common animals have become locally extinct or else quite rare.

The animals of the open plains, being most open to dispossession and harassment by humanity, have fared much worse than the animals of the hills. The plains forests have virtually disappeared in the south, and in many parts of the north, and the denuded land has been occupied, cut up, and otherwise exploited by men to such an extent that in most areas the animals have vanished. Typical of the plains country is the blackbuck, exclusively Indian, arrestingly beautiful, and the fastest long-distance runner on earth. A hundred years ago, it roamed the plains in vast herds, and was the commonest wild animal of the country even around towns and cantonments; 35 years ago, it was still to be found in its old haunts, but in sadly depleted numbers; today it is locally extinct over most of the country, and survives in small herds in a few areas. The blackbuck is the best example of an Indian animal whose decline is due entirely to hunting. Even after men crowded the plains country, it was there in large numbers, but the nets and snares (some of them horribly cruel) of the professional meat-hunters and the rifle of the 'sportsman' finished it off in most places.

The wolf, a plains animal in the peninsula, is now extinct in the south and rare even in the north. Other animals of the scrub jungles and open forests, common till recently and now uncommon or rare, are the chinkara, the nilgai (extinct in the south) and the dinky little Indian fox; among birds, the Great Indian Bustard and the florican may be mentioned. The seasonal slaughter of water-birds at large waters where they assemble in great numbers, as at Chilka Lake in Orissa and Tada in Andhra Pradesh, goes on unchecked. Migratory duck and geese, resident duck, flamingos, herons, even pelicans, are killed for the table.

Among the animals of the tree forests and the hills, the dramatic decline of the tiger in the past five or six years has attracted the most attention. It is true that the poisoning of cattle kills by villagers has accounted for quite a few tigers, but it is the hunter's rifle that has been the main cause for the decline of this grandest of all the cats, so long and intimately associated with India. Till very recently, tigers were regularly shot all over India, by licensed and unlicensed hunters—except for a negligible percentage, there was not even the excuse for their destruction that they were man-eaters or confirmed cattle-lifters. In Mysore, Hyderabad and elsewhere in Andhra Pradesh, all over Orissa, Bihar, Madhya Pradesh and Uttar Pradesh, tigers were shot for 'sport'—in the Kanha National Park of MP there is a tree from which dozens of tigers have been shot on licence. Being a slow breeder, the tiger has not been able to cope with such sustained shooting down.

In my opinion, the leopard is also on the decline, for the same reason. Other forest animals which are now uncommon in their old haunts are the sloth bear (so peculiarly *the* bear of India), locally extinct in many areas where it was common a generation ago, the fishing cat and the rusty-spotted cat over their somewhat limited ranges, gaur in some of their long-held homes, the hard-ground subspecies of the barasingha in Madhya Pradesh, the lion-tailed macaque of the southern hill-forests and the Nilgiri tahr in places. Himalayan and sub-Himalayan animals, with an entity of their own, are not specifically mentioned here.

Local populations may exhibit marked fluctuations, but no animal, not even the pig and the chital, shows an overall increase; most have dwindled considerably.

It may be thought that while this is the position outside sanctuaries (which term is used here to include all national parks in the country, however constituted), within them conditions are very different. Unfortunately, this is not so. It is difficult to give a figure to indicate the total extent of all sanctuaries in the country, because some are in the making, but allowing for this the total sanctuary area is only about 3 per cent of the total forest area, and even so all the causes of faunal decline that operate outside them obtain within the sanctuaries, too.

It is true that it is mainly in the sanctuaries that one can see many wild animals, and that the incentive of the protection accorded does keep them there to some extent, but in all sanctuaries wood and flesh poachers are a problem, particularly on their periphery. It may be argued, with much force, that this is a problem common to all sanctuaries in the world, but in the present precarious state of India's fauna it assumes a magnitude and a lethal potency it did not formerly have.

With two exceptions, in all Indian sanctuaries forestry operations of all kinds are freely indulged in, perhaps the greatest single cause of constant disturbance to the wild animals. Village rights are recognized in almost all of them, and in all cattle are grazed. The Mudumalai and Bandipur sanctuaries of Tamil Nadu and Mysore, adjoining each other and forming one wildlife unit, though territorially distinguished, are the finest stamping grounds of gaur to be found anywhere in the range of these most magnificent of wild oxen over South-east Asia. A devastating epidemic of rinderpest, which spread from cattle being driven through both sanctuaries, killed off a great many gaur here and drove the survivors right out of the area; with luck, the gaur should return to Mudumalai and Bandipur in a few years.

The presence of private pockets of land and human settlements within the sanctuaries, the recognition of the rights of villagers to collect fuel and produce and graze their cattle in the preserve, and the ever-present threat of politically motivated changes that might further affect the preserve inimically, are wildlife problems peculiar to India.

In considering these influences, two other factors peculiar to the country should be remembered. Neither at the level of the illiterate poor nor among the educated people is there any popular feeling for wildlife in India today. I believe it is in sincere ignorance of the permanent damage they are doing to the country's wildlife that the ministers and other elected authorities in many of our States are so willing to placate the 'landless poor' (whatever that means—I find it difficult to imagine the 'landed poor' from whom they are obviously distinguished) by ceding rights, privileges and even territory inside the reserved forests and sanctuaries to them. The second highly relevant factor is that as the

Constitution of India stands each State has sovereign rights over its forests, and the Centre cannot prevail upon a State to adopt a more conservationist attitude towards its wildlife.

The setting up of hydro-electric and other national projects inside a sanctuary (as in Uttar Pradesh, where the Ramganga project will drown the best developed area of the Corbett National Park) or on its borders (like the Moyar project which adjoins the Mudumalai and Bandipur sanctuaries) leads to tremendous devastation of the natural forests and, by opening up the cover with clearings and roads, renders the animals accessible to poaching and constant disturbance. Industrial plants and projects in or around a preserve have much the same effect: the dangers of pollution that they bring in have not yet been studied in India.

The position, as outlined might seem pretty bleak, but it is far from hopeless. What gives one hope is the wonderful innate richness of the country's wildlife and the fact that we have achieved real feats of wildlife conservation in the recent past. Making every allowance for the decline set out above, the fact remains that even today India is in its flora and fauna one of the richest countries of the world. And although exotic plants have invaded, and been nurtured in, the land, to the deteriment of its wildlife, we have not made the mistake that other countries have of introducing exotic animal species into India. Compare India's faunal integrity with that of Australia, where the English rabbit, the Asiatic camel and the domesticated Indian water-buffalo have run wild and are major threats to life and wildlife, or with that of England which is the only place on earth where the Indian and Chinese muntjacs interbreed in the wild.

Consider, besides, the taxonomic richness and highly individual character of India's fauna. We have more cats (taking the lesser and greater cats together) than any country in the world, and more species of deer; further, quite a few animals with a distribution over South-east Asia attain their best development here, such as the sambar, the gaur and the elephant (*Elephas maximus*); furthermore, we have a number of animals that are peculiarly our own, such as the bonnet monkey and the lion-tailed monkey, the black langur, the Nilgiri tahr, both subspecies of the swampdeer or barasingha, the chital, the blackbuck, the chowsingha or four-horned antelope, the nilgai, and the sloth bear (the sloth bear of Ceylon is taxonomically assigned to a subspecies).

The feats of preservation referred to are the saving of the Asiatic lion in the Gir Forest of Gujarat, and the great Indian rhinoceros in Assam and north Bengal. The Asiatic lion is the lion of the Bible and of Omar Khayyam, and had a wide range over Persia and neighbouring countries, and north India; it was saved only in the Gir Forest, thanks to the conservationist wisdom and zeal of princes, and the subsequent efforts of the State Government. The saving of the rhino in Assam in the face of heavy odds was an even greater achievement, but the story is so well known that it need not be told here.

All wildlife conservation is solidly based on the fact that given *Lebensraum* nature can always maintain its own balance, as between the flora and the fauna, between predator and prey species, and against the upsetting influences of population fluctuations, droughts, floods, epidemics, fires and all other such catastrophes somewhat impiously termed 'acts of God'.

All wildlife preservation is only preservation of nature against the intended and unintended consequences of human actions. Granted adequate natural habitat and efficient protection from human influences (mainly against hunting and disturbance), India's wildlife is assured of a long and great future.

In some countries, such as North America, the forest space needed has been no problem, but in India, because of public and departmental demands upon the forests, and the politically motivated willingness of changing administrations to satisfy at least a part of the public's demands, real, undisturbed sanctuary space for the fauna is a problem at present.

The growing interest of foreign and international bodies in India's wildlife might help, but not very much, I think, considering that the ultimate fate of our wildlife is in the hands of diverse and changing administrations. But if we can somehow tighten up protection and prevent further depletion for a decade or so, I believe public interest and pride in the country's wildlife will develop sufficiently to assure its future. The next ten years, I think, will decide the future of India's wildlife.

1970

61

Ecological Patriotism

IN RECENT YEARS there has been a notable volte-face in Government thinking on the great decline in our wild vegetation. Right till 1970 Governments turned a blind eye and a deaf ear to the visible and voiced devastation of our native flora. It was in that year that the representative of the Planning Commission on the Indian Board for Wildlife sternly condemned, as a wild exaggeration, the statement in the Expert Committee Report (commissioned by the IBWL) on the large-scale depletion of India's wild flora within the previous 50 years. He asserted that there had been no decline at all in our forest cover. Being responsible for that statement and knowing it to be true, I went to the offices of the Planning Commission to check the statistics on which his assertion was based. And there I learnt that what he meant was that, subject to territorial adjustments during the formation of the States, the areas held by the forest departments of diverse States had remained largely unaltered, irrespective of the loss of their vegetation, or their invasion by roads, plantations, human settlements and projects. In other words, the earth's crust had not shrunk materially since 1920!

Government views in this regard have now swung the other way, and it is about the possible disastrous consequences of their enthusiastic and well-meant efforts to clothe the denuded land with green cover that I am writing this. It is best to begin my argument with some seemingly disconnected generalizations that have a vital bearing on the issues discussed here, and to repeat that I am concerned solely about the country's natural vegetation.

Nowhere in the world have they succeeded in replanting a denuded forest with the mixed species of herbs, shrubs and trees it held originally, but, in places, denuded areas left to themselves and protected from human trespasses and activities have regained most of their pristine vegetation, at times within a generation. This has happened in our own country—for instance, in a depleted forest in Madhya Pradesh protected from human activities. I have no personal knowledge of this forest but am assured of the truth of its successful natural regeneration by reliable, knowledgeable people, among them H.S. Panwar, Director of the Wildlife Institute of India.

I myself know a spiky, foothill scrub jungle that was severely denuded and then left alone by men, which regained its vegetation in a few years. It is now a remarkable haven for shrikes, doves, grey partridges and a host of other resident and migrant birds of the thorn scrub, and the other small animals of such tracts. Outside India, too, there are records of purely natural regeneration. Even the heat-sterilized lava of volcanic eruptions has acquired soil and vegetation and its own fauna in due season.

Where conditions are not propitious, the pristine vegetation may not come up but only a secondary growth. But even so it will consist of native plants and not of exotics. Ours is a hospitable country. Plants from distant lands flourish here with an exuberance they seldom achieve at home— lantana, water hyacinth, the wholly useless *Croton bonplandianum* and the pestilent mesquite. But it is true that where the soil has not been cleared and opened up, exotics are unable to dominate and suppress indigenous plants.

The desideratum prescribed by forestry experts for India is that a third of the total land area should consist of forests—more than half in the hills and less than a quarter in the plains. Statistics are available for the present proportion of forests to the land area of each State, and in most it is only a fraction of the prescribed ratio. But even if it satisfies the prescription, these figures are illusory and misleading because the 'forests' in them include plantations, artefacts, human settlements, and large tracts already heavily depleted by over-exploitation.

India is one of the richest countries in the world, if not the richest, in flowering plants, and the diversity of our flora is truly stupendous. It does not consist mainly of trees. Our richest plant families are mainly herbs and shrubs. Trees are more demanding of soil and climatic amenities than the smaller, less woody plants. Trees will, of course, come up where they grew and were cut down, but where the substratum is less congenial, it is the herbs and shrubs that form the vegetation, and these are no less valuable in binding the soil and in offering cover and fodder to the local fauna. In sandy, arid tracts (the Thar is an excellent example), it is the hardy herbs and shrubs that sustain life and, at high elevations in our oldest hill ranges (far older than the Himalaya), there are alpine meadows over a thin crust of earth formed over a million years on top of hard sheet rock. It is these herbs that held, and have held for centuries, this precious soil inviolate against wind and water erosion, powerful forces at that height.

Like most of our current ills, the devastation of our wild flora is correlated to our suffocating overpopulation. The inability, or unwillingness, of our Government to safeguard the nation's heritage of nature, directly under their aegis, from sustained depletion by the populace, and the extent to which this is due to our democratic Constitution and the dependence of successive Governments in power on the vote-holding public, are no doubt relevant factors but are not considered in this note, which is intended as a constructive analysis and not as a post-mortem. However, I should mention an important aspect of this matter here.

Our sanctuaries constitute a minute part of our total land area, only about two per cent in a realistic assessment. But in them too protection is complaisant: cattle grazing and wood and produce collection are freely practised in them by the people around, often without licence. A decade ago, when this ineffectiveness of Government protection came up at some wildlife conservation forums, a novel supplementary remedy was suggested—that not only the officials of a preserve but also its residental and peripheral tribals and others should be induced to take on protective responsibility. If there has been an authentic instance of the exercise of protective zeal by those previously engaged in depletive activities, I have not heard of it. However, the loss of our natural forests, scrublands and hilltop vegetation is due not only to depletion by people, by non-official, unlicensed humanity. Government and Government-sanctioned projects and industries can be much more devastating, and everyone knows of the popular revolts against the permissiveness and projects of the Government that threaten the traditional way of life of remote human settlements and their surroundings—the Chipko movement and the Narmada movement.

Some three decades ago, some forest departments initiated a scheme for planting trees outside the reserved forests, as a supplementary source of firewood and small timber for the people. This was called 'farm forestry', and such plantings were in denuded village commons and around agriculture, even in private holdings. This should not be confused with the many departmental plantations (mainly of exotics like cashew and eucalyptus) also made about this time in unremunerative denuded forests and scrublands, with a view to revenue.

This concept of forestry for the benefit of the people, rather than for revenue or supply of raw material to industries, has undergone many changes of name and specification which need not be detailed here. What distinguishes it from traditional forestry is its motive and today it has expanded into what is best known by the name 'social forestry', widely practised with foreign aid in most regions, though this, too, has undergone ramifications. The idea of social forestry of all kinds is that there should be popular involvement in its effort, and that it should benefit the people by supplying firewood, timber and other similar needs by silviculture outside the forests, at places even on the fringes.

Theoretically there is no reason why social forestry should not relieve and even eliminate the depletion of our natural forests by the people that is going on uncontrolled. But that is in theory. In most parts of our country, there are human settlements around the forests, at times even within them, and every day thousands of people (mainly women) go into the forests to lop wood, even allowing cut wood to dry *in situ* before transporting it in headloads, to sell at the nearest towns—so that this destruction might be camouflaged as the collection of deadwood by the forest-side poor for cooking their modest meals! Hazaribagh in Bihar and Mundanthurai in Tamil Nadu are examples of specially-protected forests (both are sanctuaries) from which firewood is supplied to the nearest towns every day. The compensatory social forestry supplies at present are only a small fraction of what is illegally removed. It is not merely that people find it easier to cut wood without having the bother of involvement in growing it. It has become an established way of life for them, and only unrelaxed vigilance and strict protection can alter it.

Till recently, nature conservation was concerned mainly with our flora and fauna and their settings, with our wildlife degradation. Now it is more concerned with air, water and soil pollution, with human health and safety. Of course, it is essential to protect ourselves from environmental hazards but, in our preoccupation with this, we seem to have lost sight altogether of something even more important, of which we had only glimmerings even in the past—the vital importance to our national identity (and that of future generations) of conserving India's Indianness from ourselves.

With communication now instant even from distant countries, our growing association with very different countries, and with the consequent sustained repercussions of alien values on our life, our cherished cultures, philosophy and religions no longer have the impregnable insularity and vivifying potency they had. All our accretions of culture and religious tenets, and our traditions and ways of life, are of our own

creation and mutable, and to some extent artificial. Only the great heritage of nature that we have owes nothing to our contrivance, intellect or
imagination, and is beyond our creative genius, though we still have the
power to destroy it. Only that can ensure the stability and identity of our
nation and national consciousness, and endow us with truly Indian moor-
ings in life.

In recent weeks we have been hearing and reading almost every day
of the only common commitment of diverse political potentates, the
iron resolve of every one of them to safeguard the nation from all en-
croachments and destructive attempts from outside it, and also against
all forms of subversion from within. More power to these patriots, but
do they not know that a country can be lost as wholly as by conquests or
betrayals, by sustained, relentless whittling down of its age-old entity by
its people?

Afforestation is no way to conserve our wonderfully varied wildlife.
The flora, fauna and terrain are so closely interlinked in so many ways
that each tract has its own wildlife identity, different from that of others.
Even in a preserve the vegetation of which has been depleted, its original
cover cannot be restored by afforestation. Further, our wildlife is by no
means confined to different kinds of forests. Arid, sandy grounds, wet-
lands, flat country with a low, hard-bitten cover, thorn scrub, high-ele-
vation herbaceous meadows and rocky hilltops all hold their characteristic flora and animal life. Many beasts and birds (especially migrants like
the white stork and animals given to ranging far) would be lost without
open country of the kind nowadays clubbed together as 'waste land', and
the planting up of such land with trees will have disastrous consequences
on their lives.

Even social forestry is not the only way to provide an alternative to
meet the denudation of the forests by the people. The only justification
for the large-scale devastation of some of our finest forests by hydel projects is that they supply electricity, which together with gas and solar
energy, can all serve to save firewood, if our rural humanity can be induced to utilize these sources of thermal energy—a truly valuable contribution of national importance that our scientists and social workers
can make to our life. Cattle grazing must, of course, be strictly banned
in all categories of wildlife preserves. This will also prevent the constant
human trespasses now being made for collection of dung from the forest
floor.

At times a profound truth is embodied in a jocular saying, and the classic definition of a virgin forest as a tract where the hand of man has never set foot is such a saying. Provided they are of adequate area, all manner of wildlife tracts in our country have the potential to recoup if left strictly alone, even if now heavily depleted.

If only 10 per cent of our total land area, representative of our much diversified wildlife, and each of adequate area, can be effectively saved from the hand of man setting foot on them, the future of our national integrity and character can be perpetuated to generations of Indians yet unborn, and provide them with an authentic Indian setting and identity and a vital interest in life that can compensate for most ills. Surely, with 90 per cent of the land at their disposal, our Governments should be able to meet the people's demands, but so far no Government we have had has resisted the temptation to achieve popularity at the expense of the country's entity.

1991

XYZ

THE XYZ?

The XYZ, it is quite clear,
must always be a mystery:
for being ex, YZ I fear
has long since ceased to be.

We only know that it is ex,
and when alive was Y and Z—
all of which only serves to vex
our sorely puzzled head.

Diligent digs have failed to yield
two unknown fossil bones, or three,
that now, at last, might have revealed
YZ's identity.

Was it a bird? Was it a beast?
Or just a saurian of some kind?
We have no clue, and not the least
glimmerings in our mind.

The name 'YZ' does not belong
to namings of a modern nature —
it is a taxon of some long
forgotten nomenclature.

So let us drop this futile quest
for what we cannot ever get,
and concentrate upon the rest
of the long alphabet.

Nature Transcended

62

The Genus Feringhee

ACCORDING TO MY trusty old dictionary the word 'Feringhee' is 'a Hindu name for a European', and is derived from the common European name, Frank.

I had always thought that 'Feringhee' was derived from the Tamil 'parangi' which also denotes a European—used adjectivally, 'parangi' specifies a kind of pumpkin, as well as a disease that came to us from the enlightened West. However, I am unable to trace 'parangi' far back in Tamil; it seems to be a word of comparatively recent import. Apparently my dog-eared dictionary is right, after all, and the Tamil 'parangi' is also a corruption of Frank.

And it is a word with a peculiar connotation. For example, no one would think of calling an American a Feringhee, or even an Indian who apes the European sedulously, particularly in his habits of dress and eating—for such an Indian we use the term 'Dorai' in Tamil, with a sneering intonation. Even to indicate a European in a purely racial and detached manner the term Feringhee is rarely used—perhaps I should say that it 'was rarely used', for it is essentially a word of the past, of the days of the rise of European powers in India.

In many shrines and pavilions belonging to the period of the Vijayanagar Empire and later, we find unmistakable depictions of Europeans, figures wearing trousers (usually of strongly ribbed corduroy) and a hat. These are never carved in heroic attitude or size, but are subsidiary figures. These are Feringhees, for as I understand the word it was invariably used in a somewhat derogatory sense, to deny the importance of a figure rapidly gaining stature, or already of heroic proportions, in those days— never in praise of the European in India.

In fact, a few of these carvings and effigies are positively spiteful. Tippu Sultan's Tiger (now in a museum in England) is probably unrivalled as an effigy of hate—a clockwork tiger of metal, shown in the act of devouring a European soldier, the clockwork movements lending a grue-some verisimilitude to the depiction. This royal toy, incidentally, was made for the Sultan by a Feringhee!

However, few of the representations of the European in India are inspired by such hatred. The Feringhee in my picture* will appeal even to Europeans, for there is nothing that is not good-natured in its delightful caricature. The face is cleverly carved from the fibrous outer covering of a peeled coconut shell, the fibres cunningly separated on the upper lip and chin to bristle into fierce moustachios and a beard; the sawed-off, unpeeled terminal part of the coconut forms a snug-fitting lid, which makes, by its natural conformation, a perfect tricornered hat, and even the pipe struck between the teeth is of the fibrous outer covering, neatly chiselled into shape. This is a contemporary depiction, but what it portrays is not the modern European, no longer so sure of the supremacy of Western culture and civilization after two world wars, but a full-blooded Feringhee, circa 1880, bursting with colonial zeal—the Feringhee, in short.

What will Indian history say, a century from today, of this colourful character? Our history then will be sufficiently removed from the present for objective appraisal, and I think it will rightly be much more a record of ourselves than of European domination in India. There will, of course, be a chapter or two in it about that domination, but I am afraid the Feringhee as an individual will be ignored, even forgotten. So, long before that history is written, I would like to pay my tribute to him.

I am thinking not of any one old-time European when I say that, but of the genus Feringhee, perplexing as it was varied. And I am not thinking of distinct type-specimens, highly differentiated from one another, of Hume, Ross, the Kiplings (father and son), Gamble, 'Eha', Dunbar Brander, Sanderson and Forsyth—I am also thinking of hundreds of Feringhees whose names even I do not know, but who are all, somehow, personified for me by this coconut-shell effigy. And I must add that I am not interested in their official lives or doings, if some of them had such a life. History, which takes note of achievements and calamities, and painstakingly of much less dramatic happenings spread out over years, can look to all that. What fascinates me about the Feringhee is himself.

What a remarkable character he was! As a rule he led an insular life.

*Not reproduced here.

He did not mix with the people of the country, for whom he had a name, quite as distinctive and peculiar as the term 'Feringhee'—he kept aloof from the 'natives'. And I'm afraid he kept aloof from his own kind as well. The idea that Europeans in India formed a solid and mutually tolerant clique is a myth; they quarrelled as bitterly among themselves as other men did, and some even found refuge from their brethren in the company of the 'natives'—they went native, to use a phrase that belonged to that era.

Many may differ from me over this, but I think the Feringhee (by and large) completely missed the culture of the country—except to the extent to which he unwisely indulged in curries and pilau. He never did get to know or appreciate the highly evolved music and dance of India, and though occasionally his comprehension of Indian art (with a heavily historical bias) was better, he rarely got much beyond folklore in literature. I know there were Europeans in India who claimed considerable scholarship in Indian languages—without going into the depth or reality of their scholarship, or their mastery of their own, native English (which, frankly, I think was wretched), I may safely say these men were exceptional, and that anyway they were not sufficiently true to type to be called 'Feringhees'.

It is true that some Feringhees did assume, within their limited territories, airs more properly left to God, but many of them loved that bit of the country where they lived, and spent much of their spare time (and, one fears, much of their official time as well) exploring it. But for the Feringhee, there would have been no rich lore of natural history in India. And there would have been no Ooty.

Nor is this all. They have left behind a wonderfully varied and valuable heritage of their own culture that deeply influences our lives to-day. You may disagree, but I think the scientific outlook that is developing in India today is mainly due to the pioneer work (often in the face of real difficulties) of many Feringhees in many parts of India—much more than to the abridgement of horizons in the sphere of modern communication. I am quite willing to confess that my life has been profoundly influenced by Feringhee values—you may, probably, deny this influence in your own, though I am writing this in the language of the Feringhee and you are reading it!

What we will do with this rich heritage from a historically recent past, how much of it we shall assimilate into our culture and what we shall reject, are all questions of raging controversy today. I do not know the answers to those questions—I doubt if anyone really does. But I do think we would be very foolish to pass by things of solid value to which we can so easily help ourselves today.

1959

63

A Letter to the Editor

W HEN I WAS young, I had one sure test for incipient senility. When people started writing in to the correspondence columns of newspapers, they had left mental youth, and even middle age, well behind.

The way I argued it, such letters showed lack of faith in one's prowess. A strong man fights his fights decently and in private. With maturity he may bring a certain cunning into the fight, to supplement valour, but when he starts making public appeals it is plain squealing, a confession that he can no longer look after himself and has degenerated into a querulous complainant. Furthermore, the fact that he has time for such correspondence (let us take it one letter in ten gets published) shows that he has reached the age of superannuation.

Later, I could see that this argument was somewhat immature, for those who write to the Editor are not complaining of injustice to themselves as a rule, but fighting an issue on principle. 'Pro Bono Publico', 'Vox Populi', 'Fairplay' and 'A Retired Headmaster' have nothing to gain by public ventilation of grievances—even 'One Affected' and 'Bare Justice' make no attempt at unmanly disguise of their personal implication, and they are fighting for the clan really, not cadging sympathy for themselves.

It is only recently that I realized that these selfless people are, in fact, the pillars of our democracy. They risk brawls in public in the interests of equity, and I think their letters, far from disclosing senility, prove their virile community spirit and mature daring. It is only recently that I have taken to writing such letters.

And, believe me, it is a losing battle. You see the flagrant injustice in something public, say, in a university examination paper, and sit down purposefully to work out pros and cons. This analysis is quite necessary in the interests of logic and length. Otherwise your letter will be rejected because it seems biased and is much too long, or, worse still, be relegated to the Points from Letters column. Of course it is hardly possible to compress arguments on an issue like this into the compass of a brief letter, but it is a question of compression or nothing.

So your arguments are reduced to main points, ignoring all subtleties, and you write them down concisely. Your preliminary draft covers two closely-typed foolscap pages, in spite of its stark fundamentality. By cutting out adjectives, clubbing sentences together and omitting a phrase here and a whole clause there, you reach one page. Then you see that you must give up some of your arguments, for the utmost the Editor will suffer is half a page. However, this does not dishearten you—surely the reader can be trusted to read between the lines and think up subsidiary points for himself; no need to state everything so fully.

It is when you have succeeded in trimming your letter of all frills and in reaching the stipulated length that you begin to see that it is all cons and no pros, and will surely give the Editor the impression of bias and inability to see the point of view of the question-setter. Only by further sacrifice of cherished arguments, and devoting one whole sentence to your apprehension of pros, can you give yourself any chance of publication. At this stage you give up the idea of a letter to the Editor. Two hours later your final draft is on its way to him.

In the morning you are surprised to find your effort at the foot of the correspondence column, below the letters of three tedious correspondents who have much to say on nothing. The sentence you fancied especially in your letter has been omitted wholesale by an Editor who has, evidently, no feeling for the niceties of prose. But you console yourself with the thought that probably some raw, sub-adult sub-editor was responsible for this.

Only next morning do you come to know what you have let yourself in for. An egocentric nincompoop has written at length, casting aspersions on your motive in writing to the paper, and justifying the question-setter in tortured sentences distinguished only by pompous vacuity. For some reason that is quite beyond you (pull in Editorial circles?) this tepid fool has been given pride of place, and his letter, in larger print than the rest, heads the column. It is clear that you must reply at once, mincing no words, and exposing this cantankerous nonentity unmistakably.

The trouble is that while you are willing to annihilate him, you do not know how. He has side-stepped your arguments and brought in wholly irrelevant considerations that the Editor has passed somehow. Moreover you cannot say what you think of him frankly, for the Editor will not permit suspicions about a correspondent's lineage or even plain statements about his depravity of mind and morals. However, by the use of sarcasm (a weapon you had always despised) and mock agreement with the adversary's views you succeed in concocting a suitable reply, which you despatch posthaste to the Editor. Only while reading the carbon copy, later, do you notice that you have made two rather silly spelling mistakes.

Next morning you find your letter again at the foot of the column and in small print. The Editor has cut out the sarcastic bits and toned down the mockery in your agreement till it seems sincere and almost apologetic. Nor is this all. Your old friend, Tuljayram, has rushed in loyally to your rescue with a letter published just above yours. At college debates people worked hard to lure Tuljayram into the opposition, for his flair for losing arguments was unbounded. You note that he has lost none of his old skill.

In a joint reply to both Tuljayram and you, published in the next issue, the contemptible adversary has used means to which you had not imagined anyone would descend. The first line of the correspondence column begins with the words that Tuljayram and you have 'rushed in where angels fear to tread' and the rest of the letter is similarly inspired by insulting innuendo. There is no point in continuing the correspondence when the Editor is prepared to publish such stuff from the opposition. Moreover, at the end of his letter there is a brief editorial note that says, 'Correspondence on this subject is closed.'

Yes, it is a mug's game all right, writing letters to the Editor. Sometimes I wonder why I play it.

1955

64

A Suggestion to Government

APEON EMPLOYED IN the Bihar Legislative Assembly who owns
45 bighas of land and an elephant which he rode to his office
one day claims that his job is a labour of love for him. (Report).

The Under Secretary owns a car
(An asthmatic old crock with its own will),
A flat, a dog, six textile shares (at par)—
But of elephants; nil.

The Secretary has a bigger car,
A wife, four daughters and a coffee mill,
A solar cooker and a Chowkidar—
But, of elephants: nil.

The Minister for Transport rides a bus,
When of his limousine he's had his fill—
In pomp and state how far removed from us!
But—no elephant, still.

Neither bus rides, nor photographs displaying
One digging earth and sweating like a lascar,
Nor badge-decked limousines, can be as paying
As just one healthy tusker!

What can convince the public of one's zeal,
One's zest for work for its own sake, and firm
Resolve to serve the Governmental weal,
So like the pachyderm?

What can affirm more massively the word
Of those who say they do not work for bread,
Than, just outside their offices, a herd
Tethered with tape of red?

Away with limousine and jeep and chariot,
Prescribed attire and regulations tight!
Present each worker in the Secretariat
A jumbo, coloured white!

1954

65

Tests in Far Places

RECENTLY I READ a newspaper report that said Jack Hobbs thought Saturday afternoon games on the village green more exhilarating and worthwhile than county cricket. It was good to know that another well-known cricketer held the same opinion as I, though of the game elsewhere. I have always thought few things more dreary and uneventful than the spectacle of Representative Indian Cricket at the crease—laborious, elderly, apprehensive, covetous, without that momentous incidence of fate and fortune that makes real cricket, dull even in death. But of course we have true, red-blooded cricket here, not at the Brabourne Stadium but in far places: only, you never hear of it, and very few (except some of those playing) watch it even. You watch and hear and read Representative Cricket all the time. It is the old, old story of vested interests suppressing authentic talent.

It is to tell you about real, rural cricket that I write this full-length account of our match with the Dam Site XI. Compare it to a Test (there is one in progress as I write), and you will have some idea of the relative merits of the two. Even in the preparatory stage we had to face problems unknown to Representative Cricket. There were the problems of Transport and Pads, and then the riddle of the schoolmasters. Anyone can captain an Indian Test XI and almost everyone has done it, but the captaincy of a team like ours calls for considerable finesse, tact and realism, besides a profound knowledge of the game. The thing I had to decide (yes, I skipper our team) was how to get the school bus (the only vehicle available—the Dam Site was 20 miles away) without being overburdened with schoolmasters. The conditions of loan, as stipulated by the spokesman of the school (strangely enough this was not the Games Master, but the History Assistant) were that we should supply petrol and include six schoolmasters in the team. Finally, I compromised at two masters and

two boys from the school, explaining that we could not possibly accom-
modate more than four, and it was such a nice gesture, didn't he think,
to give the boys a chance—it is my experience that schoolboys, placed
strategically in the outfield, can do much to repair the lapses of their
mentors. The question of pads was less easily solved. The letter from the
DS XI said they had five new balls and that we needn't bring one, that
they could spare us a bat or two it needed, but would we please bring pads
in plenty as they had only an ill-assorted pair? Well, we had three pads,
all right-legged. One should be realistic in deciding such problems. We
took all three.

We reached the Dam Site tired, dispirited and irritable. The trip over
20 miles of bumpy ghat-road had been an ordeal, aggravated by the
insistence of the History Assistant in telling us all about the historical
associations of the passing scenery—something about the packed, long
seats of the bus seemed to remind him of his native classroom. He was
still in the Vijayanagar Period when we got to the Site. I had planned to
debus some distance from the ground, at a hotel, and treat the team to
hot coffee and a brisk walk to help it arrive at the Present—but the Construction Engineer was waiting for us on the road, and took immediate
command. He had made this cricket field and wanted us to know just
how he had done it. I must say we were disappointed when we did get
to the field—we had imagined all this lavish use of bulldozers, tractors,
theodolites and steam-rollers would have produced something better
than the uneven, baked brown waste before us.

We inspected the pitch at once. This is of vital importance; it estab-
lishes one's status as a cricketer, and the Lawyer and the Doctor (our
opening batsmen) and I always insisted on acquainting ourselves with
every dent and bump on the pitch before play. An olive-brown mat
covered the pitch and hid it completely—we were sure there were hollows beneath its taut, flat stretch, in places known to the home side. We
could hardly ask them to remove the much-nailed-down matting and let
us have a look at the parched earth underneath, but this was unnecessary.
I know a way of putting the other side in first and we could do this, if we
wished to, and locate the hollows by close observation, while they batted.
As we returned to the galvanized-iron shed that served as pavilion, the
Doctor nudged me and pointed furtively to the steps beyond. A great
hulking figure was sprawled on them, smoking a lonely cigarette, and at
its feet lay five new balls, in a semicircle. I had never seen such over-
developed shoulders and arms on anyone. 'Fast bowler,' whispered the

Doctor in my ear, and as I watched the figure bent down, picked a bent nail from the ground, the kind of nail used for pegging down the mat, and straightened it casually between its fingers. That settled it: there could be no question of our facing this man on a pitch with secret hollows.

At the pavilion we were introduced to the DS XI. There was the expert in underwater engineering, the Engineer in charge of Bridges, Loco-Engineer, Roadways, Electricity, ten engineers of various sorts. Then there was their captain who was no engineer but the local grocer. He reminded me irresistibly, then and many times during the match, of several well-known Indian Test players, simultaneously. He spoke in soft tones and held his arms behind him. He didn't like cricket. He was good at tennis, but here there were no tennis courts. He liked tennis balls: they were not so hard. As he spun the coin for the toss, I made a loud, inarticulate sound in my throat; then I clapped him on the shoulder, and announced we would put them in. There were no protests.

The score at lunch is what counts in an One-day Test, and at lunch the position was terrible. They had made 53 for 3, and Roadways and the Fast Bowler were together, going strong. Electricity, who opened their innings with the Fast Bowler, had gone early, short-circuited by treading on his wicket, and Bridges had fallen to a catch by one of the schoolboys. Construction had been run out, and when Roadways came in the chalk-marked score-board had read '15'. And now it was 53! The engineer had contributed little to this handsome total, but Vulcan was scoring steadily. He was patient with an inexorable patience, and played each ball with the middle of his little bat, ever so gently. Never once did he hit at the ball, but the mere repercussion from such massive impact sent the ball flying for twos and fours, and there seemed to be no way of getting him out. After lunch I held a confab with the Lawyer (who kept wicket for us) but he was unusually without suggestions. We had discovered no hollow places under the mat so far, and none of our bowlers seemed keen on bowling any more.

Finally I tossed the ball to the schoolboy who had held the catch, half in desperation and half in reaction to the urgent hints of the History Assistant that he (the historian) might be given a try. This move produced startling results. From the first ball it was obvious that the scholar would be hard to play. He sent down the same innocuous stuff that our stock bowlers did, but his run to the wicket and delivery were disconcerting in the extreme. He took a corkscrew run to the bowling crease and arrived there with a jump, both feet in the air and interwined, both arms also in the air and interwined. Taken aback by this grotesque display, the batsmen were completely deceived by the impossibly projected ball. He beat both batsmen repeatedly but with no luck, for he bowled on the leg-side edge of the mat and was consistent in his direction. Finally, in response to the Lawyer's frantic waves to the right, he sent down a ball of the offside edge of the mat, and surprised by this Roadways jabbed at the ball and pulled it into his wicket. Encouraged by this our new-found star bagged two more quick wickets, both engineers dragging the ball into their wickets from the offside edge of the mat. The score-board now read 70 for 6, which was not so bad, considering all things (Wides—13). But at this stage Vulcan discovered the answer to our tactics.

He had been brooding heavily for some time, and he walked down the wicket and informed the engineer at the other end, who was nicely set for pulling the ball into his stumps, that all they had to do was to leave the ball alone and not play at it. I was astonished at this display of ponderous thought, and I did not like it. For naturally this did for our young hope: it was as much as he could do, with that tortured action of his, to keep the ball on the matting, and he seemed to be suffering from one of those strong aversions to the stump area which afflicts all bowlers at times. The score crept up steadily at the other end (and by wides) and at 80, they were still 6 wickets down. Things were looking gloomy again, and I was toying with the idea of calling on the other schoolboy, when one of these things happened that make cricket the glorious game it is. Vulcan had allowed another ball from our scholar to go past, and the Lawyer, gathering it, appealed suddenly and loudly. The umpire at the bowler's end wanted to know what he was appealing for, but knowing that the burden of proof lies on him who sets up a chain, our wicket-keeper would not commit himself. 'How's that?' he repeated. 'Not out,' said the umpire firmly, and almost on the point of returning the ball to the bowler, the Lawyer turned round and filed a Second Appeal, to the umpire at square-leg. 'How's that?' he asked again. Up went the umpire's finger, and the Lawyer turned in triumph to Vulcan: 'You're out,' he announced. This brought a chorus of protests from the batsmen and Umpire 1, but the Lawyer just refused to take cognizance. He pointed out that the jurisdiction of both umpires was concurrent, co-equal and independent and that a decision by either was binding and valid. At this point Vulcan stumped off to the pavilion, unable to stem the flow of legal argument, and thereafter we had no trouble. They were all out for 96, with three hours left for play.

I was far from happy, however. I cannot remember many occasions when our team has passed the 50-runs total, but that had not worried me. After all, with so much practice, we could take defeat like cricketers and sportsmen. What oppressed me was the thought that a ferocious fast bowler, vexed by what he thought was an unfair decision against him, might develop pace unsuspected even by himself. It was plain that the Doctor had similar thoughts. He inspected his Emergency Bag (he never went anywhere without it) gloomily and as he tied the pads to his legs with borrowed handkerchiefs (pads rarely have buckles in our cricket) I could see that the man was in low spirits. However, our other opener, the Lawyer, seemed unaffected—a thing that I could not understand at first, but enlightenment dawned on me as I turned round and saw Vulcan pulling on the wicketkeeper's gloves. Of course he was their wicket-keeper. To this day neither the Doctor nor I can explain why we took it for granted that he was a fast bowler—it was one of those apprehensive mistakes that go to make cricket, such things are in the game. They had no fast bowler, not even a medium-paced one. But there were two engineers (one of them was the Underwater Expert) who bowled leg-breaks with a brand-new ball. By the time we had made 13 runs, for 3 wickets, the sub-aquatic wretch was turning the ball a good yard from the leg.

Old Doc was still there, placing the ball unerringly over the slips off the edge of his bat, and while he was there I had hope. But someone had to keep him company, and as I untied my pads to hand them over to the next batsman (having been bowled by a grub), I pondered deeply over this. Their captain, standing nonchalantly and with eager, outspread hands, four yards from the bat at silly mid-off, was responsible for our collapse even more than the leg-spinners. Unnerved by his imminent presence, our batsmen tried to play strokes behind the wicket, and so got bowled. I wished we had someone who could hit the ball good and hard to the off, but as the fifth wicket fell (one of the schoolboys putting up a catch to Vulcan), I could think of nothing constructive to say to the next batsman. Things were made worse by the incessant encouragement of the History Assistant, who kept on providing parallels from famous battles where defeat had been suddenly turned to victory at a late stage. It was impossible to concentrate on a major problem with that sort of talk going on, so I sent him in next to get rid of him.

He missed the first ball comprehensively, then lunged forward at the next and spooned up a tame catch to the vigilant silly mid-off: the fields-man leaned forward, clutched at the ball with both hands, missed, and got it plumb on his kneecap. Play was held up for a few minutes while the Doctor massaged his knee, and thereafter he retired, limping, to deep square-leg.

Several of our former Test Players believed that it was quite all right to hit the leg-spinner against the break, and it was evident that the historian belonged to this old school of thought. He swiped with a cross bat at every ball, and the ball flew off its edge to the most unexpected corners, leaving the fieldsmen baffled. The score shot up to 20, and then the schoolmaster got a ball right in the middle of his bat. The ball went soaring to square-leg, straight to the tennis player. He clutched wildly at the oncoming missile, missed, and got it on his toe—he hopped about in agony, while the callous batsmen took seven runs, before it occurred to mid-on to retrieve the ball. This was an unexpected slice of luck, but their captain was determined it should not be repeated. He limped away to third-man.

When the Doctor sliced the ball into his wicket as he always did in the end, the score was 60 for 6, as pretty a total as one could wish for, and assured that we could not be disgraced, I gave no covetous thought to victory. But the historian was still there, swiping furiously at every ball, and at 73 for 8 wickets he was still there, still swiping. Only the other schoolmaster and the other schoolboy remained, but already we were aware that the win on foreign soil, which had eluded us all these years, was possibly within reach. I implored the second schoolmaster to stay in somehow, and leave things to his colleague, but he played every ball with a foppish straight bat, essayed cover-drives, and was soon back, bowled round his legs while attempting a glance.

Schoolboy II, last man in, raised our hopes again. He was slashing at every ball with a vim and vigour that was refreshingly historical. The score began to rocket upwards, propelled by this dual onslaught of sweep and slash, and then, before we knew it, it was 90. We held our breaths and hoped. Vulcan missed a ball and two byes were added to the score. Then the schoolmaster flourished his bat in a terrific sweep, and the ball rose off its edge vertically—upwards and still upwards it soared, till it seemed a mere speck, and then descended swiftly right behind the bowler, right over the tennis-playing skipper's head. He flung his arms above him, braced his body for the shock, and embraced the ball as it hurtled down on him. We had lost the match, as usual.

But who cared? We were as excited and happy as children, and we gave the History Assistant a terrific big cheer, and the slashing schoolboy, and the tennis-playing grocer. We congratulated the Dam Site XI with a grace born of practice, and I made a feeble pun about how they were a damned sight too good for us, and the Doctor laughed loyally. Only when we were back in the bus, and headed for home, did this spirit of joy depart, almost physically. For we were suddenly aware that there was a long gap, a long wide gap, between now and the days of Krishna Deva Raya, and we were in for it.

1951

66

The Revenge

THE LAWYER AND I almost purred in satisfaction as we discussed the prospects. The Dam Site XI, which had beaten us narrowly on their own grounds, were due at our place next day, and the poor chaps had not the ghost of a chance this time. For one thing they had been considerably weakened by visitations. Their best leg-spinner, an underwater engineer, had developed a whitlow on his right index finger and was out of action, and their next best (also an engineer, as all of them were) was down with the 'flu. And we had it from the same reliable source that two visiting bosses, the Chief Engineer and the District Engineer, had expressed an urgent desire to play the dear old game they had played in their lost youth, which disposed of two able-bodied dam-men automatically. Further, we had to reckon additions to our own strength besides the enemy's losses. Now we had the Find, and the Doctor's Form.

The Find was a schoolboy, certified a moron by the History Assistant (a regular member of our team now) and a pretty hefty one at that. He had a long, fluent, sinuous run to the wicket and bowled at a terrific pace. The History Assistant, who lived somewhat in the past, called him 'Spof-forth, the Demon', and the moron really did deserve the name. His only defect was a strong, native inability to distinguish between the bowling crease and the runner's popping crease, beyond—but this was a disability shared by many famous fast bowlers, and we had already explained remedies to the lad.

Anyhow, even allowing for a fair proportion of no-balls, we were confident the dam-men could not stand up to his onslaught. And then, of course, we had the Doctor's new-found form.

The Doctor, who opened the innings with the Lawyer for us, had always been our most consistent scorer. He had been a fine footballer in his youth. A tall, well-built man with a very quick eye, he brought soccer goal-keeping distinction to his batsmanship, and had perfected the technique recently. His reach made all bowling accessible to him without leaving the crease, and besides a variety of defensive pokes and pushes he had developed a magnificent sliced-drive that rarely failed to get him a four. This shot, played at a ball pitched outside the off-stump, was usually on a forward lean, but he could play it off the backfoot, too. It was unique in that the ball, sliced good and hard, rose high over gully's head and swerved violently away from third man for a four. If that fieldsman was moved squarer, for a catch, old Doc had an answer to this move: he played his stroke a trifle late so that the ball went rocketing over first slip, to where third man had been. The only logical way to get him caught off this shot was to field three third men, some fifty yards deep, from fine to squarish—but the immutable traditions of the game permit just one third man, and so Doc was safe. He was sure to score heavily.

The first thing I noticed, after we had welcomed the DS XI and ushered them into the pavilion, was the Doctor's preoccupation. He was sitting on a bench beneath a tree nearby, wholly lost in a thick book. I knew already that he had been summoned as an expert witness in a criminal case so that this passion for books was no surprise, but one likes one's star batsman to have no medico-legal distractions on the day of the big match. I held a conference with the Lawyer, and we decided to put the visitors in, after winning the toss in my usual manner, so as to give the Doctor time to shift his mind from medical jurisprudence to gyrodynamics, and our Demon Bowler a go before the wicket lost its veneer of hardness.

Nor were we mistaken in our reckoning, though no one was prepared for the sensation of 'Spofforth's' first over. Unaccustomed to handling the shiny new ball, and with his thoughts on his feet, he sent the first three balls spinning viciously to long-off, who fielded them splendidly while the umpire signalled wides. After this we rubbed the ball in the earth till it was rough enough, and our Find came off. He was no-balled, he was erratic, the ball kicked well clear of the stumps even when he did pitch it at them, but his pace completely demoralized the dam-men. When their innings closed, for 53 runs, we had reason for satisfaction, though we felt we had given away too many sundries. Besides wides and no-balls (total, 15) the stubborn pride of our wicketkeeper in refusing to have an old-fashioned 'back stop' had cost us 23 runs in byes.

However, the Lawyer, taking the strike after lunch, seemed determined to make amends. From the first ball it was obvious that he was at his ease. His late-cuts and leg-glances were pretty in the extreme, though unproductive of runs. By one of those curious accidents of cricket, the Doctor got no chance to face a ball for the first 25 minutes, and the score was still 5 for no loss. Then the Doctor faced their opening bowler, who sent down straight up-and-down stuff to an offside field, and I sat forward expectantly. Very soon it was apparent that there was something very wrong with old Doc. His bat, instead of descending in a flashing arc on the ball, was stiff and perpendicular and immobile, while he lunged forward and back from the waist; every ball beat him and many hit his pads. The spectacle was so unedifying that we wished the man would get out, but by a miracle the ball kept missing the stumps. It seemed incredible that a dose of medical jurisprudence could have transformed a dashing player of the sliced-drive-to-third-man into this groping nonentity—then I had an inspiration, and stepped across to the bench beneath the tree. There was a thick, brown-paper wrapped book on it, the same that the Doctor had been reading with such concentrated interest, and one look into it explained everything. Of course it was no medico-legal book: it was *The Jubilee Book of Cricket*, with the school rubber-stamp on it, bristling with faded pictures of famous batsmen of the past playing forward and back with geometrically straight bats. Instantly I accused the History Assistant, and he confessed to the deed—he had brought it along to show our fast bowler a photograph of Spofforth to inspire him, and now—this was the result. Too often one learns a lesson belatedly in this game, but others can profit by such mistakes. I warn all captains of cricket teams to see to it that illustrated books on the game are not left anywhere within reach of impressionable batsmen.

Have you noticed how often it happens, when a batsman is playing confidently and another is groping about vulnerably, that a wicket falls? The Lawyer was bowled middle stump with the score at 7, and after making three consecutive cover-drives (unfortunately they went straight to the fieldsman) I was back in the pavilion, to change the batting order. This did little good. The score at 17 for 7 was positively depressing, but what was worse was the Doctor's metamorphosis. He was still there, still poking weakly about with his left elbow held high and stiff, still missing each ball. Then a ball caught the edge of his perpendicular bat and streaked away between second slip and gully. Third man was moved squarer at once, to cover the gap—a foolish and thoughtless move. The movement gave old Doc his lost cue, and almost mechanically and in response to the stimulus he slice-drove the next ball late and expertly, to send it soaring to the boundary over the wicketkeeper's head. Thereafter the spell was broken, and there was no holding him back. The well-known stroke, in all its variations, blossomed out of his bat with the rush of a held-back spring, and almost in no time we had won the match, for no further loss.

Which just goes to prove, once again, what a great and glorious game cricket is, how unpredictable in its vagaries—and how suicidal it is to move third man from a fine to a square position.

1952

The Truth About an
Old Lady

S RAIGHTAWAY I SHOULD make it clear that this is no sort of criticism of the recently produced Tamil talkie, 'Avvaiyar'. It cannot be, for I have not seen this picture—those that have say it is outstandingly good, and no doubt it is so. But the acclaim it has won has a curious quality.

Auvvaiyar is a recurrent feminine figure in Tamil literature, whose life the picture purports to depict. What is remarkable about the acclaim is the number of eminent men retired or retiring from politics, the judiciary and other high walks of life, but with no great pretence to knowledge of Tamil, who have come out in emphatic print over 'Avvaiyar'. According to these incognoscenti (I coin the word solely for purpose of classification) the picture is true to life, 'historical', and a vivid portrayal of a specific poetess whose 'limbecks,' though 'dry of poison', still held a potent morality. The pity of it is that just now, when classical Tamil is at a discount and moral armaments at a heavy premium, the words of these good people will be accepted by thousands unquestioningly.

Was there really one Auvvaiyar with an unmistakable identity? Of course not, for there were three of them at least, so far as we know. It should be realized that the word 'Auvvaiyar' is not a personal name, not a proper noun so much as a respectful term of reference to an old lady. 'Auvvai' in Tamil is only a mode of reference or address to a woman— it does not connote motherhood or venerable age in itself and is an address no longer current in the Tamil country. But in Kannada the word is still in use; in colloquial Kannada you may say 'auvva' when speaking to a girl of 15 or to a grandmother of 85. In Tamil today we employ the word 'amma' in the same way precisely. The suffix 'yar' merely denotes respect—not necessarily to antique years but to a person of some maturity. 'Ammaiyar' is common in Tamil now as a title of dignity in referring to a lady—'auvvaiyar' has the identical connotation.

So, to three women verse writers who were respected in their time and afterwards the title 'Auvvaiyar' was given. Who were these three and what do we know about them?

The earliest Auvvaiyar seems to have lived some 2,000 years ago. No sizeable work that can be definitely ascribed to her survives, but there are occasional verses and other pieces. From the diction, prosody and stray references to contemporaries in these verses we can say that she lived about the time of poets (and patrons) of considerable antiquity and that she belonged to the Sangam period which was, approximately, 2,000 years ago. Her work has the quality of authentic poetry and is not moralistic.

The next belonged to the age of Kamban, Pukhazhendi and Ottakkoothar—a period that I may term the golden age of court poets, and which is now fixed at about the thirteenth century AD according to a Tamil scholar whom I consulted. This Auvvaiyar has more popular identity than her predecessor or even her successor, and seems to serve as a link between them, since it is difficult to be positive that neither of them had anything to do with some of the verses usually credited to her.

She seems to have been far advanced in years (her predecessor, also, appears to have been quite elderly), cantankerous, and much given to the 'venba' form of verse which attained its zenith during this period. A number of occasional verses attributed to her show that she had a fine contempt for mere opulence, a bitingly sarcastic tongue, and a willingness to fell the mighty.

At this stage two things should be explained. First these qualities were by no means peculiar to Auvvaiyar II. Many Tamil poets (some of them men capable of magnificent poetry) possessed them, and vituperative verse is quite a feature of Tamil literary traditions. Kalamegha-p-pulava and, to cite a recent example, Ramchandra Kavirayar may be mentioned among those prone to instant repartee in verse. Even today, when verse is a lost art, men of traditional literary blood are apt to relapse into verse if deeply provoked.

Secondly, I am not relying on the versicular duels between this Auvvaiyar and Kamban in saying that she had a quick and caustic tongue. The well-known passage of arms between them that is sustained by a pun on the Tamil name of a sort of greens is too elaborate and apt to hold conviction—I don't suppose any Tamil scholar would care to guarantee the genuineness of this and similar verses, or affirm that they cannot be interpolation. But even otherwise the Auvvaiyar of this period seems to have been a formidable old lady, as evidenced by her addresses to niggardly patrons and men of pride. There are many such, but one will do for sample. When Aazhvaan of the village Koraikkaal was larger in his promises to her than in the performance, this was her comment:

> First it was an elephant; then a horse;
> Then a dark milch-buffalo—
> Later an ox, and then a saree of full length—
> Then, its fabric frayed in every thread
> The gifts of Koraikkaal Aazhvaan developed
> The retiring feet of a toad
> And disappeared altogether from view!

This verse is one of the mildest written by the lady and has lost much in translation, but I chose it because it displays a certain poetic fancy. This quality distinguishes many of the pieces attributed to this poetess, and saves them from being just slick verse. For instance, speaking of the things that are hardest to suffer in life she says:

'Poverty is cruel, and especially is it cruel in one's youth.' I have always been struck by the deep understanding of youthful zest and aspirations that this line evinces—the rest of the verse is conventional.

I am not quite sure if this verse does not belong to the earlier Auvvai. However, many occasional verses prove that the Auvvai of the thirteenth century was not overmuch given to didactic sentiments and smug moralization—some of them betray her zest for food and her sapient acceptance of sensuality. Here is a verse which is from the stylus of this Auvvai according to the scholar whom I consulted (diffidently, I beg leave to differ from the pundit, for its diction and form seem, to me, to belong to the Sangam period) which is worth quoting whoever wrote it, for it is typical of the attitude of many Tamil poets to life. Asked by a prospective patron who had lived in a negative, cautious sort of way to write a verse in his memory, Auvvai says:

> How shall I, who have sung of the Trinity and the three kings,
> Sing also of you!
> You, who have not even seen
> The red battle-fields where war elephants die,
> Nor listened enraptured to the sweet pure strings of the Yazh;
> Nor have you fondly embraced
> Sweet-voiced, tender-breasted young love,
> And the insistent words of poets have never moved you:
> Nothing you know of elegant attire or of good food,
> You neither give nor take.

That, the concept of worthwhile manhood as a thing that is at least capable of sensuous pleasures, is surely human and poetic, and anything but didactic.

The third Auvvaiyar was a writer of complacent moralistic dicta. She seems to have been the latest of the three, and it was she who wrote 'Aaththi-Cudi', 'Kondral-Vendan' and other alphabetical moral precepts for the young—the first of these begins with the line 'Desire to do good.'

It is difficult to write that sort of thing and still be a poet. It is interesting to note that centuries later a man of indubitable poetic worth, Subramanya Bharathi, wrote a 'New Aaththi-Cudi'—I don't think even his best friends will count it among his masterpieces. In fact, only one poet, Thiru-Valluwar (according to traditions he was the brother of Auvvaiyar), has written such didactic verse that has also true poetic quality (often when it is factual and not moralistic). Making allowances for all this, it is still hard to discover any poetic virtuosity in the work of the last of the Auvvais, however much moralists may praise its 'goodness' for children.

I might digress for a moment to point out that another well-known didactic work in Tamil, the four-lined 'Naaladiyar,' remains anonymous. It is recognized as the work of many poets, but their names are undisclosed. I can readily sympathize with the desire of those who would preach to remain anonymous—it is a safe way of tendering idealistic, irritating advice! The fact that 'Aaththi-Cudi,' 'Kondrai-Vendan' and other such works are attributed to an Auvvaiyar may not even mean that they were written by a specific, elderly lady. But the burden of proof in literary criticism, as in law, is on him that sets up anything and I have not a shred of evidence.

Then there is legend, much legend linking up the three dissimilar Auvvais of literature. It is miraculous legend (and not history of literary continuity) that unites these different people—that, and the sameness of their pen-names. Almost every miracle in the Auvvaiyar story has a verse supporting it supposed to have been written by the poetess to mark the occasion. This is dangerous ground for a reason that I shall state immediately, but I think there is ample evidence in Tamil literature not only of interpolations to sustain legend but also of subsequently manufactured miracles to explain (often unnecessarily) a mystic or imaginative passage. I understand that the picture 'Avvaiyar' so highly praised for its realism, is based largely on the legends of the Auvvaiyar story.

It is absurd to presume in these popular-scientific times that miracles have no currency—today we believe as much, and as hopefully and illogically, in miracles as man ever did. It is only the age of chivalry that is dead: the age of miracles, thank God, is still with us. But even so, is it not somewhat uninformed and incorrect in a literary way to call any depiction of the Auvvaiyar legend 'historical' and to enthuse over its realism?

1954

Verse for a Living

TAMIL LITERATURE IS of indeterminable antiquity, for nothing survives of its first few periods. All scholars agree that it is over 20 centuries old, but while traditional pundits claim that an entire age of almost a thousand years has been irretrievably lost, modern investigative scholars, sceptical of the reverential regard of these pundits for anything of great age (and lost!), place the literature later without committing themselves too narrowly to specification—but even they concede that a sizeable body of the oldest poetry has vanished without a trace.

One of the earliest works of extant Tamil, *Tholkappiam,* a highly prescriptive and comprehensive treatise of prosody and grammar, probably belongs to the second or third century AD—the identity of its author is unknown. Besides this all that is left of the ancient literature is a set of nine anthologies (compiled by different anthologists whose names we do not know, at different times) of selected poems of diverse kinds, some short, some longer and one containing ten long poems. In classical Tamil, verse was the medium of literary expression: prose was limited to glosses and commentaries, though, of course, people spoke to one another in prose of several dialects.

The foregoing is a prefatory summary. This dissertation is of the professional verse writers of the comparatively recent literature. However, to establish that there were such professionals 17 or 18 centuries ago, it is necessary to go back to these nine anthologies. In some of the nine, there are quite a few poems in extravagant praise of a king or chieftain. Some of the poems in *Paththu-p-paatu* (the anthology of ten long poems) feature the travelling minstrels called *paanar,* who went about from the court of one chieftain to that of another singing their lays to the accompaniment of musical instruments (and dance, at times) for the sake of reward. These are in a form peculiar to old Tamil termed *aatrippadai*, in which minstrels who had already benefited by the generosity of a chieftain tell their kinsmen in detail the way (sometimes long and difficult) they must traverse to reach that three-handed patron. The composition of verse and its communication to patrons was already a traditional means of making a living in the period of these primal anthologies—and no doubt much earlier. It was a calling that was continued right down the ages, through the proliferations of the Tamil language, even up to the first decade or two of this century.

Old Tamil is direct, terse and limited in its vocabulary: it has the strength and freedom from profusion and rococo flourishes of brevity, and because of its elliptic brevity, also an ambiguity that makes the rendering of it into other languages without stultifying interpretations and annotations difficult, often even impossible. With the growth of its vocabulary and the development of sophisticated and contrived verse forms, the scope for versification in which virtuosity prevailed over poetic verve was enhanced considerably. By about AD 1500 forms featuring rhythmic jugglery, clever puns, difficult and ornamental structure, and similar artifices had been developed, and they lent themselves to the composition of flattering addresses and to impressing prospective patrons. This piece is about such addresses and their authors.

The line of demarcation between these peripatetic verse writers and court poets is almost invisible at times. Both depended upon patrons, but on patrons of very different kinds—the former on prospective benefactors of whom they had only heard, who might or might not reward them, and the latter on personally known potentates and on a more settled basis.

However, neither of these professionals was given merely to adulatory verse. Both have written much that is of considerable literary merit—brief, piquant addresses to the gods with a mythological base, rhythmic verses that depend on their words being split without metrical dislocation to yield two wholly different meanings (both these are untranslatable, because they rely on puns in Tamil and on mythological allusions), short amatory poems sustained by vivid but archaic similes, bitter, and also detached and wryly humorous, reflections on their own abject state (the latter also sustained by mythological analogies), lyrics, odes and epics. Kamban (*circa* AD 900), who wrote his celebrated *Ramayanam* (the most famous puranic epic of Tamil), was a court poet and did not lack patrons. Kaallameghappulavar (the suffix *pulavar* means 'poet'), renowned for the spontaneity of his poetic verse and sleight-of-word skill, was an out-and-out freelancer—incidentally, one of the many zestful quatrains he wrote some five centuries ago is a delightful dig at Kamban, who had once shortened a long vowel in a name without literary sanction to conform to metric requirements—in the parody familiar Tamil words have their long vowels shortened to reduce them to gibberish! Court poets and unattached verse writers were not the chief source of the literature: a long line of religious and philosophic poets, mystics and authentic amateurs have contributed substantially to it, in varied metres.

Naturally, it was only from the affluent that these professionals without backing could hope for reward, and these prospective benefactors were of varied kinds. Not all were equally rich, and some had amassed riches by the simple expedient of being stingy. Many were not particularly literate and, worse, some were verse writers themselves and had their own fads and fancies. Further, most were not to the manner born, as princes and potentates, but were merchants and landholders. Luckily for the itinerant vendors of verse, the obligation traditionally imposed on men of wealth and status towards the arts still persisted—*noblesse oblige.* But this, by itself, frequently did not suffice. Adventitious incentives to move prospective patrons were necessary.

Some highly artificial set verse forms, already evolved, were utilized with necessary amendments, when a patron approached was unlikely to appreciate original effort. One was the *santhappaa* in which consecutive lines had the identical words and number of feet: by splitting the words skilfully without altering the metric flow and rhythm of the lines, different meanings were disclosed. Another, probably borrowed from Sanskrit, was the *rathabandhan,* in which the verse, when inscribed, had the shape of a *ratha* (a temple chariot). A third was the *ulaa*—the word literally denotes a stroll. In it, the central figure (the patron) is out for a stroll, and upon catching sight of him beautiful maidens fall headlong in love with him, and languishing, grow thin and pale, with their luxuriant coiled tresses now hanging loose in untidy strands and the bangles slipping down their wasted hands. By deftly substituting the name of the hoped-for benefactor for the name originally there (they had the skill for this, all right) an address suitable for the occasion could be had. It was not imagined that a successful merchant, elderly, bald, and wrinkled with strenuous years spent in the acquisition of capital, would fancy himself as the young, irresistible figure in an *ulaa*, or that a broad-acred landholder adept in the collection of lease rent could appreciate the intricacies of a *santhappaa*, but both would know they had been conventionally praised, and that some acknowledgment of this was expected.

A tradition sedulously nurtured by these poets was that the refusal of aid to them would have unpleasant consequences. Curses and abuse on the frustration of fond expectations are as old as humanity itself, but these men built it up as a regular reprisal—if denied reward, they threatened to 'sing abuse' (the Tamil term, *vasai paadal*, means precisely that), which would be disastrous. Belief in the potency of sung abuse was warmly encouraged by these poets, and many of the patrons they approached had an uneasy uncertainty about its effects—no doubt it did serve to loosen tight fists on occasion.

Vastly as they differed among themselves in their poetic and scholarly attainments, and personal attributes, these professionals had one thing in common which modern poets lack—all of them followed, literally, an outdoor pursuit, and had much experience of hunger and fatigue, the open air and the countryside. In those days there were no trains and the only means of conveyance was the bullock cart, which they could not afford. They walked. Often, the patrons they went in pursuit of lived 40 or 50 miles away, and they trudged for days till they reached their destination. Some have written of the hardships endured in their quest through thorn scrub and jungle. This well-known stanza of Kaallameghappulavar is addressed to the Mudali of Aamoor, a remote rural settlement:

What ages have we walked, till the white bones
show through our soles! Ignorant of the way,
gone on and on, when prince among immortals,
the Mudali of Aamoor is right here!

Verbal dexterity, and knowledge of prosody and verse forms, were essential to the profession these men practised, but physical endurance and stout-muscled calves were not less necessary. It was not only money that they sought of patrons. Some have asked for shawls for cover against the cold, and the present of a milch-cow has been gratefully acknowledged. A few have sung even of the outrageous generosity of a potentate who had rewarded their verse with the gift of an elephant—I think the animal must have been purely metaphoric, for men seeking aid for their own subsistence could never have provided for so hearty an appetite. It seems strange that none of these marathonists has asked for durable footwear.

The supplicatory appeals of these poets often featured stark, graphic accounts of their destitution, sometimes in symbolic terms. There were two men named Chockanaathappulavar who lived about the same time, both accomplished poets, and the one belonging to the village of Balapat-tadai wrote this address to the patron, Bhoja:

> Bhoja, when as a thunderstorm you showered
> gold-rain upon the spread of earth beneath,
> not a drop touched me, for my poverty
> shielded me wholly with its deep umbrella!

I was told that this conceit is probably borrowed from a very similar verse in another language, but no details of the authorship and probable date of that other poem are available for verification. However, I doubt if any other language has anything like this poem of Madhurakavirayar addressed, not to the well-known patron Kaallaththi, but to his own indigence:

> Long have you wandered with me, like an abiding shadow—
> what, O my poverty, will you do tomorrow?
> When I reach Kaallaththi's seat where will I be and where you?
> Come, stay with me today.

A few have written, not of their own distressed circumstances, but of a professional poet's lot, with much bitterness. These do not lend them-selves to close renderings in English—and all renderings here are close—for, in spite of their power, they are either sustained by allusions to inci-dents in mythological stories about the gods, or by being set in a milieu whose social values are now wholly obsolete—and anyway their metric ebullience and perfection are untranslatable. Padikkaasuthambiran, a gifted and original poet of the early eighteenth century, has written one of the bitterest of them:

> Foredoomed, with many callings there, we chose scholarship witlessly, think-
>   ing it great..
> We did not learn the street magician's art, dance the pole-dance, or practise
>   sleight-of-hand.
> Not born full-breasted prostitutes, we did not, abandoning accursed Tamil,
>   enter service with women as their go-betweens.
> To what a wretched life have we been born!

Ashtaavadhanam Saravanaperumal Kavirayar, who had exceptional skill with rhyme and rhythm, was the court poet of Ramanathapuram in the nineteenth century. He has a set of seven vibrant stanzas about niggardly householders visited with the trader in verse. These are two excerpts:

> Who is it striding down the street, with palm-leaf slats in hand?
> Great heavens! It looks like a poet—go quickly shut the door,
> and leaving it ajar a crack, keep watch till he has gone
> far down the street and safely turned the corner at its end.

This is a conversation between a wealthy citizen and the visiting poet:

> 'Whom visits me?'—'A poet'—'And where are you from?'
> 'From Vadakasi'.—'What brings you here?'
> 'Your fame has brought me here.
> Hearing of you we have composed sweet verses in your praise.'
> 'You were not wise. Which of my long line of forefathers has
> listened to verse? A slight unknown in all my ancestry
> is what you bring! Go far away before there is bloodshed.'

Tamil poets have never been unresponsive. The simplest meal provided by some modest householder has been lavishly praised, and its two elementary dishes described in loving detail—grudging and meagre hospitality has also provoked response! The munificent patronage that they, and their fellows, had enjoyed at the hands of kings and chieftains has been remembered and superlatively extolled, but it is no royal benefactor but a Muslim ship-owner that has had the warmest and most extravagant tributes paid to him. This was Seethakkaathi Marakkaayar (early eighteenth century) who had a love of literary Tamil and an unfailing sympathy for poets. They praised him when he was alive, and they praised him long after he had been buried—they even wrote that with his death poetry was also dead. Padikkaasuthambiran has many stanzas on the patron—this is one of them:

> Spent with his blaze the sun is red: the eyes
> of women redden in the toils of love:
> the poet's heart grows red reading the classes—
> and Seethakkaathi's hands are red with giving.

So much for the roses—the thorns are also there. Quite a number of vituperative verses have been composed through the centuries by poets denied reward for their offerings, especially when the denial was by someone with pretensions to status and culture. Except for being in a standard verse form, most of these are just plain, uninhibited abuse, but there were specialists in this line, too. Kaallameghappulavar was an acknowledged master of instant repartee, and has written some foul-mouthed insults and curses in immaculate metres, but these are not addressed to any patron. He seldom approached patrons and except for a rare stanza in praise of some benefactor (like the Aamoor Mudali) has not written of them at all.

Ramachandra Kavirayar (who lived in Madras towards the close of the nineteenth century) was a talented poet, noted for his power of invective, but his 'sung abuse' is difficult to translate. One of his verses is about a patron named Mazhuvarangan, on whom some sycophant had conferred the grandiose title 'Bhoopan', meaning 'lord of the earth':

> Why does the milk-hedge need a protective thorn fence?
> Why does one need a bridle for a donkey?
> Why take an axe to break thin, dried up twigs?
> Why scents for garlic, or for salt-earth seeds?
> Why should this idle, worthless outcast need
> The pompous title, Mazhuvarangan Bhoopan?

Even in comparatively recent times, there have been men feared for their facile mastery of verse and vituperative verve, among them Muthukuttippulavar of Ramanathapuram, Vasaikavi Aandaan Pulavar ('Vasaikavi' means 'abusive verse'!), and Avinasippulavar of Tirunelveli. The last has utilized a sacred classical form of loving addresses to the gods termed Pillai-th-thamizh, in which the deity is imagined as a very young child just learning to clap hands and indulge in similar infantile activities. Exploiting the fourfold pun on the word *kottu*, which means clap, sting, beat and shed or spill, and addressing a patron called Venkataraman who refused him aid in the Pillai-th-thamizh form, he has urged Venkataraman to clap hands while scorpions and wasps sting him, funeral drums beat around his house and his nearest and dearest shed torrential tears of grief.

Vituperative responses have also been much more cultured and subtly barbed than such fiendish addresses. The finest example of such verse that I know is by a poet whose name is unknown and who, to judge by his verse, probably lived early in the nineteenth century. This gem was discovered, inscribed on an isolated palm-leaf slat, nearly a hundred years ago by my father (A. Madhaviah, the Tamil scholar, poet and novelist) and, to the best of my knowledge, has never been published before. It is addressed to a petty chieftain named Kumaraswami Pandian ('Pandian' is a generic clan-title of southern Tamil Nadu) in whose praise this anonymous poet had composed a *santhappaa* and a *rathabandham*, verse forms likely to impress the semi-literate. He was rewarded with eighteen pice for his pains (roughly equal to 38 paise). The response refers to two celebrated instances from the past of impulsive generosity to an indigent poet. The chieftain Mothaipperiyavan was so enchanted by the verse that a poor poet took to him that he gave his daughter's hand to the young man in wedlock and bestowed a part of his holdings on him.

It is said that when Seethakkaathi was about to be buried, a footsore poet in need arrived from some distant place, and lamented the power of his poverty that had killed so great a patron. And as the richly bedecked body was being lowered into the burial pit, its right hand was flung out towards the sorrowing supplicant, and realizing the significance of this accidental happening, they took the diamond ring from the patron's finger and gave it to the poet:

> Long ago, Mothaipperiyavan gave a beautiful maiden,
> and later Seethakkaathi stretched out his hand from the grave.
> Tell me, free-handed Kumaraswami,
> you who have given for these songs all of this sum of eighteen pice,
> what will you do tomorrow for your creature needs and daily rice?

1995